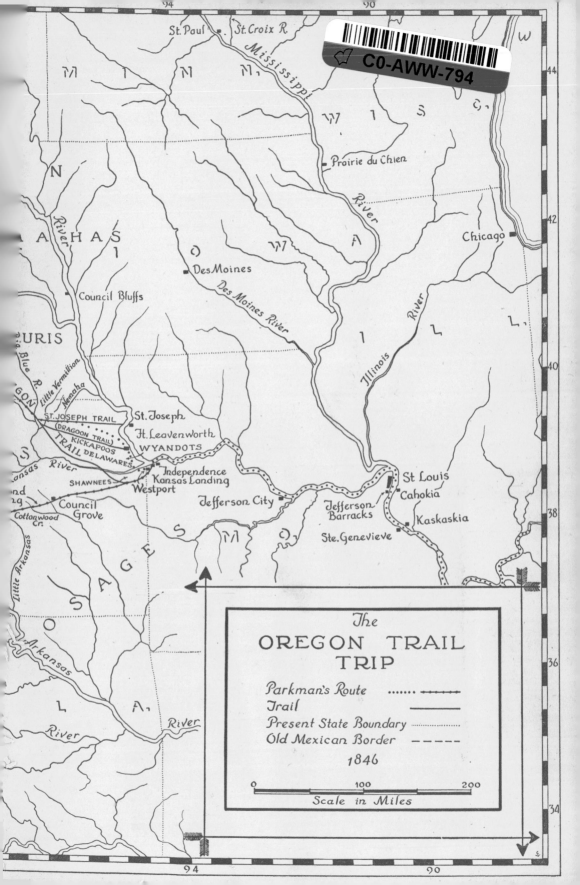

The
OREGON TRAIL
TRIP

Parkman's Route ······•→•→•
Trail ——————
Present State Boundary ·················
Old Mexican Border — — — —

1846

0   100   200
Scale in Miles

THE
JOURNALS
OF
FRANCIS PARKMAN

VOLUME II

Buffalo Hunt—Surround, 1832
One of George Catlin's paintings of life in the Far West from the lithograph by McGahey
(Coverdale Collection of North American Indians, No. 136)

THE
JOURNALS
OF
FRANCIS PARKMAN

Edited by **MASON WADE**

Author of

FRANCIS PARKMAN: HEROIC HISTORIAN

ILLUSTRATED

VOLUME II

NEW YORK AND LONDON

HARPER & BROTHERS PUBLISHERS

MCMXLVII

22444
10 - 7

TABLE OF CONTENTS

VOLUME II

LIST OF ILLUSTRATIONS

VOLUME II

The Oregon Trail Journal
1846

Introduction

PARKMAN'S Oregon Trail trip was the greatest of the journeys
that he undertook in preparation for his lifework, and the diary
kept on that arduous expedition is the most notable of all his journals.
Its importance is twofold: it casts an invaluable light on *France and
England in North America* as the chief source of Parkman's understanding of the Indians, the third party in the great struggle for the continent; and it is a major document of Western history, for 1846 was
a vital year in the development of the West and Parkman was thrown
into the company of many of the great men and movements of the
time. Alone among the journals, this informal record is more important than the book for which it furnished the raw material, since
The Oregon Trail was diluted triply by the circumstances of its
composition, and for all its reputation is inferior to the notes upon
which it was based.

It must not be forgotten that *The Oregon Trail* was Parkman's
first book, begun when he was only twenty-three and finished, under
singular difficulties, three years later. In a new preface, written a
quarter of a century after the book first appeared in 1849, Parkman
discounted the dangers he had run with these words: "My business
was observation, and I was willing to pay dearly for the opportunity of exercising it." He did pay dearly for the knowledge he
obtained, for he went back to Boston from the West a sick man. It
seems clear that the journey brought about the breakdown of a
constitution already strained by unwise attempts to strengthen it.
The summer in the West was intended as rest and recreation from
too much study, for Parkman had supplemented his law studies with
extensive historical research. He returned home with his already
strained sight weakened still further by exposure to the pitiless glare
of the sun and to the harsh alkali dust of the Plains. He had acquired

an impaired digestion and the insomnia to which he was to be a lifelong victim; and he had further advanced the arthritis that later crippled him and prevented him from ever again leading the strenuous outdoor life he loved so well. Most serious of all was an obscure mental disorder, which Parkman thought was brought on by this general collapse of his health, but may have been the basic trouble of which the other ailments were merely symptoms. In its train came hypochondria, which haunts the book, while the journal possesses an entirely different spirit. But just as a starvation diet and the exercise of the strong will which was his greatest asset had brought Parkman through the onslaughts of illness on the journey, when "a horse, a rifle, a pair of pistols, and a red shirt might have offered temptations too strong for aboriginal virtue" had he yielded to invalidism, so upon his return home he conquered his "Enemy" by acting on his favorite principle that "to tame the devil, it is best to take him by the horns." Condemned by baffled doctors to complete repose and unable to use his eyes in the historical work he yearned to do, he wrote *The Oregon Trail* by dictation, a procedure of which he soon caught the knack and which he found as "easy as lying."

The journal lost much, however, in the process of thus being transmuted into book form. Parkman was forced to rely upon others to act as amanuenses and to revise his work. His companion on the journey, Quincy Adams Shaw—who significantly bore a triply sacrosanct Boston name—was one of the cousins who read the notebooks aloud to Parkman as he underwent medical treatment at Staten Island, Catskill, and at the Brattleboro Spa, and then took down the version which he dictated after recasting the narrative in his head. Shaw made the Oregon Trail trip for sport, adventure, and his health, while Parkman went chiefly as a student; and doubtless Shaw's outlook helped to shape the book into an adventure story, "A Summer's Journey Out of Bounds," as the original subtitle runs, and into the record of "a tour of curiosity and amusement," as it is described on the opening page: "The restlessness, the love of wilds and hatred of cities, natural perhaps in early years to every unperverted son of Adam, was not our only motive for undertaking the present journey. My companion hoped to shake off the effects of a disorder that had impaired a constitution originally hardy and robust; and I was anxious to pursue some enquiries relative to the character and usages of the remote Indian tribes, being already familiar with many of the border tribes."—*The California and Oregon Trail* (New York, 1849), Ch. II. Much valuable material about the Indians and about the fur traders, soldiers, emigrants, mountain men, and sportsmen they encountered thus was lost; and also most of the immediacy and vigor of the original notes. Parkman had yet to shed the rhetorical impedimenta with which Harvard had encumbered his style; and he was self-consciously trying to be literary, under the romantic influence of his own literary idols, Byron and Cooper, and those of Gaylord Clark, in whose *Knickerbocker Magazine* the first version of *The Oregon Trail* appeared as a serial from February 1847 to February 1849, complete with Byronic epigraphs. Still more of the original quality was lost by the editing of Charles Eliot Norton, who revised the *Knickerbocker* version for book publication in accordance with the literary amenities as then understood by right-thinking Bostonians. On September 12, 1848, Parkman, beset by illness, accepted Norton's offer to read proofs for him, though it is evident that he was critical of Norton's style, for in the same letter he urged his friend to "put a little pepper and allspice" into a contribution to the *North American*: "It will not harm its respectability, and perhaps will make it more welcome to the taste of some of its readers." But Norton was constitutionally incapable of taking this injunction to heart, and *The Oregon Trail* as we know it was carefully bowdlerized of much anthropological data and many insights into Western life which seemed too crude to his delicate taste. Harvard's future professor of fine arts was not the best imaginable editor for one of the great firsthand records of the West, though Norton did a service to history by correcting some of Parkman's remarkable distortions of French names.

What happened is best illustrated by examples, aside from the many minor changes occasioned by Norton's low shock-point, which toned down or omitted Parkman's references to the prevalence of heavy drinking and loose sexual behavior in the West. But more serious than this bowdlerizing was the attempt to make literature out of history, at the expense of the latter, for which Parkman himself must bear the ultimate blame. In the journal Parkman thus described his impression of the American Fur Company upon his arrival at Fort Laramie:

Fort Laramie, June 16th. Prices are most extortionate. Sugar, two dollars a cup—5-cent tobacco at $1.50—bullets at $.75 a pound, etc. American Fur Cmp'y. exceedingly disliked in this country—it suppresses all opposition, and keeping these enormous prices, keeps its men in necessaries on these terms.

In the book this vivid picture of fur trade practices became merely:

Fort Laramie is one of the posts established by the "American Fur Company," which well nigh monopolizes the Indian trade of this region. Here its officials rule with an absolute sway . . .

Again, the journal offers this incisive account of Parkman's second visit to Fort Bernard, where an emigrant party has just arrived:

June 28th. Yesterday rode down with Paul Dorion, who wished to swap a wild horse, to Richard's fort. Found there Russel's or Boggs' comp'y., engaged in drinking and refitting, and a host of Canadians besides. Russel drunk as a pigeon—some fine-looking Kentucky men—some of D. Boone's grandchildren—Ewing, Jacobs, and others with them—altogether more educated men than any I have seen. A motley crew assembled in Richard's rooms—squaws, children, Spaniards, French, and emigrants. Emigrants mean to sell liquor to the Miniconques, who will be up here tomorrow, and after having come all the way from the Missouri to go to the war, will no doubt break up, if this is done. Paul very much displeased, as well as the Canadians.

In the book this became:

Two large villages of a band of Dakotah had come three hundred miles from the Missouri, to join in the war, and they were expected to reach Richard's that morning. There was as yet no sign of their approach; so pushing through a noisy, drunken crowd, I entered an apartment of logs and mud, the largest in the fort: it was full of men of various races and complexions, all more or less drunk. A company of California emigrants, it seemed, had made the discovery at this late day that they had encumbered themselves with too many supplies for their journey. A part, therefore, they had thrown away, or sold at great loss to the traders; but had determined to get rid of their very copious stock of Missouri whiskey, by drinking it on the spot. Here were maudlin squaws stretched on piles of buffalo-robes; squalid Mexicans, armed with bows and arrows; Indians sedately drunk; long-haired Canadians and trappers, and American backwoodsmen in brown homespun, the well-beloved pistol and bowie-knife displayed openly at their sides. In the middle of the room a tall, lank man, with a dingy broadcloth coat, was haranguing the company in the style of the stump orator. With one hand he sawed the air, and with the other clutched firmly a brown jug of whiskey, which he applied every moment to his lips, forgetting that he had drained the contents long ago. Richard formally introduced me to this personage, who was no less a man than Colonel R——, once the leader of the party. Instantly the colonel, seizing me, in the absence of buttons, by the leather fringes of my frock, began to define his position. His men, he said, had mutinied and deposed him; but he still exercised over them the influence of a superior mind; in all but the name he was yet their chief. As the colonel spoke, I looked round on the wild assemblage, and could not help thinking that he was but ill fitted to conduct such men across the deserts to California. Conspicuous among the rest were three tall young men, grandsons of Daniel Boone. They had clearly inherited the adventurous character of that prince of pioneers; but I saw no sign of the quiet and tranquil spirit that so remarkably distinguished him.

In the journal Parkman gives this sharply-drawn picture of Smoke's village of Sioux fording Laramie Creek:

This morning, Smoke's village appeared on the opposite bank, and crossed on their wild, thin, little horses. Men and boys, naked and dashing eagerly through the water—horses with lodge poles dragging through squaws and children, and sometimes a litter of puppies—gaily-attired squaws, leading the horses of their lords—dogs with their burdens attached swimming among the horses and mules—dogs barking, horses breaking loose, children laughing and shouting—squaws thrusting into the ground the lance and shield of the master of the lodge—naked and splendidly formed men passing and repassing through the swift water.

In the book the sharpness of impression is lost amid too much detail and a certain romanticization, in the approved manner of Cooper and Irving, which Parkman later condemned:

The stream is wide, and was then between three and four feet deep, with a very swift current. For several rods the water was alive with dogs, horses, and Indians. The long poles used in pitching the lodges are carried by the horses, fastened by the heavier end, two or three on each side, to a rude sort of pack-saddle, while the other end drags on the ground. About a foot behind the horse, a kind of large basket or pannier is suspended between the poles, and firmly lashed in its place. On the back of the horse are piled various articles of luggage; the basket also is well filled with domestic utensils, or, quite as often, with a litter of puppies, a brood of small children, or a superannuated old man. Numbers of these curious vehicles, *traineaux*, or, as the Canadians call them, *travaux*, were now splashing together through the stream. Among them swam countless dogs, often burdened with miniature *traineaux*; and dashing forward on horseback through the throng came the warriors, the slender figure of some lynx-eyed boy clinging fast behind them. The women sat perched on the pack-saddles, adding not a little to the load of the already over-burdened horses. The confusion was prodigious. The dogs yelled and howled in chorus; the puppies in the *traineaux* set up a dismal whine, as the water invaded their comfortable retreat; the little black-eyed children, from one year of age upward, clung fast with both hands to the edge of their basket, and looked in alarm at the water rushing so near them, sputtering and making wry mouths as it splashed against their faces. Some of the dogs, encumbered by their load, were carried down by the current, yelping piteously; and the old squaws would rush into the water, seize their favorites by the neck, and drag them out. As each horse gained the bank, he scrambled up as he could. Stray horses and colts came among the rest, often breaking away at full speed through the crowd, followed by old hags, screaming after their fashion on all occasions of excitement. Buxom young squaws, blooming in all the charms of vermilion, stood here and there on the bank, holding aloft their master's lance, as a signal to collect the scattered portions of his household.

So much for the literary consequences of the way in which *The Oregon Trail* was written. Much more important was the loss of historical information of considerable importance. Until the journals came to light, it was impossible to make a satisfactory itinerary and chronology of Parkman's trip, for many of the essential details of the journey were omitted in the book version. It was also impossible to identify many of the people that he met; and it so happens that though Parkman was far more interested in Indians than in whites or halfbreeds, he met an extraordinary number of Western notables.

The Oregon Trail has often been criticized on the grounds of how much Parkman missed, as well as of how much he reported. The journal proves that he missed less than has been assumed on the basis of the omissions that his friends led him to make in both the magazine and book versions. Neither Shaw nor Norton saw the value of many a note on the Indians which later served Parkman well, and neither was concerned with the making of the West.

Parkman's primary purpose in taking the Oregon Trail trip was to study the Indian. This he made clear in his foreword to the first edition:

The journey which the following narrative describes was undertaken on the writer's part with a view of studying the manners and characters of Indians in their primitive state. Although in the chapters which relate to them, he has only attempted to sketch those features of their wild and picturesque life which fell, in the present instance, under his own eye, yet in doing so he has constantly aimed to leave an impression correct as far as it goes. In justifying his claim to accuracy on this point, it is hardly necessary to advert to the representations given by poets and novelists, which, for the most part, are mere creatures of fancy. The Indian is certainly entitled to high rank among savages, but his good qualities are not those of an Uncas or an Oudalissa.

During his college years Parkman had formed the intention of writing the history of the American forest and of the American Indian. The Appalachian forest, the scene of that Old French War which he at first thought would be the focal point of the history he proposed to write, was now thoroughly familiar to him; but in the East the Indian had died out, or had been hopelessly corrupted by white civilization, or had been transferred to Western reservations. Parkman's earlier encounters with the Abenakis of the Penobscot, with the Iroquois of the Mohawk, and with the Ojibwas of the Great Lakes, had not given him the knowledge of primitive savage life which he required. Only in the West could that knowledge still be obtained; for beyond the western boundary of Missouri, then the frontier of the United States, the remnants of the Eastern Indians had recently been settled on reservations; while on the Plains and in the Rockies the Western Indians lived much as they always had done, still little affected by casual contact with mountain man and fur trader and emigrant. The culture of the Plains Indian was very different from that of the forest-dweller of the East, but his psychology was much the same, and Parkman used his acquaintance with the Sioux to unlock many an Iroquois mystery. He was fortunate in going West when he did, at almost the last moment suitable for his purpose; for the opening of the West had begun, and with the rising tide of emigration and the establishment of fixed trading posts in the mountains the doom of the savage and of his ancient way of life was assured.

In his great triangular sweep through the prairies and the plains, Parkman had an opportunity to observe many different Indian tribes at first hand. His route took him across the prairie and the plains from Westport (Kansas City) to Fort Laramie in eastern Wyoming, along the first part of the Oregon Trail; then he spent some weeks hunting with a Sioux village beyond the Laramie Mountains in the Laramie Basin, and in the eastern foothills of the Medicine Bow Mountains. Returning to Fort Laramie, he traveled southward along the Front Range of the Rockies to the Pueblo and Bent's Fort on the Arkansas (near La Junta, Colorado) by one of the oldest Indian trade routes, which crossed the sites of Cheyenne and Denver. Then he turned eastward, following the Mountain Route and then the main Santa Fe Trail across the plains to his starting point, leaving the Arkansas at the Big Bend, Kansas, and crossing the prairies to Westport by way of Council Grove. On the steamer from St. Louis, where he had met Shaw and acquired part of his outfit, to Westport, the jumping-off place for his prairie journey, Parkman encountered the degenerate Kansas or Caws, who had become thieves and beggars. About Westport and near-by Independence, he found the missionized Shawnees and Delawares, Eastern Indians recently installed on reservations. The Shawnees had become farmers and half-civilized, under the influence of their Methodist Mission; but the Delawares were the Indian Ishmaels of the Plains, extremely useful to the whites as scouts and hunters, since their hand was against that of every other Indian. Near Fort Leavenworth he saw the semicivilized Kickapoos, whose white trader kept both a loaded revolver and the poems of John Milton close at hand.

With considerable good fortune Parkman passed scatheless through the country of the Pawnees along the Platte, for they had become master thieves and cattle lifters on the Oregon road which to their surprise was being thrust through their ancient homeland. The region about Fort Laramie had long been a neutral ground, where buffalo and trade goods lured each summer both the Sioux (whom Parkman calls the Dakotas) and their enemies the Shoshones (Snakes) and the Crows; though when Parkman came upon the scene, the Sioux had for some years been trying to make Laramie Plains their own. While hunting with the Sioux to the west of Fort Laramie—Parkman's Black Hills are the fir-covered Laramie Mountains, not the Black Hills of Dakota—he feared an onslaught of the Gros Ventres, who had allied themselves to the Blackfeet of the Rockies and were the toughest fighters and raiders of the region. The far more powerful and populous Sioux told him tall tales of their enemies' prowess. Turning southward to Pueblo and Bent's Fort, he encountered stray Cheyennes, whose center was the latter establishment, after the trader William Bent married Owl Woman of their tribe. On his way back to Westport along the much-traveled Santa Fe Trail, Parkman missed the Comanches, the cruelest and most murderous of the Plains Indians; but he did encounter the southern Arapahos, no less dangerous than their northern relatives but somewhat intimidated when he met them by the passage of the Army of the West on its way to Santa Fe. Here Parkman also fell in with the southern Pawnees. Any of these tribes would have cheerfully wiped out or "counted coup" on so small a party as Parkman's, or at best would have as cheerfully robbed it. But Parkman had great good fortune in what was an extremely foolhardy adventure.

Parkman and Shaw ran a very real risk of death because of their dislike for the company of fellow travelers; and only luck and the wisdom of their guide, Henry Chatillon, a master mountain man, brought them through unscathed. To be sure, the Pawnees were more interested in robbing the whites than in killing them. But the theft of weapons, provisions, and horses on the Plains often meant merely a less merciful death than that from arrow, gun, spear, or knife. Chatillon would never have led so small a party into the Indian country, and must have thought that Parkman and Shaw planned to join an emigrant train. But they had no love for the "offscourings of the frontier," and when they reached the Forks of the Platte they parted with their British companions, reducing their number to four. Again, they set off southward from Fort Laramie without companions for the most dangerous part of their journey. And at Bent's Fort, instead of waiting for the formation of a regular party, they merely picked up casual reinforcements and set out for home. The Arapahos and Comanches had richly earned a reputation as violent and dangerous—they were true "hostiles," in the phrase of the trails. The Sioux were as yet well disposed towards the whites, but Parkman might have been casually killed while in their company with but two other white men, if it had not been for Henry Chatillon's high standing with the tribe, into which he had married.

Parkman had two further assets for his firsthand study of the Indians. In St. Louis, before setting out on his trip, he had talked at length with Thomas Fitzpatrick, one of the greatest of the mountain men, who probably knew the Western Indians as well as anyone. And then, as they pushed westward across the prairie and into the true High Plains, beyond the 98° meridian, Parkman found that Henry Chatillon was an encyclopedia of Indian information. These circumstances made Parkman's encounters with stray individuals or small groups of various tribes more profitable than they would otherwise have been; for Fitzpatrick had provided him with a general frame of reference, based on a rich experience of the whole West, while Chatillon fitted additional pieces into it and helped Parkman to interpret what he saw. It was from Fitzpatrick and his old companion Jedidiah Smith that Albert Gallatin, the pioneer of American ethnography, had gathered many of the basic concepts of his *Synopsis of the Indian Tribes within the United States* (1836).

But Parkman's great and unique experience in the West, which he owed to the fact that Chatillon was the son-in-law of an Oglala chief, was that of living with the Sioux as they pursued their normal life. His three weeks with the Sioux village in the foothills of the Rockies made him the first American man of letters to possess any real firsthand understanding of the Indian. Washington Irving's *Astoria* and *Captain Bonneville* are remarkable recreations of the experience of other men, but Irving's *Tour of the Prairies* is no *Oregon Trail*. Parkman destroyed Fenimore Cooper's highly romantic concept of the Noble Savage—one who had lived with the Dakota Sioux had few illusions about Indian nobility of character—and enriched American literature with the most lifelike Indians it was to know for years to come, although Parkman's Indians are a little too inevitably "snake-eyed" or "lynx-eyed" for the less romantic modern ethnologist. How revolutionary the Indians of *The Oregon Trail* were in the literary world of the day is indicated by the fact that Herman Melville was thoroughly upset by Parkman's view of them as not much better than brutes, and publicly informed him that "Xavier and Elliott despised not the savages; and had Newton and Milton dwelt among them, they would not have done so."* To Francis Bowen of the *North American*, Parkman's encounters with the Indians figured merely among "the other incidents which usually lend variety and interest to a journey to the Rocky Mountains" in these "pleasing and truthful sketches." Bowen found Parkman's book far superior to Edwin Bryant's *What I Saw in California*, but quite obviously it did not evoke in him the same enthusiasm as Irving's *Tour*, in which he found the "finest qualities of Addison and Goldsmith, without the free language of the one or the shallow judgment of the other."† In 1849 the East wanted from the West either elegant romance or information useful to the prospective gold miner, and it ignored Lewis Garrard's *Wah-To-Yah and the Taos Trail*, a better job of writing than Parkman's far more celebrated book, but too truthful and uncouth for the taste of the times in its lively picture of the West.

Parkman's experience on the Oregon Trail trip served him well in dealing with the past in which the Indian had played so great a role; the basis of many a statement in the histories may be found in some incident or observation recorded in the Oregon Trail journal. The Sioux might well be called the Iroquois of the West, and as such they were particularly apt subjects for Parkman's study. They were the most typical of the Plains Indians, and one of the best tribes, though inferior both physically and mentally to the Crows and Cheyennes, and mentally to the Arapahos. Thanks to their primary

---

* Unsigned review of *The California and Oregon Trail* in *The Literary World*, IV, 113 (March 31, 1849), 291. I am indebted to Mr. Bernard DeVoto for calling this review to my attention.

† *North American Review*, LXIX (July, 1849), 175.

importance to the fur trade and their stubborn resistance to white encroachment after 1865, they became for most Americans the symbol of the Indian. A Sioux was the model for the Indian-head nickel, and the Sioux war bonnet has been thrust by artists upon many an Indian who never saw such a headdress.

The Sioux confederated better than any other Indians except the Iroquois, and matched them in their belligerency and bravery. In their gradual progress from their original home in the forests about the Lake of the Woods to the Plains, they conquered or drove out every nation they encountered, except the Ojibwas, who forced that southwestward movement when their European weapons, provided by French and English traders, proved superior to the Sioux bows and arrows. The Sioux, like the Iroquois, were a confederation of tribes, made up in their case of seven main divisions, each divided into bands and sub-bands. Four of these main divisions, grouped under the name of Santee, lagged behind in the great migration and centered in Minnesota; while the Yankton, Yanktonai, and Teton divisions pushed on west of the Missouri and adopted the cultural characteristics of the Plains Indians.

The Oglalas, with whom Parkman sojourned, were the principal band of the Teton Sioux. Their 5,000 souls made up half the nation, though they constituted only one of its seven divisions. The Oglalas led the southwestward movement in the late seventeenth and eighteenth centuries; they were the first of the Sioux to cross the Missouri, about 1750, and the first to reach the Black Hills of South Dakota, about 1775. After crossing the Missouri, they began to use horses and to hunt buffalo, which they followed westward in many small bands; from this, they derived their name of Scattered or Divided People. They pushed the northern Cheyennes and the Kiowas out of the Black Hills, and by the end of the century they were waging war on the Arikaras to the north, the Kiowas and the Crows to the west, and the Omahas and Poncas to the south. In 1795 they had a great struggle with the Cheyennes, to whom they later showed more tolerance than to any other Algonkin tribe.

Parkman was familiar with Jonathan Carver's description of the River Bands of the Sioux, whom the latter had found in 1766 near the Ste. Croix River of Minnesota. These laggards in their nation's migration fought with the British in the American Revolution and the War of 1812, while their Western kinsmen gradually gave up the practice of wintering east of the Missouri and formed new ties with the St. Louis French, with whom they traded at the mouth of the Bad River. From 1785 to 1820 the Oglalas had no less than three wars with the Crows, whom they cut off from the East and from British traders at the Mandan and Hidsata Villages on the Upper Missouri. Consequently a north-south trade developed along the Front Range of the Rockies about 1815, when the Kiowas began trading horses and Spanish goods with the Crows at Horse Creek on the North Platte.

During the first quarter of the nineteenth century the Oglalas continued to roam the Black Hills north of the Bad River, trading with the St. Louis French and becoming friendly with them, though not above raiding traders bound upstream, as in the case of the Astorians in 1811. In 1823 they aided Colonel Henry Leavenworth's expedition against the Arikaras of the Missouri villages, who had attacked W. H. Ashley's fur brigade, but the Sioux were not impressed by their first contact with the U. S. Army, which to their disgust refused to wage war in the ruthless Indian style. In 1823, when they signed a treaty with the Americans who had gradually taken over the Teton fur trade from the French, the Oglalas numbered 1,500, of whom 300 were warriors. One of their three sub-bands was then headed by Bull Bear (Mato-Tatanyka), who later became the head chief of the Oglalas. In 1832 they were visited by the artist George Catlin, who mentions Parkman's acquaintance, the Whirlwind, in his *Manners, Customs, and Institutions of the North American Indians* (London, 1841), a book with which Parkman was familiar. About 1835 half the Oglalas were grouped into four sub-bands under Bull Bear, known as Bear People, while the other half of the tribe, known as Smoke People, followed Chief Smoke. As the American Fur Company's monopoly of the Oglala trade broke down, they moved southward toward the Platte, drawn by the liquor which was the most effective weapon in these fur trade wars.

They first came to Laramie Creek in 1834, lured to Fort William by John Sabille and C. E. Gilpin, traders for Sublette & Campbell, who sought to break up the practical monopoly of the American

Fur Company's Oglala Post, conducted by Thomas L. Sarpy on the South Fork of the Cheyenne, near Rapid Creek. This move brought them into conflict with their old enemies the Pawnees, with whom Bull Bear quarreled over the buffalo hunting—the best within five hundred miles—near the forks of the Platte, which marked the western boundary of the Pawnee country. By 1840 Bull Bear's warriors were hunting west of the Laramie Mountains, while Smoke's took over the Platte Forks range. The two Oglala bands came into frequent contact, for the fine horses which Smoke's people obtained from the south were an attraction to Bull Bear's followers. Both bands were on good terms with the whites, but had formed different alliances among the neighboring tribes whose war and hunting parties frequented Laramie Plains, long a crossroads of Indian trade. The northern Arapahos and Cheyennes, whose territory lay to the south of Laramie, were well disposed towards Bull Bear's people, while the Crows to the north were their bitter enemies. Another trade war flooded the region with liquor in 1841, and in November of that year Bull Bear was killed in Smoke's camp on the Chugwater during a drunken brawl. The Oglalas then split into two factions, a division which endured for forty years, despite the unifying effect of growing anti-white feeling as the swelling tide of emigrants spoiled the grass, timber, and game of the Sioux' favorite hunting grounds. The Grattan massacre at Fort Laramie in 1854 was a forerunner of the trouble to come, and after 1865 the Sioux were the terror of the expanding frontier. General Custer was sent out against them in 1876, when the invasion of the Black Hills in Dakota by gold seekers brought them out on the warpath. After the massacre of his command, the Sioux were gradually forced northward into Canada, where many of their descendents remain today, reunited with the remnants of the western divisions of their people.

Parkman was fortunate in meeting the Sioux just before they turned against the whites, though they were in social anarchy as a result of the fur trade wars and Bull Bear's murder. He was still more fortunate in that his guide Henry Chatillon was married to Bear Robe, Bull Bear's daughter, and thus was allied to the great leader of the Oglalas, for whom no real successor had yet been found and whose prestige still was great. Though personal fitness and popularity determined chieftainship more often than heredity, where descent did operate among the Sioux, it was from father to son; and the elder Bull Bear's fame had been great enough to overcome his son's lack of qualifications for leadership. In any case, among the Teton Sioux the authority of the chief was limited by the band council, without whom, as Parkman observed, little or nothing could be accomplished. War parties were commonly recruited by individual warriors, such as the Whirlwind, who had the reputation of being successful leaders. The dispersion of the Sioux into small bands made it difficult for them to muster a large war party for action against another tribe, as Parkman saw when the grand alliance of the Oglalas and the Miniconjous against the Snakes fell through. The only unity of the seven divisions of the Sioux was in language and in the fact that they did not commonly wage war upon each other. Even the Teton Sioux were united solely by a common dialect and by the Plains culture which set them apart from their Santee kinsmen, who still followed the forest way of life.

The chief characteristics of the Teton Sioux culture were their utter dependence upon the buffalo, which not only supplied their food but their clothing, shelter, and utensils of all kinds; their use of the horse and the *tepi*; their custom of using "soldiers" to maintain order in camp and in the cooperative buffalo hunt; and their cult of the sun dance. They used the short bow, which held its own for buffalo hunting on horseback, as Parkman bears witness, until the invention of the repeating rifle in the 1870's. They practiced little agriculture, and made no pottery or textiles. The Crows were better workmen than the Sioux, and the Nez Percés made better bows. Like almost all the Plains tribes, the Sioux used the *travois* (from the French *travail à cheval*), an A-shaped frame of poles bound together by sinews and drawn first by dogs and later by horses. They made little use of wild seeds and grass in their diet, but their development of pemmican, sun-dried buffalo meat packed in fat and sometimes flavored with pounded wild cherry stones, gave them a balanced diet ideally adapted to their life. They were among the few Plains Indians to eat dog, and, as Parkman discovered to the alarm of an already queasy stomach, a dog feast had ritualistic significance for them. Their use of the by-products of the buffalo—skin, bones, hair, horns, and sinew—was often ingenious; but their whole culture depended too much upon this one beast, and when it failed them, they were doomed. While the buffalo roamed the Plains in thousands, the Sioux squandered their only resource; and only when the whites had driven it into extinction did they realize that they, too, were threatened with a like fate. Then they turned and fought the new-comers who had destroyed the source of their civilization. In the 1840's the Sioux were slow to recognize that they were being exposed to a new form of the white encroachment which had forced them from their original home in Canada. It was fortunate for Parkman's purpose that this was so, and that the Sioux were as yet unwilling to go on the warpath against the whites, as the southern Arapahos did that very summer and as the Cheyennes soon would.

It is clear that Parkman had an invaluable opportunity to study the Indian way of life. It is also clear, from both the journal and the book based upon it, that at twenty-three he was not equipped to make the most of that opportunity. Bred in a romantic conception of the savage which is clearly reflected in his frontier tales for the *Knickerbocker* in 1845, he was too shocked by the contrast of the reality with his concept to appreciate fully what he saw. Ethnology was an infant science in America in 1846, and Parkman had hardly begun to think in its terms. The journal is full of vivid impressions of Sioux life, but little deep penetration of Indian thinking is evident. Parkman's understanding of the Indian grew with the years, as he pieced together what he had observed with the findings of later students. In 1846 he was too much under the influence of Henry Rowe Schoolcraft, then considered the leading authority on the Indians, and too full of enthusiasm for that worthy's romantic fictionalization of Indian thought. By 1851, when he opened *The Conspiracy of Pontiac* with a long chapter on the Eastern Indians, he had become familiar with sounder authorities, and had had the opportunity to reconsider his own observations in the light of their views. Fifteen years later, when writing *The Jesuits in North America*, his understanding of the Indian had matured, and he used his knowledge of the Sioux to good advantage in dealing with the Iroquois and Hurons. As student and critic he had closely followed the great advances during his lifetime in Indian studies, keeping in touch with men such as Adolph Bandelier, Lewis H. Morgan, E. G. Squier, and John Bourke who were carrying on investigation in the field. Notes which had meant little to him as he scribbled them in the Oregon Trail journal now took on new significance as he turned over the faded pages; and they formed the basis of many a conclusion advanced in the later histories. But the journal remains the best measure. of Parkman's youthful understanding of the Indian and the West.

It is also one of the great historical records of our national past, for, aside from its bearing on Parkman's work, the Oregon Trail Journal is an invaluable document of Western history. The same good fortune which had lavishly endowed Parkman with a great Boston name, social position, means, and the best education his environment afforded, also gave him the most ample opportunities to witness history in the making that any young historian could imagine. In 1845 at Mackinaw he had encountered Robert Stuart, an old Astorian; and in New York before setting out for the West, Parkman met Ramsay Crooks, another original Astorian who since 1822 had been administrative head of John Jacob Astor's American Fur Company, and was given all the aid and advice that master of the fur trade could supply. He also had an interview with Schoolcraft. Then he passed westward along the old Alleghany frontier and down the Ohio with the trickles of the westward movement which united at St. Louis to form a great stream. In the old metropolis of the West he had discussions with Pierre Chouteau and Pascal Cerré, patriarchs of the Western fur trade, and with Thomas Fitzpatrick, who soon was to become the first Indian agent for the Plains tribes. At West-port he joined forces with a party of three Britishers, supposedly traveling for sport and adventure, but probably not uninterested in the threat that the swelling Oregon emigration represented to Britain's claims in that disputed region, where Joint Occupancy by the two countries was about to be terminated. One of them, Romaine, had accompanied the Jesuit missionary Father De Smet into the buffalo country with Bidwell's historic Oregon party of 1841, while another, Captain Chandler, had seen service in Canada and may have been one of the British agents who abounded in the West as American war talk over the Oregon question rose ever higher. In Westport Parkman also encountered Daniel Boone's grandsons, who were following the family tradition of ever looking to the West; and Passed Midshipman Woodworth, who was carrying dispatches to the Columbia River, notifying the Oregon settlers that Joint Occupancy was about to be terminated. This hotheaded young officer on leave, drunk on the potent brew of Manifest Destiny, was talking loudly of his plan to raise a body of volunteers and capture Santa Fe—a little matter soon to be taken care of by the trader James Magoffin at President Polk's request. At Fort Leavenworth Parkman dined with Colonel Stephen Watts Kearny, who in the previous year had marched his dragoons over much the same route as his guest was to follow, in order to quiet the Indians by a show of force; and that very summer was to lead the Army of the West to Santa Fe and California. On the Oregon Trail Parkman met the ill-fated Donner Party, one of the chief groups of the emigration in that year, and some of the notables of the California uprising which brought the flag to the Pacific. At the Pueblo and on the Santa Fe Trail he encountered some of the forerunners of the Mormon migration, searching for a New Jerusalem free from the persecution of the Gentiles. At Fort Laramie he swapped horses and stories with Paul Dorion, the grandson of the half-breed voyageur who had accompanied Lewis and Clark as far as the South Mandan Villages and who had shared the rigors of Wilson Hunt's journey to found Astoria. He met many of the leading mountain men and traders: Louis Vasquez, Jim Bridger's partner; Pierre Papin, the famous *bourgeois* of Fort Laramie; Jim Clyman, returning disgruntled from the Oregon settlements; Sublette, Sabille, Richard, Bissonnette, Robidoux, and many more. Returning by the Santa Fe Trail, he saw the rear guard of the Army of the West on the march, in the form of Sterling Price's Missouri Volunteers and Andrew Jackson Smith's Mormon Battalion, and he met Marcellin St. Vrain, of the great Southwestern firm of Bent & St. Vrain. He was one year ahead of the great rush to Oregon, of the Mormon trek to Salt Lake, and of the first great swelling of the emigrant tide to California. But while Parkman was on the trail the destiny of the West was being fixed in an American pattern: Frémont was declaring the Bear Flag Republic and preparing the annexation of California, while Zachary Taylor was advancing into Mexico and winning the victories of Palo Alto, Resaca de la Palma, and Monterrey, which paved the way for the collapse of Mexican power in the Southwest in the following year.

But the significance of most of this was missed by the young Bostonian who had long suffered, as one of his Harvard classmates put it, from "Injuns on the brain." He lived so much in the past that he ignored too much of the present, though there is more of the pageant of the West in 1846 in the Journal than in *The Oregon Trail*, which Parkman first conceived merely as a record of adventure rather than as the history which he later saw it truly was. By force of environment and heredity he was blind to the profound social forces at work in the West; by tradition and taste he was contemptuous of the masses, and so he found the company of foreigners more congenial than that of the men who were making America out of the wilderness. He had only amused contempt for the democratic spirit of the emigrants and for the Jacksonianism of the West; he had no understanding of the forces behind the westward movement, which upon reflection he likened to the savage hordes of Huns who swarmed over Europe in the last days of Rome. The Mormons were mere miserable fanatics, "a very dangerous body of men," in his eyes. The easy friendliness of the West grated on his Bostonian reticence, and he was happier with the Indians and with the French-Canadian halfbreeds, to whom he could adopt a superior attitude, than with his fellow Anglo-Americans, who would not tolerate such an attitude. This was all very well for his basic purpose, since it made him concentrate his attention on the savages and leave us this invaluable record of their primitive life; but the missed opportunities are such as to make the Western historian weep, and to add *The Oregon Trail* to the long list of unfinished masterpieces of American literature. Fortunately, some measure of the great book that never was written can be recovered from this journal.

The diary of the Oregon Trail trip is written in pencil on the blue paper of three small notebooks, 4 by $6\frac{1}{4}$ inches, with leather spines and marbled boards. The first volume carries Parkman from New York to Fort Laramie; the second is chiefly devoted to his stay with the Sioux in the Laramie and Medicine Bow Mountains, though it continues the record until the Pueblo and Bent's Fort were reached on the southward leg of the journey; and the third, very scrappy and sketchy because of Parkman's illness and weariness, covers the eastward journey along the Santa Fe Trail to Westport. The route followed by Parkman is shown in as much detail as possible on the endpaper map in this volume, while a chronological itinerary of the trip is provided. There is also another small leather pocket notebook, which contains 1845 law school notes, references to historical books and papers, a diary of a brief historical research trip to New York, Philadelphia, and Baltimore in January 1846; some notes on the early part of the Oregon Trail trip, and accounts of the expenses of the expedition. This notebook is printed as an appendix. In a pocket of this notebook were found the passport issued to Parkman and Shaw by Pierre Chouteau, Jr. & Company, the successors of the American Fur Company as the overlords of the West—and some weather-worn calling cards. No Boston gentleman could go adventuring among the Indians and mountain men without such tokens of gentility!

1846

Volume I

New York,[1] *March 29ᵗʰ, 1846.* I met at Mr. Bellows'[2] a Mr. Kay,[3] a Philadelphia bookseller, a man who, though successful in his calling and very conversant in his business, is one of the Fourierites—a queer combination of worldly shrewdness with transcendental flightiness. His face bespoke it all—it was thin and sallow, and comical in the extreme. He exposed the secrets of the bookselling trade, which he thought the most trickish going.

The little, contemptible faces—the thin, weak, tottering figures—that one meets here on Broadway, are disgusting. One feels savage with human nature.

March 31ˢᵗ. Saw Mr. Schoolcraft.[4] Indian phlegm and apparent immobility may, in part, arise from temperament, but it is also the result of long training. If the child cries, or becomes angry, the mother says, "You will never be a warrior." Under such influences he grows up, accustomed not to suppress the emotion, but to conceal it. The man is encased in this impenetrable exterior—within he may be full of hatred, malice, and suspicion, but none of this appears. He is a statue!

He lives in constant fear. The world, to him, is full of spirits—or of the Great Spirit manifested in a thousand forms. He is surrounded with evil and with good—every voice of nature has its hidden meaning to his ear.

March 31. Mr. Stoddard, the cracked man, who copied my papers, and then tore them.[5]

Harrisburg,[6] *April 1.* The bridge swept away—the fields strewn with logs and debris of the woods by the freshet. The river swollen, but already much subsided—it was calm but swift, and dimpled with eddies. Looked at it at sunset—rafts and canoes floating rapidly down—flat boats passing the ferry with Conestoga waggons—a beautiful scene at that hour.

Man lounging by the river bank. Is it not true, that the lower you descend in education and social position, the more vicious men become?

Carlisle,[7] *April 2nd.* Crossed the Susquehanna in a flat boat filled with quiet, stupid, stout Dutch—men, women, and pretty girls. Some old, octogenarian veterans, and two young, fat dandies with checked breeches and frogged wrappers. The whole was a striking contrast to a corresponding group of Yankees. In the wretched cars, too, the same phlegm and stolidity were apparent—their minds were gone to sleep.

Carlisle is eighteen miles from Harrisburg. As you go to it, the Blue Mts. sweep away on the right—behind them is Sherman's Valley, with —— Gap opening into it. Opposite is a corresponding range, called also, I believe, the Blue Mts. You are traversing Cumberland Valley—level and rich.

The ancient barracks of Carlisle stand in the midst of broad meadows—overlooked from far off by the Blue Mts; and not far distant is the town.

The same range, sweeping southwardly, makes a lofty wall across the west—not enough to exclude the savages who prowled around the place in 1763. Around these barracks Bouquet's[8] army was encamped, and behind those hills lay the scene of their dangerous enterprise!

Carlisle, April 3rd. Mr. Officer *versus* Waldstein, the German optician. Officer wished to bargain for a pair of spectacle glasses: A cheap article was the thing for him. Damn it, he had been a dealer himself, and had put in many hundreds, yes and thousands, too, of glasses. He was an impertinent, obtrusive fellow, always talking, and seemed to take pleasure in exposing his own meanness.

The population here is said to be chiefly of English and Irish descent. The men at the tavern seem to be chiefly lawyers, and are of decent appearance.

Chambersburg, April 3rd. Shippensburg is situated in a country less level than that around Carlisle. The Southern Blue Ridge is nearer, while the northern presents a wide gap. The country is broken into low hills, and continues so to Chambersburg. The day was beautiful.

Pittsburg[h], April 6th. Left Chambersburg in a shamefully crowded coach at 12 o'clock at night. Soon reached Loudon among hills, at the ascent of Cove Mountain. The morning rose beautifully among the mountains. Were passing Cove Mt. Cove Valley near at hand. Tuscarora Mt. on the right—a long range. Soon came upon Sidling Hill. These mts. are not high and run in long parallel ranges. Juniata Crossings, where the bridge passes the Rayston Branch of Juniata. Bloody Run, the scene of Col. Smith's[9] exploit, in a valley beyond Sidling Hill. Bedford, in a valley at the foot of Wills Mt. Dunnings Creek near by.

Passed the Alleganey—the woods quite leafless and lighted by the slant sun. Late in the night reached Ligonier. This was, I suppose, the identical road cut to meet Braddock's road in 1755, and the same by which Bouquet passed.[10] Leaving Greensburg, we came in a few hours to a very rough, hilly country—no mountains. It was a succession of hills and hollows, like waves. Bushy Run was not far on the right, in a deep hollow. Very few people had heard of the battle, and no one could show the scene of it.[11] Turtle Creek was about eight miles farther, and the latter place is some 13 or 14 from Pittsburg. It runs through a very deep hollow, across which the road passes, descending and ascending the banks. A bad place for an Indian surprise. Thence to Pittsburg, the road was more level, till at length the town appeared, on its peninsula, surrounded by the river bluffs.

Steamboat, Ohio River. Yesterday visited Braddock's Field. It is as described by Sparks.[12] B. crossed at a riffle, called Braddock's Riffle, several hundred rods below (above ?)—marched first over flat, and then gently sloping ground to the foot of a knoll, where there is a spring at which the men stopped to drink. The ascent to this knoll is steep; marching up, the army found itself between the two ravines mentioned by Sparks. These flank the knoll or hill—the one on the left is comparatively shallow, with gently sloping sides, but that on the right is a deep, abrupt trench, and from this, as the bullets indicate, the heaviest fire proceeded. The army could scarce have advanced from between these fatal ravines, for beyond the knoll the ground rises into very abrupt hills. A sword was, however, found not long ago, high up the slope of one of these. Bones are still easily to be seen on the field. Returning, I rode down the beautiful shore of the Monongahela—spring was just advancing.

The man who showed me the field could not be persuaded to take any recompense.

Visited, with Mr. Biddle,[13] Bouquet's redoubt, and saw the scanty remnant of the pavement of Fort Pitt.[14]

Grant's Hill is very near the extremity of the peninsula, on the Monongahela side. Where Ft. Du Quesne[15] stood was quite level— but some distance behind, the country rises into hills—and the opposite shores of both rivers presenting lofty declivities, the situation of the town is very fine. The Ohio, too, is flanked by lofty eminences.

The physique of the Pennsylvania country people is very fine, but they strike me as dull and stupid. One of the stage-drivers com- pletely realized my idea of an Indian trader—bluff, boisterous, profane, and coarse. As I watched him, I could not help recurring to certain female friends, and wondering how beings so opposite in all points of person and character could belong to the same species.

"Human nature is the same everywhere"—so says everybody, but does not education make most essential distinctions? Take a Words- worth, for instance, and how little will you find in him in common with the brutish clods who were my fellow passengers across the Alleghanies. Or take any ordinary man of high education, and what sympathies can he have with such?

Read some good history of Penna. and observe out of what com- bination of nations and religions the present population sprang.

"La Belle Riviere"[16] deserves its name. High up, the shores are hilly and picturesque—below, the country is more level.

April 9ᵗʰ. My careless, frank, lighthearted New York acquaintance, P. M.

The man who, on some delay occurring, saluted me with: "I shan't see my wife tonight," this being our first acquaintance. Poor fellow—he was neglected in his youth, and though of a susceptible turn of mind, had—according to his own account—plunged into every kind of excess. About six years ago, he "got religion"—and he lately married. His constitution is injured by hardships when an engineer on a railroad, and he seems of a melancholy temperament; but is most frank and unreserved in his disclosures. He is on his way to see his new wife in Cincinnati.

A precious set of gamblers and ragamuffins on board.

April 10. Passed the rapids at Louisville in the steamboat.

The English reserve or "offishness" seems to be no part of the western character—though I have had no opportunity of observing a gentleman of high standing. I observe this trait in myself—today, for instance, when a young fellow expressed satisfaction that he should accompany me to St. Louis, I felt rather inclined to shake him off, though he had made himself agreeable enough.

My acquaintance, P. M., for whose extensive travels I found it hard to account, is a lecturer on Gouraud's system of Mnemotechny[17] —for which his agreeable person and manner well qualify him.

Spring is beautifully awakening as we descend the Ohio—a hundred shades of green are budding out along the steep declivities; and around the scattered houses are peach trees in rich bloom. It is pleasant to look upon all this, after contemplating the deformity of minds and manners that prevails hereabouts.

April 11ᵗʰ. Passed the site of Fort Mass[i]ac,[18] situated on low, wet land. The banks of the Ohio grow more low as we descend, and now the forests rise from the very margin of the water—it is a wide expanse, with here and there an island.

At night, at Paduca[h], three flat-boats of West Virginian emigrants came on board—they had built their flatboats on Holston River, near which they lived, and had been from the 1ˢᵗ of March descending to the mouth of the Tennessee. The boats were like floating houses—the same, probably, with those originally used in navigating the Ohio. The men were good-looking and hardy, though not so large as the West Pennsylvanians. Some were dressed in red rifle-frocks, and they tell me that Indian leggings are still occasionally used in the Valley. All their domestic implements had an old-fashioned air: chairs with bottoms of ash-slivers—gourd dippers—kettles—anvil—bellows—old bureaus—clothing—bedding—frying pans, etc., etc., were rapidly passed into the steamer. Several old, long-barrelled, flint-locked rifles followed. Conversing with the men, I found them intelligent and open, though apparently not much educated. They were going to Iowa.

We are on the Mississipi, with its rapid muddy current, and low, forest-covered banks.

The men of the emigrant party are manly, open, and agreeable in their manners—with none of the contracted, reserved manner that is common in New Englanders. Neither have the women, who are remarkably good-looking, any of that detestable, starched, lackadaisical expression common in vulgar Yankee women.

The true philosophy of life is to sieze with a ready and strong hand upon all the good in it, and to bear its inevitable evils as calmly and carelessly as may be.

St. Louis, April 15ᵗʰ. A crowd was gathered round the door of the Planters' Hotel,[19] and in the midst stood Henry Clay,[20] talking and shaking hands with any who chose. As he passed away, he asked an old man for a pinch of snuff, at which the mob was gratified, and the old man, striking his cane on the bricks, declared emphatically that Clay was the greatest man in the nation, and that it was a burning shame he was not in the presidential chair. So much for the arts by which politicians—even the best of them—thrive.

April 16ᵗʰ, St. Louis. Quin[21] not yet arrived. Infinite difficulty from contradictory accounts of the Indian country. I went over to Cahokia yesterday—in the midst of a beautiful level country, part forest, part prairie, the whole just awakening into life and bloom. A warm spring day. Herds of wild ponies running about. The forests here are not like ours—they are of a generous and luxuriant growth, and just now fragrant with a multitude of buds and blossoms, and full of the song of birds. They are fettered and interlaced by grape-vines that overrun the whole, like so many serpents.

Cahokia is all French—French houses, with their far-projecting eaves and porches—little French horses—and a little French inn. Madame Jarrot's[22] house is the chief establishment of the place. Calling on the old lady for historic information, I entered a large hall, with a floor of polished oak—oak panels—a large fire-place, and two stair-ways in the rear leading up to the chambers. This hall was the reception room—the only part of the house I saw—but it smacked sufficiently of the Olden Time.

Passed Midshipman Woodward [Woodworth][23] is here (St. Louis), on his way with despatches to Columbia River. He has a wild plan of raising a body of men, and *taking Santa Fe.*

Apr. 19th. How infinite is the diversity of human character! Old M. Cerré[24] of nearly eighty—lively, bright, and active—the old man goes about rejoicing in his own superiority to age—wrapped up in himself, unobservant, impenetrable, impassive. His companion was the reverse—young, silent through bashfulness, observing all, feeling all, and constantly in hostility to external influences—though resolute and determined, acting ever under the burden of constitutional diffidence. How hostile is such a quality to a commanding character. It is the mind as it stamps its character on the bearing and manner, that carries weight—the bold, unhesitating, confident expression has authority—not the forced, sharp, painful expression of resolution, struggling against diffidence. Some men have a sort of power from their very vanity—they are too dull, too impassive to feel a repressing influence from other minds—and thinking themselves the greatest men on earth, they assume a port and voice that imposes a sort of respect. Others there are who, with many of the internal qualities of command, can never assume its outward features—and fail in consequence.

How wide and deep and infinitely various is human nature!—and now the contemplation of it grows more absorbing as its features disclose themselves to view.

Pontiac,[25] says tradition, was killed near Cahokia.[26]

April 20th. Yesterday I went over to the Cahokia side—a beautiful Sunday afternoon. Numbers were passing over for amusement. A lank, half-idiot German was strolling up the banks of the muddy creek, just beyond the landing, with a long spear catching frogs; and two boys were laughing at his ineffectual attempts. I walked up its banks into the woods—it was nothing like our swift and clear mountain waters—all was teeming with life, animal and vegetable, just awakening in the warm spring sunshine. The creek was slow and sluggish—a haunt, in the season, for fever and ague—the luxuriant woods overshadowed it, interlaced with vines like snakes, and all bursting into leaf and flower—full, too, of birds, who would come down to splash and wash themselves in the water—and fragrant with the fresh smell of young leaves and blossoms. The pool was full of frogs and great turtles, sitting on logs, and among slime—now and then a water-snake, with his head lifted high, would writhe his way across—and as you passed by some sheltered cove, the whole water would be alive with minute fishes, skipping out of it in their terror.

The country overflows with game. In returning, I saw on board the boat some twenty sportsmen. Some had a dozen or two of duck slung together—others as many fish as they could carry—perch, bream, gar-fish, buffaloes, cat-fish, etc. The sportsmen were chiefly Germans. No wonder that the French at the old settlements led a merry life of it.

Old Mr. Thomas Fitzpatric[k],[27] the well-know[n] hunter and frontiersman, wrote to Lieut. Abert,[28] of the Topog. Engineers, a letter expressing his opinion of the origin of the western tribes—the following is its substance:

There are two great roots from which all the Indians of the territory east of the Rocky Mts. are derived, "with the exception of a few tribes which have no resemblance whatever to the others, and are the Pawnis [Pawnees], Ari(c)karas, Mandan, Chiennes [Cheyennes], and Kiawas [Kiowas]. These tribes, I think, have originally belonged to the extreme southern parts of the union, or far in Mexico."

Of the Inds. derived from the two roots spoken of, some of those of the first and most numerous stock are the Sioux, Kanzas [Kansas], Osages, Otoes, Iaways [Iowas], Mahas [Omahas], Punkas [Poncas], Saxes [Sauks], and Foxes, "and besides these, there are numbers of others that have a close affinity to them."

"The other root is the Ir(r)oquois, to which belongs the Shawnees, Delawares, Chippewas, Tuscaroras, Mohawks, and indeed, all the N. York and Canadian Inds., together with those bordering on the Lakes, etc."

The Crow language is a dialect of the Sioux.

The Camanches [Comanches] properly belong among the Shoshome [Shoshone] or Snake Inds., as their language is exactly the same; "and with them I would also place the Otaws [Utahs], Ponacs [Bannocks], Sandpitch [Sanpets], Pintas [Pintos], Tinpana [Timpaivats], Utas [Utes], together with all the very numerous small tribes in the great desert west of the Salt Lake, and lying between the Columbia on the North and the Colorado on the south, all of which belong to the Shoshome nation."

On the north fork of the Columbia, the tribes differ entirely in language and character from the above. They are, the Cotonary [Kutenais], Flathead, Collespillum [Kalispels] or Pond de Veil [Pend d'Oreilles], Spogan [Spokan], Nez Percé, Kinsé, Wallowalla [Walla Walla], "and many smaller tribes, all of which speak a similar language, but so harsh and guttural that few of our people have made any progress in attaining it."

The Chinooks belong to the coast Indians, "who differ very much in language and appearance from those of the interior, and, I believe, ought rather to be classed with the Islanders of the Pacific than with any of the inland tribes."[29]

The date of the above is from St. Louis, Feb. 5, 1846.

April 22ⁿᵈ. Rode out to Jefferson Barracks.[30] A beautiful April day— a mingling of clouds, showers, and sunshine, in which the landscape looked most fresh and verdant. This was not a forest country, though there are fine oak-openings at intervals; and across the Mississipi is one great ocean of woods. From the hill overlooking Vuides Pouches [Vide Poche][31] the scene was lovely—the French settlers plant fruit-trees everywhere amongst their picturesque-looking houses, and these were all in bloom. The French are content to live by the produce of their little gardens, knowing nothing and caring nothing for the world beyond their little village. Returning, we were overtaken by a tremendous but momentary shower.

Mr. Fitzpatrick speaks of the high discipline he has seen on war-parties. The chief's authority is absolute. Among the Crows,[32] where he thinks that the government and discipline are better than else-where, this is particularly the case. He has seen the young men erect the chief's lodge for him, cut off the choicest parts of the meat and bring them to him, waiting till he had eaten before they satisfied their own appetite. Boys, even the sons of the highest chief, will attach themselves to a distinguished war-leader and consider them-selves honored in discharging the meanest offices for him. This con-tinues till they have themselves made some *coup* in war, when the apprenticeship ceases. He thinks that the warlike spirit is the stimu-lant that saves the Indian from utter abasement, and mentions, in proof, the wretches whom he met near the Great Salt Lake, who were without this motive.

There is no *permanent* aristocracy—the meanest man may raise himself by talent, and the highest born sink into insignificance from the want of it.

The power of the peace-chiefs arises from their influence over their "soldiers" or counsellors (*comites*).

He thinks them *not* brave—though he mentions some extraor-dinary instances of courage—as that of a Crow whose favorite horse was stolen by a Blackfoot. The Crow went into the B. village where his enemy was sitting at evening before his lodge, with the horse at his side. He was singing his songs, and playing with the haltar which he held in his hand. The Crow took it from him, tied it round the horses' nose, mounted him and rode off, the B. thinking all the while that it was one of the young men of the village who wished to prove the merits of the horse.

Mr. F. is staggered by some of their *medecine* feats. There was a very famous medecine man in a Crow village, who, on going on a war-party, had fasted, retired, sung his songs, etc.; and prophesied that if within two days it rained the party would be unsuccessful, but that otherwise they would return in triumph. They departed—the weather was then fair and had long been so—but on the afternoon of the second day, a tremendous thunder-storm came suddenly up. All the village was instantly in the greatest commotion. The storm passed, and a horseman was seen approaching. He was the *only survivor* of the party.

*April 25*th, *St. Louis.* I have seen a strange variety of characters— Dixon, the nonentity—Ewing, the impulsive, unobserving ardent Kentuckian, who lays open his character to everyone, and sees nothing of those about him—the quiet, sedate, and manly Jacob(s), his companion. These two are going to California.[33]

*April 27*th, *St. Louis.* Rode out at the eleventh hour to see old Pierre Chouteau[34]—three miles from St. Louis. Found his old, picturesque, French house in the middle of the woods—neat Negro-houses, with verandahs—bird cages hung in the porch—chickens chirping about the neat yards. The old man was not well—and could not tell me much. He, however, described Pondiac [Pontiac] as a man six feet high, of very commanding appearance, and, whenever he saw him, splendidly dressed.[35] He used to come to St. Louis on visits.

His son, Liguest P. Chouteau,[36] told me the following, as coming from his father. Pondiac held a high command among Montcalm's Indians.

He was killed at Cahokia, at the instigation of the English. The Spaniards requested his body, and buried it at St. Louis. Mr. L. P. C. promises to look into the church records for the mention of it.[37]

*April 27[8]*th. On board steamer *Radnor.* All our equipments embarked. A number of Kanza[s] or Caw Indians on board. Their gravity seem[s] to me rather *vacant* than *dignified.* When they speak, their gestures are lively and natural.[38]

*April 29*th. On board the boat are a party of Baltimoreans—flash genteel—very showily attired in "genteel undress," though bound for California. They make a great noise at table, and are waited on by the Negroes with great attention and admiration. Also a vulgar New Yorker, with the moustache and the air of a Frenchman, bound for Santa Fe.

The Mississipi is channelled through a rich alluvial soil, giving away and caving in every moment. The small creeks, swollen by the rain, pour down a torrent of muddy waters, trees, and refuse that sweep under the banks at the rate of four miles an hour.

Entered the Missouri in a dreary rain.

The weather is now clear—the banks are loaded with a luxuriant growth of cottonwood, elm, etc. At one of the landings was a grove of trees six feet through, that would have been a noble ornament for a park. Snags are frequent.

A young man on board from St. Louis, bound for Santa Fe, has one brother on the Atlantic, another on the Pacific, and a third on the Mississipi, while he is going to the [Rio Grande] del Norte. So much for American wandering.

Rocky limestone bluffs, with here and there lofty and noble forests.

The river changes constantly—young forests are springing up— old ones are swept away—an old tree completely enveloped in young grape leaves. Sand-bars and new channels constantly forming.

April 31ˢᵗ. The wretched Caw Indians on board were hired, for a pint of whiskey, to sing. The chief, a mean-looking old fellow, expecting a friend at Jefferson, painted, took his sword, and wrapped his blanket about him. In this attire he went ashore, and saluted his acquaintance—a white man—with great cordiality. One of the others indulged in a little fooling with a fat Negro, who danced while the Indian sang.

Henry Chatillon[39] mentions an Ogillalah [Oglala] chief of great authority, who made nothing of killing his subjects. In a drunken revel he would place his robe in the midst of them, and not one, even then, would dare to disturb it, for fear of the consequence. He was killed, not long ago, by the friends of some of his victims.

May 1ˢᵗ. The Indians are playing cards about the deck. They have a paper for begging, and one of them sat on the deck collecting contributions yesterday.

May 2ⁿᵈ. The landing at Independence[40]—the storehouses—the Santa Fe waggons—the groups of piratical-looking Mexicans, employees of the Santa Fe traders, with their broad, peaked hats— the men with their rifles seated on a log, ready for Oregon. Among the waggons behind, some of the Mexicans were encamped. The Baltimoreans got shamefully drunk, and one of them, an exquisite in full dress, tumbled into the water.

Speyer,[41] the Santa Fe trader, has an immense number of goods on board.

Walked a mile or two into the woods at evening—had felt a little "hipped."[a] The reawakening of old thoughts and feelings, recurring along with the whole train of subsequent observations and experiences, is very agreeable. I felt as I had felt many years before, but I was no longer the same man, either in knowledge or in character.

C. W. of St. Louis, who harnessed his mule into his waggons, and drove off for Santa Fe, bent on seeing. He seemed about eighteen years old, open, enterprising, and thoughtless. He will come back a full-grown man.

Westport, Mo., April [May] 5ᵗʰ. Rode to the village of Westport[42] from the landing, where we put up at the solid log house of Col. Chick.[43] A beautiful morning. Hipped and wavering. The Indians passed us, travelling towards their homes. Mules and horses in abundance.

Rode from Westport to find the Sac [Sauk][44] encampment. They had gone—but we had a sight of the great green ocean of the prairies; for the forest terminates at this place, where also is the boundary of the State of Missouri.

A lofty forest, all fresh and verdant in the spring—then a tract of shrubbery and crab-trees full of fragrant blossoms—and then the great level expanse of prairie. The Kansas Inds., arriving again at their native haunts, stopped and sat in a circle on the grass to have a talk. Shawnees dressed in shirts and handkerchiefs passed us on horseback. Their reserve, together with that of the Del[aware]s and Wyandots, is near here.[45] They are farmers, and demi-civilised. The Dels. have the reputation of being very brave and enterprising, and are called "Grandfather." They are constantly wandering and fight-

[a] Depressed.—Ed.

ing in the direction of the Mts. The Wyandots are considered very intelligent.

The emigrants, encamped at some distance, are choosing officers. W[oodworth] seems to be making a fool of himself. We have joined Chandler's party.[46] Bought an excellent horse, for which I paid too much.[b]

Col. C[hick] is an excellent old man, and his house stands nobly on the bluff above the river. The weather is beautiful—the scenery noble—we are in the very region of enterprise—all promises well.

April [May] 6th. Yesterday rode on Hendrick across the Kanzas River to visit the Wyandots, lately removed from Sandusky. The ground but partially cleared—a trader lives amongst them, who conducted us to a school, kept up by the tribe out of their annuities. They are called "Uncle" by the other nations, and have not the wandering propensities of the Dels. and Shaws., their neighbors.

Bought two mules[c] today at Wes[t]port, and rode over on Pontiac from Kanzas to bring them down. Quin and I each took one, by a haltar twisted round the pommel of the saddle. The thunder had growled incessantly all the afternoon. Just after we set out, a terrific storm began. The lightning was very bright, and followed on the instant by crashing peals of thunder, louder than I ever heard. The woods were half obscured by the torrents of rain, which swelled the brooks so rapidly that passing was difficult in one or two place[s]. We drove on our horses—the mules trotted behind—and we scoured along rapidly, till at last we saw the logs of Col. Chick's house and barn up the side of the hill, and rode to the primitive little stable, completely drenched.

The freshness and fragrance of the crab-tree groves along the edge of the prairie, just before the storm came on, was delightful. I rode Pontiac at a gallop among the paths and openings, exalting in the possession of a fine buffalo horse.

May 7th. Rode by vile roads, through the woods, to Independence. The clouds in this region are afflicted with an incontinence of water

b $60.—1846 Account Book.
c For $75.—1846 Account Book.

—constant alternations of showers and sunshine—everything wet, bright, and fresh. Plenty of small game and gorgeous birds. At Independence, every store is adapted to furnish outfits—the public houses were full of Santa Fe men and emigrants. Mules, horses, and waggons at every corner. Groups of hardy-looking men about the stores, and Santa Fe and emigrant waggons standing in the fields around. While I was at the Noland House,[47] the last arrival of emigrants came down the street with about twenty waggons, having just broken up their camp near Independence and set out for the great rendezvous about 15 miles beyond Westport. What is remarkable, this body,[48] as well as a very large portion of the emigrants, were from the extreme western states—N. England sends but a small proportion, but they are better furnished than the rest. Some of these ox-wagons contained large families of children, peeping from under the covering. One remarkably pretty little girl was seated on horseback, holding a parasol over her head to keep off the rain. All looked well—but what a journey before them! The men were hardy and good-looking. As I passed the waggons, I observed three old men, with their whips in their hands, discussing some point of theology—though this is hardly the disposition of the mass of the emigrants.

I rode to Westport with that singular character, Lieut. Woodworth. He is a great busybody, and ambitious of taking a command among the emigrants. He tells me that great dissentions prevail in their camp—that no organisation had taken place, no regular meetings been held—though this is to be done on Saturday and Sunday, and the column to get under weigh on Monday.

Woodworth parades a revolver in his belt, which he insists is necessary—and it may be a prudent precaution, for this place seems full of desperadoes—all arms are loaded, as I have had occasion to observe. Life is held in little esteem.

This place, Westport, is the extreme frontier, and bears all its characteristics.

As we rode home, we met a man itching for Oregon, but restrained by his wife—at McGee's[49] at Westport, there was a restless fellow who had wandered westwards from N. Y. [New York] in search of work, which he had not found; and now he was for Oregon, working his passage as he could not supply himself with provisions.

Met at McGee's Parks, the chief of the Shawnees, who keeps a store here—a fine-looking man, scarcely distinguishable from a white. He was educated by Cass.[50] He told me the story of the wanderings of the Shawnees, and of their being attacked by the Senecas, whom they at last completely defeated. The Senecas then employed the Wyandots to attack them, as they passed down the Ohio; but the latter, instead of this, made a treaty with them. The Wyandots kept the council fire of the western Inds.

Everybody here is full of praises of the courage of the Delawares. They are by far greater wanderers and hunters than any of the other half-civilised tribes. In small parties they spend years among the most remote and hostile tribes—they will fight with a courage like desperation, and, it is said, completely awed the Spaniards at Santa Fe.

Plenty of vagabond Inds. are about here, trading at the different stores, and getting drunk.

I saw many at the store of Mr. Boone,[51] a grandson of Daniel.

May 9th. After great trouble yesterday with one of our mules, bought of Fogel [Vogel],[52] who played the deuce in the cart, and had to be changed—we got under weigh. Left Westport this morning —the cart stuck several times in the mud, and delayed us much. We passed out through the Shawnee country. Stopped at noon to eat and rest animals by the side of a creek. An old Caw Ind. in full paint came riding up, gave his hand, and sat down to smoke.

Presently the whole tribe passed along on their way to Westport, on miserable little horses. Some were in full costume, but the greater part were ragged vagabonds, with bad or vacant faces, and a very mean appearance. They crowded around, men, women, and children, the first offering their hands as they came up. Many had bows and arrows—all were adorned with wampum or beads, and often a snake skin. In the beautiful country we had passed, Shawnees were constantly riding by on a canter, upon little stubborn ponies, and with their calico shirts fluttering in the wind.

Not far from where we met the Caws, there was a religious meeting of the Shawnees. Most of those present were good-looking—much

more robust than the Caws, and well-dressed in the English fashion.
The place was the Methodist meeting house.

We traveled a few hours and encamped by the Caw River. The
horses, not used to hobbles, were in a great quandary. A vagabond
Caw sat sometime by our camp, talking by signs, and expecting some
food. This river is the boundary line of the Dels. and Shawnees.

The vexations and deprivations of such a journey do indeed
resolve a man into his first elements—and bring out all his nature.

May 10th. Left camp and crossed the Kanzas by the Ferry,[53] after
much difficulty. The cart had to be unloaded and so carried up the
steep road. Travelled only eight miles and encamped in a beautiful
prairie—abundance of flowers—the borders of the beautiful oak-
openings we had traversed—the shrubbery along the course of a
little stream—the occasional rich and sunlit groves—and the emerald
swells of the vast plain, made a beautiful scene.

This was a part of the Delaware country. Many of the tribe have
been killed in their incessant wars and wanderings. I hear but one
opinion expressed of their extraordinary bravery and enterprise. One
of them brought us in some eggs, and lay for some time talking by
our camp. He had heard of the Dels. being made women by the Six
Nations.

The horses gave great trouble in hobbling.

May 11th. A beautiful day. Travelled slowly through the country
of the Delawares. Fine, swelling prairies. Stopped for nooning at a
creek in a wooded bottom, turned the horses loose, lunched in the
shade, bathed, and conversed. Resumed our course—very hot—lines
of beautiful woods ran along the bottoms, intersecting our road, with
invariably a stream running through them—a most grateful refreshment in the heat. At one of these places we met a party of Del. Inds.
—men, women, and children—returning on their ponies from a
trapping expedition. This tribe is constantly diminishing from the
numbers that are killed in their wanderings.

Soon after, the white walls of Leavenworth[54] appeared in the
distance, and in a level meadow by a wooded stream we saw the
horses and tents of our English friends—a welcome sight.

May 12ᵗʰ. Still at camp. Rode to Fort L. and saw Col. Kearn(e)y.[55] Then, with Q., went over to Kickapoos,[56] four miles. All half-civ[ilized] Ind. villages in wooded countries are the same thing—straggling paths through woods and underbrush, with here and there a log house—a creek winding through the midst. Inds. are most provoking beings. We addressed one who was lying at full length in the sun before his house—he would not give the least sign of recognising our presence. We got from the rest nothing but silence, hesitation, or false directions. Pottawattamies [Pottowatomies][57] in a neighboring settlement, with their *pukivi*ᵈ lodges. Some of the scenery—the rich, sunlit, swelling prairies with bordering hills and groves—was very beautiful.

Returning, we stopped at the trader's. Plenty of Inds. around with their little scraggy ponies—he characterises them as ungrateful—the more they get, the more they expect, and become suspicious in the extreme. We were hot and tired; and the trader showed us into a neat, dark, and cool parlor, where he gave us iced claret and an excellent lunch—a most welcome refreshment. His mistress, a yellow woman, brimful of merriment, entertained us with her conversation.

Stopped at the Fort—sat down to the Col.'s table with Romain[e][58] and the Capt.[59]—the last Madeira, the last fruits that we shall enjoy for a long time. This over, rode to camp with Romain.

May 13ᵗʰ. Broke up camp at the meadow. Travelled several miles, and took the wrong turning to the road—none of the party had been on this route before—the ordinary emigrant route is farther south. Their [the Englishmen's] waggon stuck badly in the mud several times and had to be unloaded. At last we found ourselves *close by the Kickapoo trader's*. Struck off on a bye road—wandered over wide prairies for a long time, and at last struck the trail of two companies of dragoons who went out yesterday to build a new fort up the Missouri.[60] This was the right path. Nooned and passed on. Noble, swelling prairies varied with wooded declivities, groves, and scattered trees. Riding at the head of the line and looking back, our straggling line of horsemen and animals stretched over the plain for a mile or more, and on the horison the white waggons were slowly moving

ᵈ Bark.—Ed.

along. We have 23 horses and mules. A severe thunder-storm at camp. The Capt. very solicitous about his horses, moving about morning and night in an old plaid to watch them. Wolves seen at evening on the prairie. The thunder and the wolves, who approached at night, frightened the horses. Pondiac and several others broke their haltars.

May 14th. Great trouble at a stream. Waggon stuck. As we were on the [point of] departure after nooning, Pondiac stepped down to drink, and then trotted off on the back trail for the settlements. I followed, impeded by gun and accoutrements. He led me a chace of about 5 miles to the wooded creek where the waggon [had stuck?] —for mile after mile of beautiful prairie, swell after swell, he kept trotting on before me—sometimes I would be close upon him, and then he would start again. Tried to head him but in vain. Nearly caught him at a stream where he stopped to drink—slid from my horse but my rifle bothered me—Hendrick darted back, and I could not catch the trail rope. He stopped again at the creek aforesaid— slid down and got the rope—a joyful moment. Had much trouble in getting the reluctant brutes back to camp, which meanwhile had moved on some miles. At last, saw on the green swell of a hill, beyond a line of woods, the white tents and the band of horses in the meadow below.

May 15th. After riding all the morning, we came to what we thought was Clough Creek, the place where the old dragoon trail[61] of last year diverges to the left and leaves the new trail we have followed. No such divergency appeared. The Capt. and I went forwards as "videttes"—waited long for the party by a creek, and saw them coming at last with four dragoons. They told us we had passed the place where we should have diverged a day and a half ago—that our present road led to the Iowa village, and thence to the emigrants' road to St. Joseph's.[62] So we determined to keep on. This morning, fired at a wolf among the horses, and missed.

Sunday, May 16th. Advanced as far as a deep creek, where we had great trouble with the waggons. Nooned here—a beautiful spot, where in the woods about the stream was a variety of birds. S[haw] and I set out in advance to find the Iowa village, but without success. Struck the St. Joseph's trail. Followed it for many miles over a vast, swelling prairie with scarcely any trees in sight, where the advanced waggon looked like a mere speck on the green surface. Camped on a spot occupied about a week since by the Mormons,[63] whose cattle had eaten the grass close. Up to this time, our progress has been very slow—about thirty miles in three days. This Mormon trail is much better than the previous ones.

May 17th. Rode for nearly twenty miles before we nooned. The heat was intense. Stripped off all superfluous clothing. Very few camping places; and at these the Mormon cattle had eaten the grass. Rode on—the expanse of prairie stretched for mile after mile without tree or bush—we ascended swell after swell and could see nothing but the vast, green level. At last, turned aside from the road to a clump of trees in the distance. Camped, and Q. and I tried a bath. The water was the same that we have had lately, only worse—quite warm and full of frogs and snakes—no current, but plenty of weeds and mud. We struggled through bushes, reeds, and mud till we came to a nasty pool, rich in mud, insects and reptiles, where we washed as we could. Dor-bugs swarmed in the prairie and camp.

May 18th. This morning all the horses ran off for at least a mile, and gave us great trouble to head them back. Both Pondiac and Hendrick broke their hobbles. Nooned at an old encampment of the Mormons. Prairie without a tree for many miles—a good road, but no place to camp. Travelled about twenty miles, and then our party turned off to a piece of woods some distance from the road. The Englishmen kept on—the devil knows where. Their hunter, Sorel,[64] had kept in advance about a mile, and they followed. Sorel is dissatisfied about something.

May 19th. The Englishmen were encamped about half a mile in advance. We advanced—passed a beautifully wooded stream, which we supposed to be the Little Nemaha[65]—kept on till we had made about ten miles, and nooned. The Englishmen, as usual, were impatient to get on the moment they had snatched a dinner—we chose to remain, as our mules were much tired. So the parties were again separated. Romaine, virtually the leader of the other party, seems jealous of his authority and desirous of having all his own way. Capt. C. and his brother are of a different stamp—very good-natured, sociable fellows.[66] We let them move on and followed at our leisure. Came to camp alongside of them, having made about twenty miles (as we did yesterday).

May 20th.   Last night, were awakened by tremendous peals of thunder, quite different from any in our part of the country—beginning with a tremendous burst, they ran reverberating around the whole firmament. The rain that followed was like a cataract, and beat through the tent in a thick drizzle, wetting everything. The lightning was very intense and brilliant. Lay by today until after-noon, when the restlessness of Romaine impelled his party to move. We, against our judgment, consented to follow, not caring to appear obstinate—so broke up camp and moved off. Intensely sultry and oppressive, and when the sun came out it was terribly hot. The sky was hung with clouds, and thunder muttered incessantly. As we rode on, things grew worse, till the whole prairie and the grove grew almost black in the stormy shadow, and the lightning kept flashing vividly. The masses of cloud in front grew blacker and more ragged—the thunder more and more threatening—till both horses and men took alarm, and we all rushed forward in a medley, running or gallopping, and the muleteers lashing and shouting. We wheeled round behind a line of trees—tore off our saddles—hobbled the frightened brutes—seized the tent and thrust the pole into the ground. No sooner was this done than a sharp flash and a crashing peal came upon us, and the rain descended like a torrent.

We do not know our exact position, but we are on the Mormon trail, and probably within ten days of the Platte.

Henry says that at Laramie, a common clay pipe sells for half a dollar—a three-bit calico shirt for four dollars—a pair of the very coarsest pantaloons for ten dollars—a gallon of whiskey for thirty-five dollars, etc.[67]

The trading companies have their head quarters, whence single traders are sent out to winter in the several Indian villages, where they are usually received in the chief's lodge, and treated with great distinction.[68]

May 21st. It kept raining over night, and in the morning the road was in a wretched state. Sultry and showery all the morning. At noon, the road being a little improved, we set out. It still threatened rain. We passed the recent grave of one of the Mormons, who had been buried near the road. The other party were in advance, and discovered a cow, straggled, no doubt, from the Mormons. They gave chace and drove her back on the road, where we headed her, and various awkward attempts were made to noose her. After a while, she was let alone and gently driven along before us by the Captain. This would have done very well, had not a tremendous gust of rain come down suddenly upon us. The horses all turned tail to it, and stood stock still; and the cow ran off, back on the road. A rifle ball was sent after her ineffectually; and the Captain, in defiance of the storm, cocking one of his huge buffalo pistols, galloped off in pursuit, and both soon vanished in the diagonal sheets of rain. Presently he and the cow appeared looming through the storm, the Capt. shouting to us that he had shot her. He rode behind her, driving her along, which was very easy as she was shot through the body. As we approached the woods where we were to encamp, something was seen that looked like a tent, on which the cow was allowed to fall into the rear, for fear of lighting on her owner; but the alarm proving false, she was driven to camp, and at last finished by Romaine, who shot two bullets into the poor devil. We feasted on her at night.

May 22nd. Left camp and found the road very muddy from last night's rain. The road was still over the open prairie, with here and there a little wood about the streams. Our cart got through some of these with difficulty, and the waggon was soon "stalled" and had to be unladen—this happened several times, and the other party were so much detained that only the Capt., who was in advance, came to nooning with us. All this day we had milk from the dead cow's udders—and at this nooning-place, we found *another cow*, which we also milked and drove on with us. Camped by a beautiful stream, unknown, but supposed to be the Little Vermillon,[69] and I enjoyed a most delightful bath in a deep, clear pool, surrounded by beautiful woods, full of birds, and at that time lighted by the setting sun.

Pondiac will scarcely eat, he is so annoyed by his hobbles—the horses around the camp all night after salt, of which we had given them a little. Made eighteen or twenty miles today—cannot tell where we are, as not one of the party has been on the route.

Henry says that there is a great difference in point of *virtue*, between the women of different [tribes]—that many of them are very debauched, while the Sioux (among whom, however, he has a squaw) are comparatively very chaste. He mentions a custom among them of a woman's giving a feast, at which females are invited who, laying their hands on a gun or some similar implement, are required to declare whether or not they have been guilty of any breach of chastity. This solemn form of declaration seems tantamount to an oath. He saw a young Sioux girl cry all night because, as she stepped out, a young man took an indelicate liberty with her person.[70]

I am more and more convinced of the differences between tribes.

May 23rd. Leaving camp this morning, we had gone but a mile or two, Boisverd[71] driving the cow along, when we came to a muddy gully where our cart passed, but the waggon stuck as usual. Then came, as a matter of course, the curses, shouts, and blows of their muleteer Wright;[72] but all in vain, and the waggon had to be unloaded. A mile or two more, and we came to a belt of woods, and the long-looked-for Big Blue.[73] It was so high with the late rains—though subsiding rapidly—that we had to raft across. Romaine, with his usual activity, waded across to ascertain the depth. Plenty of wood grew on the banks, and in an hour or two the raft was made, the Canadians working like dogs in the water and out of it. Romaine was, as usual, noisy and obstrusive, offending the men by assuming the direction of affairs of which he knew nothing.[74] The fellow over-boils with conceit. Got across, after a fatiguing work—dined, and advanced about five miles. Coming to camp by a creek, we saw waggons ascending a distant swell.

Delorier [Deslauriers] was particularly active and talkative at his work—he is a true specimen of Jean Baptiste.[75]

Henry mentions the singular ceremony of the white robe. The possessor of a white buffalo robe gives a feast, at which he gives away all his possessions to his very lodge—his horses, arms, food, and all. This ceremony entitles him to much respect, and he is usually amply remunerated in a few days by those to whom he has given his property.[76]

The *medicines* of the various tribes differ. A red-headed wood-pecker is great medicine with the Sioux—a rattle-snake with the Caws, etc. The Caws I saw wore snake-skins.[77]

The custom prevails among the Sioux of a son-in-law not speaking to his mother-in-law, who never enters his lodge. He veils his face when she passes. A squaw does not mention her husband by name, but as the *father of her child* (naming him). How shall we account for these extraordinary customs?

A widow has her season of mourning, during which she gashes her legs frightfully.[78]

May 24ʰ. We have struck upon the old Oregon Trail, just beyond the Big Blue, about seven days from the Platte. The waggons we saw were part of an emigrant party, under a man named Keatley [Kearsley].[79] They encamped about a mile from us behind a swell in the prairie. The Capt. paid them a visit, and reported that the women were damned ugly. Kearsley and another man came to see us in the morning. We had advanced a few miles when we saw a long line of specks upon the level edge of the prairie; and when we approached, we discerned about twenty waggons, followed by a crowd of cattle. This was the advanced party—the rest were at the Big Blue, where they were delayed by a woman in child-bed. They stopped a few miles farther to breakfast, where we passed them. They were from the western states. Kearsley had complained of want of subordination among his party, who were not very amenable to discipline or the regulations they themselves had made. Romaine stayed behind to get his horse shod, and witnessed a grand break-up among them. The Capt. [of the train] threw up his authority, such was the hurly-burly—women crying—men disputing—some for delay—some for hurry—some afraid of the Inds. Four waggons joined us—Romaine urged them, and thereby offended us. Kearsley is of the party.

Advanced twenty-five miles to Turkey Creek. Several more waggons are just now in sight.

The great Sioux chief Bull Bear,[80] whom H. described as possessed of such authority and power, and commanding such dread in the village, was unable to restrain his party from attacking Frapp [Fraeb].[81] Comp[are] this with what Fitzpatrick says of the discipline of war-parties.

May 25ᵗʰ. One advantage arises from the emigrants—they give us milk. Put Hendrick into the cart. Soon came to an infernal gully— mud four or five feet deep—waggon stuck—oxen of the emigrants drew it out, though the mud came to bottom of waggon. Hendrick would not pull—oxen put to cart, and drew it out. Pondiac and Hendrick both came down floundering in attempting to cross. Emigrants' waggons themselves had great difficulty. Passed on to Elm Creek—a deep, rocky stream. Axle of waggon broke short in crossing, and we stayed for a new one to be put on. Proceeded after this delay—emigrants ahead. Overtaken by a thunderstorm and well drenched. Put up the tent in the mud, and the fury of the wind nearly threw it down. Cleared up beautifully towards evening.

The four emigrant waggons are farther on.

May 26ᵗʰ. Nooned on Black Walnut Creek. Put Pond. in harness. Afternoon, not well—sat slouching on horse, indulging an epicurian reverie—intensely hot—dreamed of a cool mountain spring, in a *forest* country—two bottles of Champagne cooling in it, and cut-glass tumblers, full of the sparkling liquor.[82] A wide expanse of perfectly flat prairie—rode over it hour after hour—saw wolves—and where they had dug up a recent grave. Turkey buzzards and frequent carcases of cattle; camped on Wyatt's Creek. Twenty miles or so.

May 27ᵗʰ. Are doubtful where we are. Set out from camp, and travelled eight or ten miles. Henry went forward with S.'s gun to shoot a prairie hen—came gallopping back to say that he had seen

antelope and borrow my rifle. His hasty approach made some of the
party think the Pawnees were on us. He could not kill any, but found
some curlew eggs. Nooned on a nameless creek and set out again—
bad rain, like last night—evening cleared up beautifully—we suppose
ourselves on the Little Blue. Mules suffer much.

Among the Sioux, a species of penance, or act to secure the favor
of the manito[u], is to fasten a buffalo's skull to a hole through the
sinews of the back, and to run until it tears out—or rots away (comp.
Mandans).[83]

May 28th. Wolves all night. Camped on Little Blue. Saw wolves and
two antelopes in the morning. Grave of a child 4 yrs. old—May
1845.[84]

Henry hunted in vain for antelopes. Nooned on Little Blue. Made
a very long afternoon march—hour after hour over a perfect level—
not very well. Sorel wounded an antelope. After twelve miles riding,
approached Little Blue again. Immense masses of blue, lurid clouds
in the west shadowed the green prairie, and the sun glared through
purple and crimson. As we drew near the valley of the stream, a
furious wind, presaging a storm, struck us. We galloped down in the
face of it—horses snorting with fear. Rode to the ground—up went
the tent and on came the storm.

May 29th. Left camp—saw plenty of antelopes and fired at one
across the river. Kept along the Little Blue, and just before nooning
had great trouble in crossing a tributary creek [Pawnee Creek?].
As we (we) were dining, Henry brought in a fine antelope—a very
welcome acquisition as our bacon is almost gone. Afternoon—
more antelope and turkeys. Scenery very beautiful and prairie-
like. The Capt. very merry, riding off in all directions and running a wolf over the prairie. Bones of game scattered in all
directions, indicating a surround.[85] Moved rapidly and merrily
—camped on a beautiful plain, hard by the woods that fringe
the Little Blue. Flowers—prairie peas—*pommes blanches.*[86]

Mounted guard for the first time last night—three hours. Middle watch to me and Delorier tonight. Delorier is a true Canadian—all his acts and thoughts are subject to the will of his *bourgeois* [boss].

Met yesterday in a rough meadow by the Little Blue two Delaware Inds. returning from a hunt—one of them a remarkably handsome fellow.

May 30th. Made a very hard day's work—came more than thirty miles from the Blue to the Platte. We had all along mistaken our route, thinking that we were less advanced than in fact we were. Soon after leaving the Blue, saw two men, Turner and another, come back from the emigrants[87] in search of an ox. They set us right, telling us we were 26 miles from the river. Just before seeing us, they had met six Pawnees, who wanted to change horses, and laid hand on the bridle of one of them, till threatened with a pistol—the only weapon they had. They told this to Sorel, and then foolishly continued their journey. Nooned early at a bad creek. Antelopes. A level plain—the low, blue line of the Platte Buttes in the distance. Badger holes. Towards sunset, drew near the Buttes—a range of low, broken, sandy hills—and after a long and gradual ascent, saw the Platte from the summit—apparently one vast, level plain, fringed with a distant line of forest—the river ran invisible in sluices through the plain, with here and there a patch of woods like an island. Camped late—an emigrant came to us, on his way to look for Turner—he told us that Robinson's party were encamped three miles off—that the four waggons that had joined us, and got ahead a few days ago, were in advance—and that a large hunting-party of Pawnees were encamped close to them.

This afternoon, passed a very large Pawnee trail, and a small foot-trail recently travelled.

May 31st. Early this morning, the Pawnees, about 30 in number, passed a short distance from our camp—a hunting-party—no women, these being probably planting corn at the village. Rather mean-looking fellows, each with a bow and arrows—led horses, loaded with dry meat. The chief walked behind—I gave him a piece of tobacco, which very much pleased him.

When three or four miles from camp, overtook the emigrants—

Robinson's party of about 40 waggons—who had just set out. Turner had got in safe. One fellow had inscribed his waggon "54°48'"[88]— a mean set, chiefly from the east. A very cold, raw, disagreeable day, with a violent freezing wind, which benumbed us—rain soon followed, which wet us through. Keathley [Kearsley], with the 4 waggons that had joined us, was ahead about a mile. Disorder in both these parties.

Went twelve miles and camped—miserably cold and dismal—wet through, with no means of getting dry—a set, cold rain. Wrapped ourselves up as we could and went to sleep in the tent, while the emigrants kept on.

The Pawnees say that buffalo are two days ahead.

June 1. The emigrants were encamped a mile ahead of us. Started early and passed them. Weather clear, but astonishingly cold and bitter. Road through the flat bottom of the Platte, with the low line of sand buttes just visible on right and left. Keathly's four waggons which had joined us, and left us when the axle broke, were ahead— soon came up to them. At nooning, the weather changed—the sky was filled with dark windy clouds, and sharp, cold gusts of rain kept coming on. We started, however, again passing Keathly, who had kept on, and travelling always in the face of an infernal bitter driving mixture of icy wind and sleet. Once it came so furiously, driving in horizontal lines, that all the animals turned tail to it and could not be moved—cart, waggon and all turned about. With Pontiac in the cart, we came 25 miles, and camped near Plum Creek.

There are plenty of emigrants ahead. Among the different bands that we have passed, there is considerable hostility and jealousy, on account of camping places, etc.

June 2nd. Soon after leaving camp, saw in the prairie a little mound of earth with a buffalo skull on top, and two horse skulls with other bones at the sides. Henry thought that it was a place where the Pawnees had buried a favorite horse. Passed a large village of prairie dogs. The 4 emigrant waggons keep along with us. Many antelopes—three of them killed. Buffalo wallows, and fresh traces of the animals. A broad, level bottom, with lines of low buttes on each side. Nooned early, and set out again very soon, much to *our* dissatisfaction. Q.'s wilfulness is roused, and he wishes to push on alone to Laramie. Travelled long over the level bottom—no wood—nothing but musquitoes, mud, buffalo-wallows, and their dung. Camped on this flat. The weather is become warm.

June 3rd. Cold and gusty again. Travelled slowly for 10 miles over a most monotonous plain. After nooning, Henry went off to look for buffalo. I gave him Pont. to ride, and accompanied him on Hendrick. Passing towards the hills, we saw on the intervening flat plenty of wolves and antelopes, and at last H. discerned a black speck slowly ascending one of the distant hills. It was a buffalo cow, and we set of[f] at a gallop after her—the wind blew directly towards her, but as we entered the hills, we saw several buffalo in a distant ravine, who scented us and began to ascend the hills in Indian file, appearing and disappearing in the gorges. Presently more and more appeared, but all, getting wind of us, got in motion. Henry's blood was up. We spurred along through ravines, and getting to leeward, managed to approach one little herd of cows. I held the horses—Henry crept over the hill and fired. I saw the buffalo come running down the hollow, and soon perceived that we had shot one. Skinned and cut her up, and then saw another herd, at which Henry again fired and brought down another cow. By the time we had finished dissecting her, a devil of a cold, penetrating, driving storm of sleet came upon us, and as, with the meat at our saddles, we rode from the hills and over the prairie to find the camp, we were well drenched. An infernal storm—temperature about 32°. Rode through a village of prairie dogs, and envied the little varmints their snug habitations. At camp, learned that Sorel and others had been unsuccessfully chasing them.

June 4th. This morning rode off towards the hills with Q. and the Capt. to look for buffalo—no success. Returning, met Henry on his little poney Wyandot; he came to say that 11 boats were coming down the river from Laramie. Gave my letter to Q. to be delivered, and rode back two or three miles after the waggons to get a letter H. had given me, intended for Papin,[89] the *bourgeois* of the boats. On my return, found the boats lashed to the bank waiting—flat-bottomed

—with 110 packs each—one month from Laramie—aground every day, for the Platte is now low, and is very shallow and swift at best. The crews were a wild-looking set—the oarsmen were Spaniards [Mexicans]—with them were traders, F[rench] and American, some attired in buckskin, fancifully slashed and garnished, and with hair glued up in Ind. fashion. Papin a rough-looking fellow, reclining on the leather covering that was thrown over the packs.

I saw Woodworth here—his party are close behind.

Papin reports that the Mormons are a few miles ahead—that the Pawnees have taken 10 of their horses, and whipped one of their men into camp—that the Sioux have been out in force, and driven off the buffalo—all this alarms the Capt. exceedingly.

In the afternoon, made 10 miles or so and encamped on a beautiful spot. Hills not unlike those of Sicily.[90]

Henry says that (that) the Pawnees are much more subordinate to their chiefs than the Sioux—that a chief of the former can with impunity whip one of the young men, but that if a Sioux chief does it, he is sure to have some of his horses killed. The Crows are under better regulation than the Sioux. Observe how this is in the Sioux village, and comp. with Murray's acct. of Pawnees.[91]

June 5th. Shaw and Henry went off for buffalo. H. killed two bulls. The Capt. very nervous and old-womanish at nooning—he did not like the looks of the hills, which were at least half a mile off—there might be Inds. there, ready to pounce on the horses. In the afternoon, rode among the hills—plenty of antelope—lay on the barren ridge of one of them, and contrasted my present situation with my situation in the convent at Rome.[92]

June 6th. Emigrants' cattle all driven off by the wolves for many miles—their guard having fallen asleep. This detained us; and Q. and I, with Henry, went off to run buffalo. Rode 6 miles—saw a herd of bulls and several of cows—set after the former full-drive. Could not bring Pont. close up—wounded, but killed none. Q. shot one. Got separated from the others—rode for hours westwardly over the prairie—saw the hills dotted with thousands of buffalo. Antelopes

—prairie-dogs—burrowing owls—wild geese—wolves, etc. Finding my course wrong, followed a buffalo-track northward, and about noon came out on the road. Awkward feeling, being lost on the prairie. Waggons not yet come—rode east eight miles and met them. At the same time saw H. and Q. coming down from the hills. They had been looking for me 3 hours. Camp near Side Fork.[93] Only *bois de vache.*[e] Very much fatigued, having ridden some forty miles.

June 7th. Nothing special occurred. Walked all day along South Fork—no wood in sight—all prairie, and distant hills. The lagging pace of the emigrants—the folly of Romaine—and the old womanism of the Capt. combine to disgust us. We are resolved to push on alone, as soon as we have crossed the South Fork, which will probably be tomorrow. Saw rattlesnakes and other curious snakes.

June 8th. Sorel, Romaine, and two of the emigrants went off yesterday morning for buffalo, and did not return at night. At nooning yesterday, four men came to us from the Mormon (?) party ahead, saying that, a few days since, ten of their horses had been run off in broad daylight by several hundred Indians, at whom they had fired, and that lately they had lost a hundred and twenty-three cattle, of which they were then in search. Some of our emigrants also thought they had seen Indians when after their cattle—so that there was some anxiety as to the four men. The Capt. declares, "It is a serious business, travelling through this cursed wilderness." This morning, we set out to cross the South Fork, intending to wait there for them.

Approaching the ford,[f] we saw the party of emigrants encamped opposite—they have not cattle enough to carry them on, and are in great trouble. Nooned and made the fording—a picturesque scene— river half a mile wide and no where more than three feet deep— swift and sandy—had some little trouble. On the farther bank were collected a crowd of the emigrants—rather mean-looking fellows, much less respectable than those with us. Romaine and the rest

[e] "*Bois de vache*" or "buffalo chips", sun-dried buffalo dung, was the standard fuel on the treeless prairies.—Ed.
[f] Lower California Crossing, near Brulé, Neb.—Ed.

came in just before, having followed the buffalo too far, and camped.

The Capt.'s eternal motto: "Anything for a quiet life."

June 9th. Nothing worth note. Advanced about 16 miles. Tomorrow we shall push on alone.

June 10th. The Capt. last night sat with a group of the emigrants, telling his peculiarly elegant stories, to the great edification of the audience. Bade adieu this morning to him and the rest. He considers our leaving "an extraordinary proceeding"—and seems to look on us as deserting them in a dangerous crisis. They seem to have thought that we were obliged to remain with them for protection. They say their party ought to be *larger*. Wright, the muleteer, plainly hopes in his heart that our horses may be stolen. Travelled fast—passed round the head of Ash Hollow[94] and the other ravines—nooned by a mud puddle—and in the afternoon descended from the sand hills by an abominable sandy trail to the North Fork [of the Platte]. Road here not much better—sand—sand—sand; recent marks of a large party on the road. Travelled late—Quin hurt by a kick from Hendrick—came up with the emigrants camped in a circle—fires, tents, and waggons outside—horses within. The bottom covered with their cattle. They visited us at camp—a very good set of men, chiefly Missourians. Extinguished fire, and went to sleep.

June 11th. Set out early, and dragged some ten miles through an abominable sandy trail along the Platte. Scenery monotonous to the last degree. Very hot—the sand flies outrageous. Nooned on a pleasant spot and lay sleeping some three or four hours, when Henry awakened us with the announcement that people were coming. They were the van of the emigrants—first came a girl and a young man, on horseback, the former holding a parasol—then appeared the line of waggons, coming over the sand hills. We saddled in a trice, pushed ahead, and kept on. The girl and her beau apparently found something very agreeable in each other's company, for they kept more than a mile in advance of their party, which H. considered very imprudent, as the Sioux might be about. Distanced them, and camped by a *clear, swift stream*. Nothing but *bois de vache* ("prairie chips") for several days.

June 12th. Rode to Lawrence Fork[95] and nooned. Passing on, saw in the distance a half-subterranean house which Frédéric[96] had made to winter in, in charge of some furs to be sent down in the spring. What a devil of a solitary time! Chimney Rock[97] in sight. Henry entertained us with accts. of his adventures at one of the *blows-out* given by the bourgeois at the Yellow Stone, when the traders come in the spring. It was very characteristic. This is the custom at all the forts.[98] Overtook a company of emigrants, Americans and foreigners, encamped with whom were five men from Laramie,[99] going down. Crept into one of the waggons—wrote letters—and gave them to these people. Then advanced to Roubideau's [Robidoux's] party,[100] camped a mile or two in advance. Camped by them.

A Sioux received a present from another, who expected to get his favorite mule in return. The Sioux gave it accordingly, which so aggrieved the squaw who had been accustomed to ride it (the previous present being a dress for another of his squaws) that the two women fell fighting. The Sioux flogged them both; but being unable to separate them, and exceedingly exasperated at losing the mule, he grew so furious that he went out and vented his passion by killing seven of his horses. What a bump of destructiveness! This is the sort of passion that often drives an Ind. to his exploits of desperate courage.

H. says that the Crows are not jealous like the Sioux—that among the latter, the owner of a good horse often has him killed by some envious neighbor, which is not the case among the Crows.

The Oregon men returning to the settlements—the vulgar-looking fellow in the white shirt and broad-cloth pants, who gave us the acct. of the Oregon settlements and govnt. [government].[101] His companions around their campfire. What a character of independence and self-reliance such a life gives a man!

June 13th. Roubideau left the emigrants and joined us. Travelled 8 miles & nooned on Platte—then came 15 or 16 farther and camped by the spring at Scott['s] Bluff.[102] All these bluffs are singular and fantastic formations—abrupt, scored with wooded ravines, and wrought by storms into the semblance of lines of buildings. Midway on one of them gushes the spring, in the midst of wild roses, currants, cherries, and a hundred trees; and cuts for itself a devious and wooded ravine across the smooth plain below. Stood among the fresh wild roses and recalled old and delightful associations.

Henry tells a story of an attempt to murder the men at the Blackfoot fort, eight years ago, by the Gros Ventres for the sake of liquor—betrayed by a squaw.

Sometimes among the Sioux a peculiar cap is placed by a medicine man on the head of a chief or warrior in a war party, thus binding him either to be killed or to make a *coup*.[103]

A war party turned back because they saw the spirits of the dead casting rocks at them.

A feast is often given to a dead chief—the pipe is offered him, and food buried for his use.

Some Inds. give themselves out to be invulnerable.

Roubideau says that the Navaho(e)s near Santa Fe make glazed pottery and beautiful ponchos.

The Apaches,[104] in the White Mts., steal the cattle, dresses, women, etc., of the Spaniards, and defy them in the midst of their towns. The latter hired an American[105] to protect them, who raised a band of Dels., Shaws., and Americans, and chastised them.

June 14th. A fellow who had been back to look for stray cattle, remained and camped with us—a true specimen of the raw, noisy, western way. "Hullo, boys, where do you water your horses?"—this was his style of address. We put up no tent—after dark, it suddenly rained—we set up the tent in pitch darkness, and huddled into it as we could.

In the morning, H. and I rode on in advance. H. saw an Ind. village in motion over a distant bluff. Soon an Ind. came gallopping up. It proved to be Smoke's village.[106] Some of them soon joined us, and rode or walked along with us. Passed two [parties of] emigrants, who in the night had camped just in advance of us—chiefly from Missouri, and many of them singularly rude and intrusive. Forded Horse Creek[107]—found the Inds.—twenty lodges—ready to camp. Old Smoke on the bank, with his white horse, his pack horse with

Saint Louis, 25. April 1846

To any person or persons in
our employ in the Indian Country, —

This will be presented by
our friends Mr. F. Parkman and Mr. Quincy A. Shaw, who
visit the interior of the country for their pleasure & amusement,
and whom we beg to recommend to your kind & friendly attention—

If these Gentlemen shall be in need of anything in the
way of supplies &c. you will oblige us by furnishing them to
the extent of their wants, as also to render them any & every
aid in your power, of which they may stand in need

Very truly yours &c
P. Chouteau Jun. & Co,
John Clapp

Signature of Mr F. Parkman — F. Parkman
do Quincy A. Shaw — Quincy A. Shaw

Oregon Trail Passport
Issued by John Clapp of Pierre Chouteau, Jr. & Company, St. Louis, to Parkman and Shaw
(Parkman Papers, Massachusetts Historical Society)

the lodge poles, and his finely caparisoned mule. Nooned here, and feasted the Inds. on sweetened tea, buffalo meat, and biscuit—then passed the pipe. Emigrants passed on to get rid of Inds. Camped ten miles further on.

The camp was a picturesque scene. The squaws put up temporary sun shades, and scattered their packs and utensils about—the boys splashed in the river—the horses were picketed around. The shield and three poles hung up for each lodge—medicine—Smoke's was pure white. One old fat man[108] rode along with us, professing great friendship for the whites, and boasting what he would do against the Crows, a party of whom are out.

June 15th. Camped on a very pretty bottom on the Platte. Rode over the sand as far as a little, unfinished log fort, in the midst of a steril[e] prairie, built by Sapi [Sarpy][109]—log houses in form of a square, facing inwards—two Sioux lodges in the open area—*corale* behind, and plenty of shaggy little ponies feeding on the bottom. The *bourgeois* Richard received us politely, and ushered us into a log room, with a rock fireplace, and hung with rifles and their equipments, *fanfaron* bridles, garnished buckskin dresses, smoking apparatus, bows & quivers, etc. The men lounging around on robes—passed the pipe—an Ind. seated in the corner—Reynard [Reynal?][g] filling the pipe in the chimney corner—a voyageur, with hair glued in Ind. fashion, lounging on a bedstead.

Nooned by the Platte, having invited our entertainers to a cup of coffee. Previously we arranged our toilets, washing in the mud of the Platte, which, from its late rising, was perfectly opaque. Gave our feast under a cotton wood tree, and rode towards the fort. Laramie Mt. [Peak], Sybil [Sabille] & Adams's deserted fort,[110] and finally Laramie[111] appeared, as the prospect opened among the hills. Rode past the fort, reconnoitred from the walls, and passing the highest ford of L[aramie] Fork [River], were received at the gate by Boudeau [Bordeaux],[112] the *bourgeois*. Leading our horses into the area, we found Inds.—men, women, and children—standing around, voyageurs and trappers—the surrounding apartments occupied by the squaws and children of the traders. Fort divided into two areas—

[g] See below.—Ed.

one used as a *corale*—two bastions or *clay* [*adobe*] *blockhouses*—another blockhouse over main entrance. They gave us a large apartment, where we spread our blankets on the floor. From a sort of balcony we saw our horses and carts brought in, and witnessed a picturesque frontier scene. Conversed and smoked in the windy porch. Horses made a great row in the *corale*. At night the Inds. set up their songs. At the burial place are several Inds. laid on scaffolds, and a circle of buffalo skulls below. Vaskis [Vasquez], Cimoneau, Mont[h]alon, Knight,[113] and other traders and hunters are here.

Roubideau says that twenty Iroquois warriors, from Canada, were not many years since on the Upper Missouri, and were braver and more enterprising than any other of the Inds.[114]

Volume II

[The front end papers of the second notebook contain these jottings:

"Jack and the Captain (!)."

"An Indian's character is more rigid and inflexible than that of other savages. A Polynesian will become a good sailor, a good servant, or a good farmer. An Ind. is fit for nothing but his own mode of life. Neither has a Polynesian the same dark, sinistre, and uncertain character. Once received into his village and you are safe."—Ed.]

Fort Laramie, June 16th. Prices are most extortionate. Sugar, two dollars a cup—5-cent tobacco at $1.50—bullets at $.75 a pound, etc. American Fur Cmp'y. exceedingly disliked in this country—it suppresses all opposition, and keeping up these enormous prices, pays its men in necessaries on these terms.[115]

The fort has a double gate at the main entrance under the block-house. When there was danger from the Inds. the inner gate was closed; the Inds., admitted to the space between, traded through an open window or orifice, opening from a large room now used as the blacksmith's shop.

Lodged in Papin's room and visited now and then by Inds., the fathers or brothers of the whitemen's squaws,[116] who are lodged in the fort, and furnished with meat at the company's expense.

This morning, Smoke's village appeared on the opposite bank, and crossed on their wild, thin, little horses. Men and boys, naked and dashing eagerly through the water—horses with lodge poles dragging through squaws and children, and sometimes a litter of puppies— gaily attired squaws, leading the horses of their lords—dogs with their burdens attached swimming among the horses and mules— dogs barking, horses breaking loose, children laughing and shouting —squaws thrusting into the ground the lance and shield of the master of the lodge—naked and splendidly formed men passing and repassing through the swift water.

They held a kind of council in the fort. Smoke presided, but he had another man to speak for him, and ask for presents, and when these were placed on the floor before him, they were distributed under his eye, by one of the "soldiers."[117] Several of the warriors had their faces blackened, in token of having killed Pawnees, or at least of having been on the war-party when they were killed.

Some who visited us kept looking, with great curiousity, at the circus pictures that Finch[118] has nailed up in the room.

At their camp in the even'g, the girls and children, with a couple of young men, amused themselves with a dance, where there was as much merriment and fooling as could be desired.

The emigrants' party passed the upper ford, and a troop of women came into the fort, invading our room without scruple or reserve. Yankee curiosity and questioning is nothing to those of these people.

A Sioux of mean family can seldom become a chief—a chief generally arises out of large families, where the number of relatives who can back him in a quarrel and support him by their influence, gives him weight and authority.

June 17th. Emigrants asking questions and peering all about the Fort. Q. went to one of them and asked him to sell lead—the fellow pondered with fixed eyes and compressed lips for awhile—haggled for quarter of an hour—decided to let it go at .16 a lb.—went off to get it, and did not return.

A man came up to me and said that he had 30 lbs. of lead, which he did not want and meant to throw away if he could not sell. Offered him .10 a lb. which he at once took up, and set off for his lead. He did not return, and when I found him sitting on the pole of his waggon, and asked him where his lead was, he said he had concluded he could not spare it. Such is the indecision of these people, and their fear of being overreached.

Most of them are from Missouri—coming in companies from the different counties. The bad climate seems to have been the motive that has induced many of them to set out.

They gave a feast to the Inds. this evening. They were seated in a ring, Smoke and his chief men at the head, then the young men, the old squaws, the young squaws, the children, each in their place— two or three dandies stood around outside, too bashful, perhaps, to set in the circle, The feast was distributed by the "soldiers." Previously the women had danced in a circle, singing a song in which the exploits of the Sioux over the Pawness were boasted of.

An old Brulé came to visit H. He was miserably dressed, for the Crows had lately killed his son, and in his mourning he had given away all his possessions.

The Capt. and his party have just arrived.

June 18ᵗʰ. Gave a small present to the old Brulé—this morning, he comes to ask for more. Another Ind., who was present when we gave it, was very jealous, and soon came to say that his flag was torn, and he wanted some thread to mend it.

The old Brulé had with him some rude pictures of horses, as medicine to catch wild horses.

The Sioux women are more virtuous than the Crows, etc. A girl of respectable family can only be had on condition of taking her as a squaw—there are plenty of prostitutes, who are despised.

They are strangely jealous and indignant—their appetite for presents is insatiable—the more that is given to them, the more they expect.

Smoke's lodge, and his squaw and daughter with sore eyes. The lodge of Jack Hill's[119] father-in-law, and his dandy son.

Old Lalamie[120] had two mules, and his son wanted a horse of the Englishmen. The old man did not wish to part with the mules, but finally consented to, for fear his son would kill them out of spite.

Dandies, in full dress, are lounging about in all directions. Nothing is so striking as the indolence and inaction of the Indians. They merely vegetate.

June 19th. The begging dance—monotonous enough—in the area of the fort. Led by three dandies, the young squaws moved round singing in a circle. Mont[h]alon brought out the presents and placed them in the middle—and here the characteristic self-restraint of the Inds. was apparent. The squaws did not rush forwards to look, but stood quite quietly, and looked on with apparent indifference and without showing any jealousy while one of the young men distributed them.

Bordeaux laughs very much at the suspicion and distrust of the emigrants, who are constantly asking questions, and then refusing to credit the answers.

Gifts pass here as freely as the winds. Visit a trader, and his last cup of coffee and sugar, his last pound of flour, are brought out for your entertainment; and if you admire anything that he has, he gives it to you. Little thanks expected or given on either side.

June 20th. Old Smoke had a fat puppy killed and put into the kettle for us this morning. It was excellent. H. sent a messenger for his squaw's lodge to join us, and crossing Laramie, we set out to encamp at the mouth of Chugwater. Swapped Pondiac for Paul Dorion's[121] little mare.

Our party consisted of ourselves and followers, with an additional hand named Raymond[122]; Raynale [Reynal],[123] the trader at the village we mean to visit; his squaw; and her two nephews, brothers of the messenger H. had sent. We made rather a wild-looking band. Raynale's squaw's property fastened by the lodgepole arrangement[124] to a mule—herself riding a handsomely caparisoned mule, and her

Ind. nephews galloping about on their horses, in full equipment of bows and arrows, etc.

Travelled seven miles and came upon some wild and beautiful bottoms of the Laramie, where we encamped. Abundance of strange flowers and minerals.

June 21st. Rode to Chugwater, about 10 miles, country arid and desolate, broken with precipitous buttes—Black Hills[125] in the distance—wild sage, absanth,[126] wild tanzy, and a variety of strange plants. Here and there the pickets of a deserted wintering-house. One of the restless Indians ran a large wolf into the river. Camped by its wooded banks, near a prairie-dog village.

Raynale speaks of the legendary tales of the Sioux—of their mystic associations, in one of which there are tricks played with fire.[127]

That species of desperation in which an Ind. upon whom fortune frowns resolves to throw away his body, rushing desperately upon any danger that offers. If he comes off successful, he gains great honor.[128]

To show his bravery, an Ind. rushed up to a grizzly bear and struck him three times on the head with his bow.[h] Such acts are common.

The terrible penance to gain success in war, etc.—remaining for days, starving, with buffalo skulls fastened to cords run through the sinews of the back.[129] The animal that is dreamed of when in this state is the guardian spirit.

The initiatory fast prevails among the Sioux.[130]

One wishing to be a chief feasts the nation and gives away all he has in presents. The *war bonnet* is put on him, by which he is doomed to *count a coup* or be killed.[131] This is the test of his fitness for the office.

Raynale says as follows: The Sioux are subdivided into several bands—each band has one or more head men who direct it; for instance the Ogalallahs [Oglalas] have the Man Afraid of his Horses, the Yellow Thunder, the Panther Runner, the Whirlwind, etc., as

[h] "Counted coup."—Ed.

headmen—their influence is great, both in war and peace, and was gained by descent and personal merit.

On the great war exped[ition] now preparing against the Crows, they are directors. Messengers were sent from one band, determined on war, to another, with tobacco and scarlet cloth—stating the design and the time and place of rendezvous. A council was called by the chief to whom the messenger came, who stated the intention of it, and when it was approved a similar message was sent back to express concurrence. Thus the general agreement was made to meet at La Bonté's Camp.[132]

There will be no great head chief of the exped. Each band acts under its own headman, and the result will be division. The Whirlwind was prime mover of the thing, to avenge the death of his son killed by the Snakes, whose scalp we saw at the fort[133] with tobacco attached to signify a wish of peace. Will not the Whirlwind and his band leave the rest to make war on the Snakes?

The most efficient executive functionaries of the Inds. are the "soldiers." They are appointed in a council, called, probably by one of the chiefs for the purpose—an old man rises and mentions some young one brave and meritorious enough for the office, who is called out and invested with it. They are very necessary—the[y] direct the place to encamp—they direct the movements of a "surround" and prevent the buffalo from being frightened by vagrant hunters. In old Bull Bear's day these things were all well regulated, but now all is loose among the Ogalallahs.

Bull Bear, a wise as well as brave chief, used to call together his young men when he had any design in view, and ask if they thought it a good plan. No one ever dissented. Like all the chiefs, he was very profuse in presents.

On a surround, those who first come up to the game take what they choose of the meat—all are entitled to a share, whether hunters or not. This is all that prevents many from starving. So much for generosity and public spirit.

During the war ceremonies a ring is formed, and the old men call out those young warriors whom they think most deserving for their bravery. This public acknowledgment is considered a great honor.

On a large tree near our camp, the bark is cut off for the space of a foot square, and marked with 14 pipes and 14 straight marks, to indicate that a band of Crows had come down and struck *coups*.

June 23rd. Still at the camp at mouth of Chugwater. One of the two young Inds., His Horses,[134] is sent to find Henry's squaw's lodge and bring news of the movements of the Inds. Some danger from war-parties of Crows. Q. and I rode to the beautiful bottoms of Laramie not far up. Arid prairie around. Prickly pear, and another cactus, with a beautiful red blossom.

Reverence for age. A boy veils his face before an old man. The "dandies" at the fort were ashamed to sit and smoke with their elders—and at the feast, several stood outside the ring, apparently unwilling to sit down.

Bull Bear's son aspires to emulate his father's power. His chance is good, for besides his bravery and resolute character, he has more than 30 brothers. Henry, his brother-in-law, is told that he need fear nothing, for nobody will dare to touch him, since he has so many relations growing up around him. Family connexions are evidently a great source of power.

Bull Bear's connexions were numerous and powerful. Smoke and he once quarrelled. Bull Bear ran for his gun and bow, and Smoke withdrew to his lodge. Bull Bear challenged him to come out, but Smoke, fearing the vengeance of his enemy's relatives in case he should kill him, remained quiet, on which Bull Bear shot three of his horses.

This quarrel was brought to an end by Smoke's procuring Bull Bear's death, since which there has been a constant feud between the relatives of each, patched up last year by the traders, but still rankling.

One of Henry's brothers-in-law nearly fell a victim—four of Smoke's nephews entered the room where he was, *standing before them with his face covered*. H. protected him.

June 25th. Yesterday and today still at camp. Two antelopes killed. Rode to the fort this morning—saw a band of 200 elk—found Smoke's village gone over the Platte, where many hundred lodges are. Plenty of Ill. and Michigan emigrants. Returning, found His Horses with a young son of Bull Bear—they say that Tunica's[135] village is four days distant, and that the lodge of Henry's squaw will be here day after tomorrow.

June 26. Not to lay idle at camp, rode again to the Fort. Bought flour, bacon, etc., of the Company. Emigrants crossing the river, and thronging into the fort—a part of Russel[l]'s comp'y,[136] which becoming dissatisfied with their pragmatic, stump-orator leader, has split into half a dozen pieces. Passed along the line of waggons, conversing with the women, etc. These people are very ignorant, and suspicious for this reason—no wonder—they are grossly imposed on at the store.

A few lodges at the fort—Old Lamalamie's among them. He offered me his niece for a horse. Paul [Dorion] is here. The Miniconques[137] are a day or two below. Tunica came in with one of his head men, and confirms the accts. brought by His Horses. The great mass of the Inds. are hunting across the Platte.

The emigrants had a ball in the fort—in this room—the other night. Such belles! One woman, of more than suspected chastity, is left at the Fort; and Bordeaux is fool enough to receive her.

May[138]—his nervous fiery temper, and his acct. of the French in the country.

June 28th. Yesterday rode down with Paul Dorion, who wished to swap a wild horse, to Richard's fort. Found there Russel's or Boggs' comp'y, engaged in drinking and refitting, and a host of Canadians besides. Russel drunk as a pigeon—some fine-looking Kentucky men —some of D[aniel] Boone's grandchildren—Ewing, Jacob(s), and others with them—altogether more educated men than any I have seen. A motley crew assembled in Richard's rooms—squaws, children, Spaniards, French, and emigrants. Emigrants mean to sell liquor to the Miniconques, who will be up here tomorrow, and after having come all the way from the Missouri to go to the war, will no doubt break up if this is done. Paul very much displeased, as well as the Canadians.[139]

Returning to the Fort, met a party going to the settlements[140]—

to whom Montalon *had not given my letters*. Sent them by that good fellow Tucker.[141] People at the fort a set of mean swindlers, as witness my purchase of the bacon, and their treatment of the emigrants.

News of two traders killed by Arapaho(e)s—one just going up told me, remarking that he was bound to meet the same fate.[142]

Started late in the afternoon—lost my way—wounded one antelope and killed another, and, long after dark, saw the glimmering of the camp-fire on the bottom. Q. and Henry were gone to bury the latter's squaw, who is just dead.[143] Reynal had heard guns in the course of the day, and was in some apprehension.

Today lay at camp.

Tunica, in order to excite the war, had to give away all his horses and property. He was bent on avenging his son's death—his messengers, bearing the tobacco and cloth, were admitted into the councils, where they stated his designs, and how much he would give that village if it would concur in them. The old men consulted—the tobacco was smoked, and the engagement thus ratified on both sides —hence this extensive combination, which so many causes may still defeat.

Henry says that the relations of his squaw are determined to kill a horse and bury it with her, because, as she was very lame, she would be left on the prairie without the means of travelling to the land of spirits. Q. says that the relations have cut their hair off, and the women cried incessantly. He spent the night in a lodge with about 20 of them—strict silence for hours, the faces just discernable by the fire.

June 29ᵗʰ. Q. and H. came in yesterday, saying that the squaw was about to be buried. A young Ind. with an extraordinary name, importing that his propensities were the reverse of amorous, came with his squaw and child to camp, on his way to the fort, where he means to leave the squaw in charge of Bisson[n]ette,[144] while he goes to war. His medicine, on the strength of which he has counted two *coups*, is to light the pipe whenever it is passed round. This morning, he went off. His domestic drudge packed the horses, and arranged all their paraphernalia while he stood looking on, and then jerking himself into his saddle, he went off at a trot, leaving her to follow.

July 2nd. A most weary series of delays, arising from the utter uncertainty of the Indians' movements. Day before yesterday, a party of trappers[145] came from the fort, in order to give their horses a chance to fatten before entering on their dangerous and uncertain expedition. Their hunts occupy but two months or more—spring and fall—and for the rest of the time, they are idling about the forts or on the prairie, eating, drinking, or sleeping.

They brought news of Bisonnette's arrival, and we allowed Henry to go down and see him. They also said that Bordeaux and another man had quarrelled at the fort, and B. had shown himself a coward— which I can easily believe.[146]

Tunica, after all his pain and preparations, has, it seems, been dissuaded from going to war by Bordeaux, who represented that he would destroy all his horses. So much for Indian constancy—in fact they are the most uncertain people living—their resolutions no more to be trusted than those of children. An old Ind. came here yesterday with this news.

This morning, Q., Reynal, and I rode out to meet Tunica's village—met an Ind. who said their *plan of movement was changed.* He came to camp with us—sat in Reynal's lodge, blackguarding. Soon after, young Bull Bear, with his brother, and one or two more, besides women and children, came to camp. We feasted them.

The utter laziness of an Ind.'s life. It is scarce tolerable to us, and yet is theirs from year's end to year's end. Bull Bear, a young chief, famous for his intrepidity, ambition, and activity, lies kicking his heels by the fire like the rest.

A certain ceremony, it seems, is necessary to constitute a chief—as a preliminary, he *gives away all that he possesses.*

Is an Ind. desirous to become a chief—is he mourning for a dead relative—is he making the medicine ceremony of the white robe—in all these cases, he *gives away all that he has.*

An Ind. becomes great by such exploits as stealing other men's wives, and refusing to make any present in compensation. The Mad

Wolf, Bull Bear's brother, now with us, had often done this. It is a great proof of bravery, thus setting the husband at defiance. If the husband claims a present, and it is given, the merit of the thing is gone.[147] So much for the regulation of Indian society.

An old squaw in one of the lodges is the very picture of one of Macbeth's witches. Plenty of fine children are playing about. Squaws laughing and blackguarding with one another.

July 3rd. Tunica's village here at last. Bull Bear and several of his brothers came yesterday. Today the whole village appeared, straggling down the swell of the prairie, and encamped within a quarter of a mile. Our camp was soon thronged with anxious expectants of a feast—doomed to disappointment. They sat round while we eat, looking on with eager eyes, staring fixidly at us. Tent thronged with smokers.

Afternoon visited several lodges with H. & Q. and got a pipe of Tunica.

Old Bourne [Borgne],[148] brother to the elder Bull Bear, lay sick in his lodge—one of his squaws was nearly blind—what a wretched condition is that of a sick or superannuated Ind.! Mad Wolf,[149] a young aspirant, sat on the other side of the lodge. The woman with the sore eyes was one of Q's patients,[150] and groaned fearfully under his treatment. Her sister, who assisted, was laughing heartily all the time—so much for the affection and tenderness experienced by the sick in an Indian lodge.

Last night the village resounded with the howlings of the women, who were crying for H.'s squaw—though the sick are neglected, the dead are grieved for.

Criers are old men, much respected, chosen in a council.

An Ind. gift is like a Turkish—it is revoked unless an equivalent is given.

They are singularly jealous—feed one, and the others look on with very dark eyes.

The women are full of jokes and raillery.

In one lodge were two Shienne [Cheyenne] strangers, who occupied the place of honor at the top of the lodge.

An old man sent to invite us to a dog-feast—the dish was placed before us—we eat what we wished—then took away what we thought proper, and passed the rest to our host and his family, who had looked on meanwhile.

The old joker, who kept up a constant stream of raillery—especially about the women, declaring in their presence that he had lain with them, at which they laughed, without the slightest inclination to blush. Reynal says, and indeed it is very observable, that *anything* may be said without making a girl blush; but that liberties cannot be taken with a young girl's person without exciting her shame.[151]

They keep up a constant stream of raillery and blackguarding.

All is still uncertain about the war—some of the Inds. are for going and some for returning—it is even doubtful if any of them go to the rendezvous at La Bonté's Camp. The present intention—if so it can be called—of Tunica's village is to hunt back of Laramie Mt. and then go to war. Some of the warriors are preparing their dresses against this contingency.

July 4th. This afternoon three Inds. came to camp, bringing on a mule a wretchedly emaciated Negro. He was out 33 days ago with Richard on Horse Creek—the oxen ran off—he went to look for them, and had been wandering in circles and starving every since, without gun, knife, moccasins, or any knowledge of the country or its productions. We seated him in the midst of a circle of trappers, squaws, and children—the wretch could scarcely speak. The men considered his escape almost miraculous.

Rouleau and other trappers told stories of their own hardships.

The squaws are constantly laughing. It is astonishing, what abominable indecencies the best of the Inds. will utter in presence of the women, who laugh heartily.

Old Borne thinks he shall get well—he is very thankful to Q.

An opposition doctor was howling and rattling over a sick child in an adjoin[in]g lodge.

A broken-down old man, in one of the lodges, kept telling of his past greatness and his friendship for the whites.

22444

July 6[5]*th*. Moved camp to-day, with the village, to the Forks [of Laramie Creek]—a picturesque sight. A few old men went ahead and sat down, when they wished the line to stop—and when they stopped in the bottom, the camp was formed in a circle round them.

We had, it seems, a narrow escape a few days ago. The tracks seen on [the] Chug[water] by Reynal and H. proved to be a party of Crows, as the Sioux have just found some bones and corpses flung from their scaffolds. They were some thirty in number, and probably missed our camp in the morning fog.

Saw the dance of the Strong Hearts in the village this morning—great frolic and buffoonery.[152]

This afternoon, a war parade in full dress—sat in the shade of Reynal's lodge and looked at it—listened to the constant joking and trickery of the squaws—tasted sundry messes of *pommes blanches* and venison placed before us—saw a domestic quarrel, where the rebellious squaw pulled down the lodge, packed her horse, and rode off, while the husband looked quietly on. The warriors were in full dress—a miserable old squaw squalled after them from a lodge door, exciting them to glorious exploits—as one of them rode from the ring, a crier proclaimed his name, and published his renown before the whole village.

Soon after the ceremony, an old man walked round, shouting the name of one who had feasted him, and thanking him before the village.

There seems to be good discipline on matters of war, even among the Sioux. The society of Strong Hearts has soldiers, who compel attendance on such ceremonies as this, the penalty being the cutting to pieces of the recusant's lodge. The war-dance once danced, the recruit is enlisted, and subject to the regulations of the soc.

Bull Bear, being in mourning, did not join the band.

July 6*th*. Shot a war-eagle, which was siezed upon by the Inds. before I could get up to it.

Left the village, and with the trappers went over to Bitter Cotton Wood Creek,[153] to meet Bissonnette and go with him to La Bonté's. In the afternoon, reached the rendez-vous where we were to lay and wait one day for B. Waited accordingly through the 7th July.

An Ind.'s meanest trait is his unsatiable appetite for food and presents. They are irrepressible beggars, and at meals, no matter how slender the repast may be, chiefs and warriors surround us with eager eyes to wait for a portion, and this although their bellies may be full to bursting. If one wishes to see an Ind. village, send a notice that you will feast, and they will come a two days' journey for the sake of your cup of coffee. What a life! where the excitement of an enjoyment so trifling can tempt them to such pains-taking. In fact, the greater part of a trapper's or an Ind's life is mere vacancy—lying about, as I am now, with nothing to do or think of.

Yesterday, July 6ᵗʰ. While we were nooning, a party of emigrants appeared, on which two Inds. attached to the lodge of Moran's [Morin's?] squaw, who is along with us, went off to get a treat. The whole line of emigrants stopped nearly an hour, made them coffee and gave them bread—such is their timidity and perplexity, and want of management and regulation. The Inds. are getting more and more importunate in their demands upon them.

Today, 7ᵗʰ. Rouleau and the one-eyed Canadian [Séraphin] set out on their trapping exped. to the Mts.

Chatron and a party came from the fort and reported that B. will not be here till tomorrow.

July 9ᵗʰ. Yesterday, Bissonnette not arriving, rode in intense heat to a beautiful camp on Horse Shoe Creek—swift water, limpid as crystal. Today came to La Bonté's Camp on the Platte—no Inds.—no buffalo—but plenty of flies. Camp is the laziest place on earth. The family of Moran's squaw is along with [him]. Her brother, a lazy good for-nothing fellow, sits under a shade of robes apart, cooing with his new squaw (yesterday they had a long ramble in the bushes together). Her father, an old, lean, mean-looking medicine-man, sits perched on the limb of a dead tree like a turkey buzzard, apparently looking out. His medicine-bag and apparatus is hung over the little sunshade of robes that he has made. There are plenty of children about the lodge. Moran's friend Jeangras [Gingras] brought in an antelope at about 4 o'clock—it was instantly cooked, and all fell to eating. The utter laziness of Indian life!

Jeangras met a party of emigrants, from whom some trapper from the fort stole a woman, as they were camped night before last. He approached with two horses—met the fair one at the edge of the camp—mounted her, and vanished.

July 10th. There will probably be no muster of Inds. at La Bonté's—there are no buffalo. Spent an abominably lazy day; and, as Q. is averse to returning to Tunica's village, resolved to go alone, that my object may not be wholly defeated. This afternoon, Q. rode to our last camp to see if there were any signs of Bissonnette.

July 11th. Q. did not return till near daylight, when he came in on foot, having lost his horse Sorel. I set out as soon as possible, taking Raymond with me, and a little flour and tea, with a haunch of antelope. Henry went to look for Q.'s horse, while Q. remained to accompany the cart on its proposed movement to Horse Shoe Creek.

Steered about south. Prairie scorched and arid—broken with vile ravines and buttes—plenty of agate, jasper, etc.—gigantic grass-hoppers and crickets—scorched pines along the sides of the ravines—a good place for grizzly bears. Nooned on Horse Shoe Creek, and striking the Oregon trail, reached at night our former camp on Bitter Cotton-Wood.

July 12th. Raymond saw an antelope, and went to shoot it. The animals were hobbled, but, tormented by the flies, ran suddenly off, Paul Dorion's mare breaking her hobbles. I followed in vain. Raymond, returning, ran up the high butte, and saw them careering over the prairie. He followed, and did not return for about four hours, when he came in with them, having followed them to the Side [North] Fork of Laramie—ten or twelve miles. He had had no water, and that which he drank on returning was immediately vomited.

His appetite was gone, but I made him some tea and let him rest. In his eager pursuit, he left his rifle on the ground, and we had much difficulty in finding it in the afternoon. I had good reason to be anxious during his absence, as I did not know exactly where Q. was encamped, and every day's delay made it more difficult to find the Ind. village. Camped on Side Fork of Laramie.

July 13ᵗʰ. Breakfasted on the remaining one of a pair of curlew I shot. Struck across for Laramie Creek, to find the trail of the village. Raymond got sight of an antelope down a ravine—fired, and broke his shoulder—my mare easily overtook her. Came to Laramie, and saw the print of a moccasin—crossed to a little, sandy creek, running into it from the south, where tracks of men and horses were very distinct and thickened as we proceeded, till after an hour's search we came upon one of their camps—several days old. Our search was rendered much more difficult by the furious storm of yesterday afternoon, which, descending from Laramie Mt., drove us for shelter to the depths of a dry ravine, where we crouched for an hour or more, but ill protected.

Nooned, and set out on the trail—it led towards the mts., but such was the nature of the arid, barren, stoney ground, that only here and there the faint trace of a lodge-pole was visible, as it passed over some ant-hill, or clump of prickly-pear—or sometimes a stone would be turned over by the kick of a horse. Intensely hot. Followed slowly all the afternoon, losing the trail repeatedly. Saw a heavy smoke rising from a valley this side Laramie Mt. Lost the trail at last, and encamped in a hollow bottom, where Laramie comes swiftly out of the hills, and where our fire would be invisible.

July 14ᵗʰ. Following a creek that flows from the south into Laramie, we found the traces of lodge-poles again, but soon lost them. Not long after, we found them again, and a camp, where by the number of fires we saw that we were on the trail of only part of the village. Traced it up a bare and scorching valley of the mts. where we led our animals. Descending, we came to a succession of little grassey and well watered nooks among these black and desolate hills, and presently came upon another camp. Not long after, with a dreary interval of hot and barren prairie, we came to a succession of defiles among fine abrupt mts., like the Dixville Pass.[154] Bare cliffs above— beautiful woods below—a clear stream glancing in their shadows over a bed of rock—and all alive with birds like Mt. Auburn.[155] It was a place to repay a week's travel. After twelve miles' riding we found another camp and nooned there. Several rude little forts, some twelve feet square, of interlaced logs and branches, marked the warlike character of the region. In the afternoon we ascended a narrow and most romantic pass—the stream in its bed of rocks by our sides, a dense foliage around us, and lofty beetling cliffs above. Larkspur and a sort of aster were among the numberless flowers— pleasant mementos of civilization in such a wilderness. In a basin among rugged hills, at the head of the pass, the Inds. had encamped again, and a little farther on we did the same. (Absanth everywhere.) Just emerging from the hills, saw several bulls on a distant butte.

July 15th. Started, and soon got on a prairie where the traces were totally lost—a wide stony expanse, tracked with buffalo. Medicine Bow Mts. in the distance. After some weary and anxious hours, found the lodge-pole marks, again to lose them. They pointed, however, towards the head of Laramie Creek, and thither we resolved to push. A number of little lakes, where wolves, antelopes, and large plover were congregated. Tried in vain to kill some, our meat being nearly gone. Were fast approaching a region quite dangerous on acct. of Snakes, Gros Ventres, and Arapahoes.[156] Raymond advised return. Resolved to advance till night, and soon after, ascending a butte, saw the circle of lodges, with the bands of horse, close by the bare banks of Laramie. Thanked God that my enterprise was not defeated. Groups stood in front of the lodges as we descended, and we presently saw Reynal coming to meet us. He quartered me upon Big Crow, the village having disagreed and split up, Tunica going one way and Bad Wound another.[157] Invited to plenty of feasts, as the village was full of meat, and soon after was seated in R.'s lodge, with a large group, discussing the cause of thunder, a storm having just risen.

The Sioux, like the northern tribes, say that the thunder is a bird flying over the firmament, and that once an old man saw it descend and flap its wings on a lake which caused the lightning.[158]

This ev'ng, two young men, desirous of raising a war-party, went round the village crying to the Great Spirit to give them success in killing their enemies and stealing horses. Next morning, one of them was on a distant butte, crying in the same manner.

The firelight scene in the lodge at night.

The squaws played ball before dark, and various games of hazard were going on—these, together with smoking and eating, pass away an Ind.'s time.

Heap of Hail[159] and his friend and crony.

July 16th. Today, gave them a feast—dog, tea, and bread. My host, the Big Crow, issued the invitations—a slender banquet for more than 20 guests, but nothing gratifies an Ind. like giving him a morsel of food, especially that which the whites use. Old Red Water,[160] the fast friend and imitator of the whites, spoke at some length, expressing his gratitude. I answered, Reynal interpreting. Feast distributed by soldiers chosen for such purposes, whose awards, says R., never give dissatisfaction. R., on the instigation of the Eagle Feather, took the occasion of this meeting to enforce the expediency of moving tomorrow after the buffalo; Eagle Feather seconded him, and remarked that since Bull Bear's death, there had been nothing but divisions and separations among them—they were a body without a head. Others gave their opinion, but there was no decision—a completer democracy never subsisted. When all was eaten, Red Water sang his song of thanks, made another speech, and then intimated that the company ought to leave breathing room to the whites—on which they went out. This was a soldier feast.

Old Red Water says that the large crickets so common about here, when taken in the hand, always twist their long horns, when asked, in the direction of the buffalo. This was told them by their great grandfather, and the name by which they call crickets means: "Those that show where the buffalo are."[161]

The conversation in the lodge at night—one man would keep on in a lively strain with much gesticulation for an hour together, the others not interrupting; and then another would take up the conversation. When the chief men sat down to smoke today (17th) during the march, the conversation was very gay and lively. In the evening, the squaws amused themselves with plenty of lively and vociferous games.

Big Crow, my host, took out his medicine bags and had a smoke, in ceremony, over them.

Reynal—his insatiable avidity to get hold of whatever he sees.

July 17th. Moved camp, though very slowly and in disorder. Old Redwater in a loud voice upbraided the village for their want of promptitude and having *two hearts.* The chief men marched before, as usual. Camped on a fine spring, ten miles off.

Redwater's voice soon heard in the village, proclaiming a feast that he was giving.

Old Redwater's tale, told with great animation and gesticulation: When he was very young, he was hunting beaver with three others, and he crept alone into the lodge, with a rope. When he had crept a great distance, passing several very small dark holes, he crawled into a place where it was very dark and slimy, and he felt very sleepy (here the dumb show became very expressive). Presently, he saw something white and indistinct—for some time he was so sleepy that he could make out nothing, but at last he discerned two white men and two white women. Just then he heard his companions singing outside, and feeling alarmed, he succeeded after a long while in crawling out. It felt very cold. His companions had thought him dead. He went to the place over that where he saw the four whites, and, beating with his foot, made a hole. Soon a beaver came out, which they caught, and then three more.

The old man says he has always considered the beavers and the whites the wisest of all animals; and he is now certain that they are the same.[162]

The boys playing at evn'g outside the village. Every little fellow has his bow and arrow, and they show great skill in knocking down small birds with them.

July 18th. Made two moves today, to get near the buffalo. In camping, each lodge has its appropriate place relatively to the others. At even'g, two bulls came directly upon the village and were killed within a few rods of it, by two men laying in wait. In the morning, His Horses killed a bull, which was at once surrounded and butchered, and much of it eaten raw. Some of the boys killed a fine prairie-cock. It was resolved on the march to cache the meat, and advance tomorrow to where the buffalo are, to surround.

The woman, with her legs gashed, howling through the camp, mourning for her son, killed a year ago. Her lodge was full of cries and songs of mourning.

The little Gros Ventre prisoner adopted into old Red Water's family.

Old R. W.'s unwillingness to tell his tales—he says it is against his medicine, for they are about to go to war, and it is not good to talk much at that time.

A young man of considerable repute is getting up the warparty. He called me to a feast today, and begged a little powder.

Eagle Feather came to me this morning to make me a present of an old waistcoat—his object was to get one of my shirts. A woman presented me a dish of *wasna* or pemmican,[163] expecting a knife in return. To give nothing for nothing is the Indian maxim.

July 19th. The meat being cached, the village began to move about 11 o'clock and advanced about twelve miles, encamping on a stream of which they did not know the name. Their course is westward; and they are very apprehensive on acct. of the Snakes, who they fear will attack them.

The young man[164] who feasts me so often, and asks for the paper of recommendation. He is at the head of the war scheme, and his equipment—war-bonnet, shield, bow and arrows, shirt, robe, and pipe—are very complete and elegant.

Raynal is absurdly offended, because I required Raimond to take care of the horses, instead of going to help him cache his meat.

July 20th. Made a short and early move. No sooner were we camped, higher up on the creek, than all the men and most of the boys set out after the buffalo, on account of which this westward move had been made. It is time to provide new lodge-skins. Most of them led their buffalo horses, and rode inferior animals—a wild, helter-skelter, hurrying group. No soldiers for the buffalo have been appointed, the village being so small. One or two young men rode forwards occasionally, and one or two old ones assumed the direction. After twelve miles riding, seeing only scattered bulls, some bands of cows appeared. The Inds. separated. Followed the largest party. Bulls wading hastily across a sandy creek. A general break-away after the band of cows on the other side. Soon plenty were down, and the whole scattering far and wide. Too languid to hunt with spirit, and my horse very sick. Wounded two cows, but lost them. Came back to where Big Crow was butchering, and his son eating raw meat, in which I joined and found the liver excellent. A tiresome ride back—at length saw the group of lodges, bereft of warriors, on the green bottom of the creek. Laid down on a robe, while the women and children discussed the raw meat we brought.

When the Big Crow came in, his squaw brought him water, pulled off his moccasins, and brought him a dish of meat. The village was soon filled with meat. Groups were gorging themselves around all the lodges—eating was the engrossing occupation of the time, and the result was that all night vomitings and retchings could be heard among the children of the lodges around. Old Red Water (Mene-Shula [Seela]), though over sixty, drove an arrow clean through a cow, and talked with great glee and animation of his exploit.

The Big Crow (Kongratonka [Kongra-Tonga]), my host, showed me his wounds, of which he has many. He has killed fourteen men; and dwells with great satisfaction on the capture of a Utah, whom he took prisoner; and, with the other Sioux, scalped alive, cut the tendons of his wrist, and flung, still living, into a great fire.

The Inds. are much afraid of the Snakes and Utahs, and reproved Raimond for going out without his rifle today.

July 21st. Today the squaws are busy upon the robes.

No family here lays by fresh meat for its own use—if a man gets half a buffalo, he is sure to be eased of it before night, by a congregation of hungry relatives and friends.

Kongratonka's medicine is to sing in the night, which he never fails to do, to my great annoyance.

The White Shield, the young brave who is raising the war-party, lurks around our lodge about meal times, expecting his share like the meanest of the village.

July 23ʳᵈ. Yesterday went out with Raimond to hunt. Wounded an antelope, and fired some six or eight ineffectual bullets into a bull. In the morning Reynal said he had dreamed of strangers arriving, and it happened that his dream coincided with that of a young Ind. Both were strong in faith, and the latter went out on discovery. By a singular coincidence he met Saraphin [Séraphin] and Rouleau, who, having trapped in the [Laramie] Mts., were coming to the village. They are bound to the Rocky Mts., trapping.

All the Inds. here try to dissuade them, saying that, since the death of Boot and May, the Arapahos have grown very audacious, having got over their first terror, and call the whites dogs, saying that none of them shall leave their country alive. They laugh at the government and the dragoons. The trappers are resolved to go on. There is considerable danger in the immediate vicinity of the camp, from the Snakes. Today the Inds. are out on another surround. The camp is full of meat drying on scaffolds, and the squaws are working like dogs at cleaning the robes.

Rouleau describes the fight in which Bull Bear was killed. The determined bravery and obstinate will of the chief are remarkable. He speaks of a Brulé chief of similar character—in such terror was he held that his will was absolute law. There was in this village a young half-breed, killed last fall, so dreaded that he could strike with impunity the considerable men of the village. There seems to have been in these modern Pontiacs an impetuous force of mind that entitles them all to be called great.

One day it stormed furiously. Something had displeased the Brulé chief. "*I am mad,*" said he to R. "I will make the village move." His squaw levelled his lodge, and no sooner was this done than the rest were down also—such was the force of his example.

Crying is the commonest thing in the world. Tonight an old squaw's horse foundered in the surround, and her lamentations were audible from her lodge for hours. I have often seen squaws crying on the way from camp to camp.

The White Shield came and sat before Reynal's lodge. He had a bad sore throat, which he bore with anything but stoicism. He seemed depressed to the last degree.

R. says that they bear *wounds* with the greatest fortitude, but yield at once to a stroke of sickness. The White Shield said he meant to have gone to war tomorrow—that his brother was killed last summer, and he must avenge him or die—that ten young men would follow him. His preparations are complete; and his sickness makes him very despondent. I hear the medicine drum at this moment—he is probably under medical treatment.

July 24th. Skins enough have now been obtained for the lodges—they are all stretched on the ground, and the squaws labor like dogs over them.

Rouleau and Saraphin set off this morning on their dangerous exped. Rouleau says if he only had one more horse he would not go—this is his present necessity for continuing his dangerous trapper life. He whistles, sings, and laughs with the utmost gaiety, and rides off with as careless a heart as if bound back to the Fort.

July 26th. Night before last, the White Shield put on his full war-dress; and, mounting his horse, paraded around the village, crying for success to the Great Spirit. Here and there, an old woman set up a song of glorification and encouragement. He was a very splendid and chivalrous-looking figure; but he is a notorious beggar, like the rest. Next day, he was still quite sick—the long projected war-party fell through, the warriors alleging a want of powder and arrows.

Yesterday, the skins being nearly prepared and the camp insufferably dirty, moved in the afternoon to our last camp higher up the creek, with the intention of getting the cached meat, and cutting lodge-poles in the hills.

Scarcely arrived—old men and warriors seated smoking in the middle—squaws unpacking horses and dogs—when a quarrel arose. There are in the village three of the broken and dispersed band of the Arrow Breakers—they undertook to sieze upon a horse belonging to a brave killed not long since. A brother of the deceased took the horse away from them, on which they shot him. There was a rush from all parts of the village—guns and arrows were siezed and discharged, some taking one side, some another. Some squaws set up a howling for the slaughtered horse—other ran to a place of safety with their children—and other siezed on the weapons. A fight was threatened, but it ended in smoke—soon all was quiet. (For the true cause of the quarrel, see *post*.)

When the pipe is passed from left to right, it is medicine.

All the evening, the village was filled with the mourning songs of squaws who lost relatives last year.

Immediately after the quarrel, an old squaw sang out the name of the man who had rescued the horse—the Tall Bear—in honor of his bravery.

Today moved nearer the Mts. and encamped.

During the quarrel, old Red Water, old as he is, rushed out of his lodge, gun and bow in hand, with the upmost vehemence, but tripped and lay sprawling on the ground.

The great number of societies, with their peculiar ceremonies and discipline.

July 27ᵗʰ. Last night there was a festive meeting (?) with songs, etc., in one of the principal lodges.

Moved camp to the Mts. to cut lodge-poles. Camped in the valley of a clear, cool creek—boys wandering about the rugged and broken mts., killing prairie-cocks, or perching themselves on tall rocks and looking down on the straggling array. Men cutting *shongsasa*[i] among the bushes. Raimond and I looked in vain for a beaver-lodge.

Camped in a narrow, grassy spot, hollowed among the rough hills —a most picturesque scene. Lodges no sooner up than, with characteristic hurry, forth poured half the population to get the lodge-poles, trotting, running, and scrambling on their horses, with dogs, colts, and all, along a rude, narrow valley. Squaws in full attire, twinkling with their ornaments and laughing. Two deer sprang up— Reynal fired—jumped from my horse to do the same—instantly the whole helter-skelter procession was sweeping by me. A suitable place

---

[i] "Shongsha" or "kinnikinnick" was red-willow or dogwood bark, arrowroot, or some other herb used to eke out tobacco, which was expensive and scarce among the Indians.—Ed.

found, squaws and men were all at work. Left the two men, and wandered up the mts. A hunter's paradise—signs of game incredibly thick—cold streams—rocks, pine, and spruce—all had the air of my old friends, the mts. of N. E. [New England]. Strawberries—larkspur—robins—bumble-bees. Mts. very abrupt, precipitous, and broken. Saw beaver dams in returning. Sat down in the lodge to a hearty meal of buffalo meat, purveyed by Red Water in the absence of my host, his son.

On arriving at our present camp, several women set up mourning songs for relatives killed in war, and whom they had last parted from at this spot last summer.

July 28th. Set out with Reynal on a hunt. Rode over mountain after mountain—wild and picturesque, but no game but two deer in the distance. Emerging upon the prairies, saw three bulls—gave chace—old mule took fright and threw me—could not approach—circled back to village over craggy mts.

A great variety of games and exercises among the Ind. children.

Reynal's "old woman" gave a feast to the squaws—consisting of dry bull-meat, lumps of fat, flour, and corn-meal, boiled in a kettle together. The object was (she always has some such object) to procure their assistance in preparing her lodge-skins.[165]

Camp full of new lodge-poles—men and women at work trimming them. Others gathering *shongsasa* by the brook.

July 29th. Climbed a high rocky Mt. a few miles from camp. On the way, in woody ravines where little streams came down, cold as ice, among the stones and moss, and everywhere about the rocks were scattered the Ind. boys, looking after berries or small game. They destroy all that comes to hand—young rabbits, ducks, prairie cocks—every thing; and this is their education. A savage prospect from the summit—lodges in the green valley like a circle of white specks.

Dozed away the afternoon in Raynal's lodge, thinking of things past and meditating on things to come. Here one feels overcome with an irresistable laziness—he cannot even muse consecutively.

At evening, Heap of Hail appeared with the skin and liver of an elk. He is very ambitious, and always after game; while his elder brother lazily struts about.

As the pipe passed the circle around the fire in the evening, there was plenty of that obscene conversation that seems to make up the sum of Ind. wit, and which very much amuses the squaws. The Inds. are a very licentious set.

July 30th. Broke up camp, and moved round to the pass through the Mts.—about twelve miles, to where we encamped on a bottom in the midst of them. On the way passed the site of a camp, whence last year the war-party that was defeated set out. The relatives of the slain immediately raised the mourning song, and the half-breed Shienne, one of whose relations was killed, gave away on the spot two horses. He will receive their value back again. After camping, nothing was heard but shouts of praise and thanks.

Just before reaching the ground, a large flock of sheep[j] seen on the mts. Drove up with Raimond, to look after them—plenty of Inds. in pursuit. Tied animals and scrambled over rocks and ravines till tired of the work. Returning, saw the camp just forming in the plain below, and heard the occasional shots of the Inds. who had so perplexed the poor animals as to bring several within range of their wretched guns. Reynal and Raimond followed one they had wounded, and pelted her to death with stones in a ravine. Meat tough and old. Several more frightened flocks, appeared on the mts. in full sight from camp.

July 31st. As the camp broke up this morning, set out with Raimond among the hills for a hunt. Killed an antelope. The White Shield followed, for a share in the spoils. Arrived in camp in time to join the circle of old smokers in the middle. A noble spring of water not far distant—a great basin of rocks, fringed by soft [ferns?]—water like crystal, many feet deep, and cold as ice. Escaping, soaking through the soil or creeping almost invisibly down the grassy ravine, it formed many rods below another basin, still larger and deeper—

---

j Probably these were antelope, known as "goats," rather than the bighorns called "sheep."—Ed.

equally clear, but not so cool—a natural bathing-tub and a luxurious refreshment in the intense heat.

Aug. 1ˢᵗ. Fairly among the mts. Rich, grassy valley—plenty of gooseberries and currants—dark pine mts.—an opening dell that tempted me to ride up into it, and here in the cool pine woods I recalled old feelings, and old and well remembered poetry. Climbed a steep hill—on the left, the mts. and the black pine forests—far down, the bare hills, and threading the valley below came the long, straggling procession of Inds.

They soon camped in a grassy nook, where crowded together— dogs and horses, men, women, and children—the sight was most picturesque. The men sat smoking—the women worked at the lodges—the children and young men climbed the steep rocks, or straggled among the pine-covered hills around the place. Droves of horses were driven to water—girls with spoons and buffalo paunches went down to a deep dell for water. Heat intense—sat on a shady rock and watched the scene. Climbed at sunset a high hill and looked over the mts. and pine forests. All night, the Inds. were playing at a great gambling game.

Aug. 2ⁿᵈ. Set out early, after a dog-breakfast, to take leave of the Inds. and meet S[haw] according to agreement at the fort. Looked back down the dell at the camp in full hubbub of preparation for departure, thinking it my last look. Heap of Hail accompanied us, to show us the way through the mts. Had not ridden long through the pine glades in the cool of the morning, when we raised a black-tailed deer. R. wounded at 200 yds.—I broke shoulder at 300,[166] and the young Ind. followed him into a deep dell and finished him. Butchering delayed us, and we joined the Ind. line of march. They were straggling down a deep and narrow gorge—rocks and pines—a confused, noisy, and wild procession. The mts. in front were all on fire, and have been so for weeks—a boundless and cloudlike volume of smoke obscured the whole landscape in front, except here and there the jutting ridges of bold cliffs and bristling pines, or the paler outline of more distant heights, just visible through the veil. High and stern crags on every side. But soon we descended into a milder region—one of vallies and little streams where plenty of wild fruit grew, which the children gathered.

Emerged from the mts. and camped on the scorching prairie. Hot as the devil. Employed myself in thrusting head, arms, and feet into deep, delicious "holes" of water, and watching the little fishes gliding in them—then smoked—then ate—then waited impatiently till the horses were brought up; and R. and I, taking final leave, set out for the fort, accompanied by a young Ind. Camped on Chugwater. The Ind. was afraid to stop at a spot I proposed on Laramie, because two dead men were buried there.

Aug. 3rd. Setting out before daybreak, reached the fort early, and found all there, Shaw having been there a fortnight. A civilized breakfast not to be sneezed at!

Aug. 4th. There is an old Ind. at the fort, badly wounded, who is always singing to cure himself. His "medicine," which he always resorts to when in pain, is to hand some bystander a cup of water and let him drink it.

Rouville[167] and his animated rattling conversation.

In the afternoon set out with Rouville, a trapper, and his Pah Utah squaw towards the camp of Bissonnette, on our way to Bent's [Fort]. Camped on a little run, ten miles—plenty of wild cherries.

Aug. 5th. Camped at noon on a stream perfectly dry, where we had to scratch holes in the sand for water. Traversed "Goshen's Hole"— a damned dry place, full of ravines—saw bear tracks, and camped very late.

Rouville's acct. of old Borne's life—told him by the old man. Old B. was eighteen when he dreamed of an interview with a grizzly bear—the *war-spirit* of the Inds. as the *antelope* is the *peace-spirit*. He saw the bear eating; and, waiting till he had appeased his hunger, went up to him. The bear told him it was time for him to think of going to war, but he must not do as the other Inds. did—he must fight openly, and not commit useless barbarities.

Next day he set out, went to the Black Hills, and soon discovered a Crow, before the latter observed him. As he was on the point of firing, he recalled the white bear's injunction, refrained, and called out to his enemy to step forwards and fight. They grappled—the Crow fell wounded. B. was on the point of despatching him, when he begged to speak a few words—he told B. that too much ambition was the cause of his present fate—that he had killed thirty-six Sioux, and now fell a victim to his desire to kill more—that he (B.) was a brave and good young man—that he had better renounce ambition and be content with a peaceful life. So old Borne has led a peaceful though honored life, very different from that of his fierce and ambitious brother, Bull Bear.

The Inds. shoot at the clouds to scare away the thunder. They think it an enemy, and turn out to fight it. So in case of an eclipse.

The Frenchmen—Rouville and Delorier—an amusing contrast to the Yankee temperament.

Aug. 6th. Advanced to Little Horse Creek and nooned. Tracks of bear. Afternoon reached Horse Creek, where was encamped Bissonnette, N. Sibille [Sabille],[168] and their party, along with some 40 Sioux lodges—Tunica's—and several Shienne.

Horse-races in the evening; Paul Dorion—the *ci-devant* circus rider; Rouville, Antoine,[169] and the Canadians; the swarm of Inds. on horse and foot.

Ind. Outrages: The Pawnees—their alarm—stopping Finch— alarm subsides—killed Bradley with an arrow in June—stopped Bissonnette June 4th—tried to rob Turner—steal horses—whip an emigrant into camp. Told Rouville that they would rob and kill every white who passed through their lands.

Sioux told Rouville that the Pawnees had been committing outrages for years and no dragoons had come, and now *they* meant to do the same. But few of them saw the dragoons, being afraid to come, then dissatisfied at getting no presents. Never so turbulent as this year. Declare that if the emigrants continued to pass through, they would rob them and kill them if they resisted. Broke up the pots and pans of the emigrants who feasted them. Robbed Sublette[170] and Reddick, and fired upon them. Robbed Bonn[e]y.[171] Robbed a party of eight waggons at Independence Creek in July.

Arapahos killed Boot and May this spring. Alarmed at first—afterwards grow insolent and declare that no whites shall ever leave their country. Trappers—Rouleau and Saraphin—dissuasions of the Inds. at the village.

Cayou, 52 Green St, St. Louis

Sibille told me the following story, told him by a young Shienne, very fond of talking with the whites about religion.

In a band of the Shiennes was a young man who always painted in a peculiar manner, and enjoyed much respect and influence. Once the band met on the prairie another young man, resembling in paint and in all respects the former, who advanced and demanded who he was, and why he imitated his paint. The latter, who was a divinity, embraced him, and directed that he should follow him, while the band stopped. Leading him into a deep dell, he entered the waters of a spring, where the young man followed. Presently after, they emerged, the young man bearing two dishes of boiled corn given him by the spirit, who told him to distribute two kernels to each person to eat. He then asked if they liked them—they said "yes," on which again disappearing in the spring with the young man, he came back with two dishes of seed corn. This he gave to the Shienne, telling them to plant it at the time the grass was springing up, and return after several moons.

Thus the Great Spirit gave corn to the Shiennes.

An Ind., when sick or wounded, feels obliged to imitate the movements of the animal whom he has as his guardian spirit. A wounded Sioux, sought for some days by his companions, was found in a deep hollow, scratching and growling like a bear.

Ind. speeches always prepared beforehand. Bissonnette once caught the Sioux *rehearsing* the speech they were to make to Col. Kearney on the visit they expected from him this summer.[172] One of them personated their American father.

Bissonnette's feast—coffee—corn boiled with grease—a huge kettle of pounded cherries, grease, and flour.

First a speech from him telling them to make more robes than they had made last winter. A reply from the orator, followed by a broad intimation that they had now better begin to eat—at which an old "soldier" poured out the coffee, which was at once gulped down. Then the corn preparation was devoured—then the other mixture.

Lomalomie, the "Hog"—the sick Tunica, gorging like the rest— the Shienne guests, served by the soldier with a treble share—the Crow prisoner. Pipe circulating constantly. Concluding speech of thanks from the orator.

Aug. 7ᵗʰ & 8ᵗʰ. Lay at Camp. Evening of the 8ᵗʰ, a dance of the Strong Hearts, Shienne and Sioux. This society extends through the Shienne and Sioux—Bissonnette does not know if it exists in other nations. The same is the case with other societies—the Hawk—Short Hairs, etc. Each has some animal as a guardian spirit, that of the Strong Hearts being the fox, whose movements they imitate in their very curious dance. They passed round to all the principal lodges, dancing at each, the object being a present—a begging dance. The object of all these societies, says B., is warlike.

The Stabber, a Missouri Ind., comes from the Arkansas, and brings vague reports of troops passing up, and of a victory over the Spaniards.[173] He tells his story as vaguely and unconnectedly as a child.

A Shienne came to B., saying he would like to swap a fine horse of his. He postponed the bargain day after day, coming every day to eat at B.'s lodge, till at last it appeared that this was his sole object in proposing the swap!

Bull Bear comes to see Henry. He seems to be a true friend, and regularly places himself in our tent as our "soldier."

The War-Whistle, not used by the chief as a signal, but blown by the young men during the fight. It is a "medicine" instrument, and is blown by the Inds. while undergoing the penance of the buffalo skulls.[174] A society among the Ponkas [Poncas] and Omahas, called the Thunder-Fighters, during a thunder-storm sit on a hill, whistling to the storm to frighten it.

The true cause of the quarrel I saw at the Ind. village[k] (related by Bull Bear) was as follows. A horse was given, with the usual expectation of another one, to which the giver had taken a fancy, being given in his place. This not being done, the giver tried to take back his gift, upon which the "givee" fired an arrow into the animal, and hence the quarrel.

The gross indecency of many Indian names, even of the most distinguished men.

Aug. 9th. The Inds. and Bissonnette moving, we made a move in the afternoon, and after passing through a region of wild cherries (on which, in the dearth of meat, the Inds. have been living for some time) we came to a very pleasant camp on Spring Creek.

Aug. 10th. Travelled all day—nooned on Pole Creek, which was nearly dry, and camped on a little stream beyond.

Aug. 11th. This morning the horses ran back to Pole Creek, which caused delay. We, however, stopping now and then for a smoke on the road, came to Crow Creek, and nooned. A hot and level prairie. Camped on a brook running into Crow Creek.

Aug. 12th. A long day's journey. Nooned low down on Crow Creek. Travelled till near sunset, and finding the creek dry, had to keep on to the mouth of Cache à la Poudre, which we reached at nine o'clock.

The Sioux, Crows, Arapahos, according to Henry, have every year or thereabouts medicine ceremonies, similar to the Mandans.
There is a "squaw" feast, where the married women come forwards and swear to their virtue and fidelity.[175]

Aug. 13th. Yesterday, towards evening, saw the very high Mt. called Vaskiss's [Vasquez] Peak [Longs Peak?]. This morning the air was not clear enough to distinguish it. Crossed the South Fork [of the Platte]—killed an immense rattlesnake—rode some ten or twelve

[k] Cf. pp. 462-63.—Ed.

miles—and nooned close to St. Vrain's Fort. Deserted—entered it—two bastions—built of *"doughbies"* ["dobies" or adobes]—fast tumbling in ruins—fine situation. Rode on five or six miles and camped on South Fork, not far from Vaskiss's Fort. Saw fresh trail of an Ind. village this morning.

Aug. 14th. Very dry, hot, and smoky. Passed Upton's [Lupton's] deserted fort,[176] six or seven miles from Vaskiss's. Nooned on the Fork. Made a long day's march, and camped on the Fork, where the road leaves it and crosses to Cherry Creek.[177] Saw a last night's camp of a large village—probably Arapaho. .

Aug. 15th. A long morning's march brought us to Cherry Creek, over a very hot and dry prairie. Weather too smoky to see the mts. Creek dry—camp of Mormon emigrants, who passed this way with Richard a few week[s] ago.[178] Cherries—plums—black currents—and gooseberries. No water in creek—dug holes and got some. Camped at night on the creek.

Aug. 16th. Today, nooned on Cherry Creek. Camped upon it where the road leaves it to cross over the waters of the Arkansas. A hilly country, full of pines. Rained in the night, and we had to put up the tent in the dark.

Aug. 17th. Weather cloudy, but more clear than before, and Pike's Peak was visible, with snow on the top. Henry killed a straggling bull, too rank and tough to eat. Rode about a dozen miles, and nooned on the head of Kiowa, where, the animals looking ill, we stopped the rest of the day.

Aug. 18th. Nooned on Black Squirrel Creek after traversing a fine piece of pine woods. In the afternoon, a thunder-storm gathered upon the mountains. Pike's Peak and the rest were as black as ink. We caught the edge of the storm, but it had passed by the time we arrived at Jamie's Camp,[179] where several little streams were tumbling down to the bottom in waterfalls. Before night, the black shroud was lifted from the mts. and a bright sunset greeted us.

Aug. 19ᵗʰ. As we left camp, there was promise of a warm and clear day, but white wreaths of cloud soon gathered about the mts., reminding one of Byron's description of Luli and Pargo. The white snow patches—the ravines and the black forests were obscured and revealed by turns—it was a sublime and beautiful sight.

Presently the weather grew clear, and we reached the stream of the Fontaine qui Bouille, in time to noon there.

In the afternoon a tremendous storm of thunder, rain, and hail, beginning on the mts., overtook us and drenched us well. The sun presently broke above the mts.—a beautiful [sight], and when the storm passed two fine rainbows appeared, relieved against the thick black and purple of the clouds. Camped lower down Fontaine qui Bouille.

[*Aug.*] *20ᵗʰ.* Made about 12 miles this morning and nooned as before. In the afternoon soon saw the valley of the Arkansas and, soon after, the cornfields and the low mud wall of the Lower Pueblo.[180]

The Crows choose "comrades" from among the whites and each other, and treat them with disinterested liberality. The Sioux pretend to do the same, but (in the case of the whites, at least) they expect a return, with interest, for their gifts, which are otherwise revoked.[181]

The stab given to my mule is a specimen of a Sioux's revenge.

The Pueblo is in a beautiful bottom. Found Richard there, being prevented by the war from going to Taos till the troops make a way. News of the victory at Metamoras [Matamoras]—of Kearney's march to Santa Fe—and of the road below being full of troops.

The Pueblo built like a rude trading fort. But two or three men and a few Spanish women there. Richard entertained us hospitably in the little mud room, the best in the fort, and gave us a good supper on the floor.[1]

The Mormons that came across with him are on the other side

---

[1] At this point the journal begins to use only one side of the page. Parkman's failing health is indicated by the paucity and terseness of the remaining notes, except when the fever of the buffalo hunt revived him.—Ed.

encamped for the winter, and perhaps longer, and on the 21ˢᵗ we rode over to see them. Found them at work upon their log-houses, but they suspended their labors to talk with us. Some of them completely imbued with the true fanatic spirit—ripe for anything—a very dangerous body of men. One of them had been wounded by a grizzly bear in coming here. A great many more are said to be on their way up the Arkansas.

The barefaced rascal, Bonny.

[*Aug.*] *22ⁿᵈ*, *23ʳᵈ*, *24ᵗʰ*. Spent these three days in riding down the Arkansas from Pueblo to Bent's Fort.[182]

[*Aug.*] *25ᵗʰ*. Near noon, encamped within a few miles of Bent's. All the grass about here eaten by the animals of the Mormon emigrants and the troops. Visited the fort in the afternoon. Holt[183] was in charge, the rest being absent. Several sick officers and soldiers, the troops having suffered much in coming up from the heat and the excessive use of water. The military ardor of the invalids[184] had chiefly evaporated. Simpson—Lt. Abbot, of the dragoons—Forrest, who is to go down with us. A man on the road told us that the Spaniards would evacuate Santa Fe without fighting.[185] Papers at the Fort, with accounts of the Matamoras victory. A very hot day— the area of the Fort burning hot.

[*Aug.*] *26ᵗʰ*. Sent on Delorier with the cart, to encamp a few miles below the fort, while we staid and dined there. A volunteer named Hodgman,[186] who has been at the fort sick with a brain-fever—a very "slow coach"—is to go down with us, as also two men from California, Munro[e][187] and the sailor Ben.[188] A homesick emigrant, turning back from Bridger's Fort,[189] is with them. The commissary officer at the fort furnishes Hodgman with provisions, but no gun. Holt and young St. Vrain[190] treated us very hospitably. The Bents[191] are both absent. Yesterday, 40 waggons of supplies for the Santa Fe exped. came up in very poor plight.

Several Shienne lodges are a mile or two below the Fort, the main body of the nation being on Dry Creek after buffalo.

[*Aug.*] *27th*. Left camp, rode about 12 miles, and nooned. Hodgman had trouble with his new mule. Ben very ready and active.

Afternoon, camped some eight miles below nooning place. Henry and Ellis, or rather H. alone, caught three stray dragoon horses, in very low condition and bitten by the wolves. The worst of them was taken by Ellis, we retaining the others.

[*Aug.*] *28th*. Made a morning march of 15 miles, one of our new auxiliaries in the cart. Camped on Arkansas—H. killed a crane and a fawn. Mexican *soap plant*—tarantula—lizards—very hot.

Hodgman, good-natured but helpless, has been clerk on Mississipi steamboats for eight years—has rubbed through the world for thirty—and is a boy yet. How much a man may see without learning! Ben, the sailor—his stories of California horses and horsemen. Afternoon, made a good march. River always near.

[*Aug.*] *29th*. Nooned on Arkansas. Afternoon, met a train of Santa Fe waggons, belonging to McLaughlin [Magoffin][192]—news that the buffalo were within a day and a half—the Arapaho village, just this side. Also of Pawnees on the road. They killed Swan. He was buried, but they dug him up and scalped him. McL. saw his remains, mangled by the wolves, and reburied them.

[*Aug.*] *30th*. Afternoon, met a train of government waggons. They say that the road is dangerous. They themselves were alarmed, and had made a halt of some time, a few days back. Raw, smock-faced boys, and of a sickly appearance. By a ready lie Hodgman procured "sick rations" from Coates, the master driver. They told us that the Pawnees had tried to steal horses from Ewing's[193] party, and that Ewing had fired at and killed one as he approached. Advise us to make our best speed between the Caches and the Pawnee Fork. Buffalo near.

Aug. 31st. This afternoon, saw the Arapaho village on the other side of the river. Crossed over with Henry and Q. Hodgman, thinking the whole party were going, was clamorous for my pistols, and wished to put on his cap and uniform coat, to strike terror.

Some young men who were guarding their numerous horses went with us. Village all in a stench with meat. Squaws busy with skins. Sat before one of the chief lodges, holding our horses fast, and the curious crowd soon gathered around. Bad faces—savage and sinister. In complexion form, size, and feature inferior to the Sioux. Their faces formed a complete wall around us. Distributed a few presents— traded a shield, trail-ropes, etc.—took out some awls, and had the women called to receive them. They came screaming with delight— very ugly and dirty, like the men. The whole village, lodges and all, were in keeping with the inhabitants. Near sunset, rode through the long grass and across the Arkansas to camp, where a few Inds. had arrived before us. Hodgman was engaged in trading a robe with them, and behaved so ridiculously, or rather insanely, that he amused us all. Jim[m] made great fun of him. H. traded one of the horses we found for a mule.

At night the wolves set up a most mournful and discordant howling which lasted all night. There was little sleep in camp—the men were anxious for the horses—H. was sick—Hodgman was fidgetty and restless—and I was kept awake by the burning pain of my poison[194]— the horses, too, tramped incessantly through the camp. Hodgman woke me out of a nap with a story that he had seen an Ind. in a white robe drive off three horses, which were just out of sight. Went out to see, and on the way he talked so vaguely and strangely that I perceived the fever had not left his brain. It was, I suppose, nothing but his fright.

Sept. 1. Began to see plenty of bulls. Q. and I each killed one. Wolf tracks astonishingly numerous. Nooned on Arkansas, and as we rested after dinner, saw a large band of Arapahos full drive after a herd of cows across the river. Saddled horses and rode through the sands and shallow water in time to see the ground strewed with carcases, and the process of butchery began.

We had not gone a mile, when the prairie in front was literally black with buffalo.[195] Q. and I put after them, driving them up the hills on the right. The mare brought me upon the rear of a large herd. In the clouds of dust I could scarcely see a yard, and dashed

[m] The sailor, previously mentioned as Ben, is hereafter referred to as Jim.—Ed.

on almost blind, amidst the trampling of the fugitives. Their rumps became gradually visible, as they shouldered along, but I could not urge the mare amongst them. Suddenly down went buffalo after buffalo, in dust and confusion, into an invisible ravine some dozen feet deep, and down in the midst of them plunged the mare. I was almost thrown, but she scrambled up the opposite side. As the dust cleared, I fired—the wounded beast soon dropped behind—I plied him with shot after shot, and killed—not a cow—but a yearling bull!

Tonight, the bellowing of the bulls supplied the place of the howling of wolves.

Sept. 2. Advanced among the buffalo a dozen miles or so and camped. H. killed four cows. We are to dry some meat here for the journey. Had met by the way some trading waggons; and after dinner two companies of Munroe and Platte City mounted volunteers, bound for California, came up, and some of them gathered around us—most unmilitary-looking fellows.

Saw this morning an old bull stuck in a quagmire. . . .[n]

Volume III

Sept. 3ʳᵈ. H. killed yesterday four cows, and today meat is drying all round our camp. Hodgman is taken with an astonishing flow of spirits and rattles away in the most amusing fashion. Shot an old bull in the back, as he came up from the river—his death-agonies were terrific. Shot another in the afternoon. H. killed a number of cows, and Q., who was with him, by laying behind one of them killed 5 bulls as they approached. A long line of buffalo stretched over the prairie beyond the river. The roaring and fighting of the bulls were incessant. Very hot in the day, but cloudy at night. Put up the tent, but about 9 o'clock a furious tornado came up, with driving rain; down went the tent upon us all; we held it up as we

[n] Three lines illegible here, because of smudging or erasure.—Ed.

could, and got completely drenched, bedding and all. Hodgman
kept on singing and rattling away, but the predicament was uncomfortable enough.

Sept. 4th. Still at camp, drying meat. Clouds of turkey-buzzards,
hawks, and crows, with here and there an eagle, around the carcases.
Wolves in abundance—they are fighting and howling all night.

Sept. 5th. At camp. Hodgman is very amusing—he has seen a great
deal of *life* and dissipation.

[*Sept.*] *6th.* Left camp and made half a day's journey, when we
stopped to dry meat. No sooner had we left camp than it was
thronged with wolves and clouds of buzzards. Henry killed several
cows when we stopped. I shot some bulls back upon the prairie.
Mounted guard.

[*Sept.*] *7th.*° A beautiful day. Fired at bulls as we rode along. Hodgman ran one at a slow lope! At noon I shot one; and in the afternoon
Q. and I ran some.

[*Sept.*] *8th.*° Cold and dreary.
    On the 6th two companies of volunteers of Price's rgt.[196] came up
to our camp—a set of undisciplined ragamuffins.

[*Sept.*] *7th* (see above).

[*Sept.*] *8th.* Cold and raw. Nooned on Arkansas. More of Price's
regt. came up—St. Louis county—much less raw in appearance
than the former. They had lost horses, and bought some of us. Their
questioning was most pertinacious and tedious. Our amusement is
plaguing Hodgman, whose good-nature is unperturbable—equal to
his gluttony and helplessness. In the afternoon, picked up three
stray horses of the volunteers, saddles and all! We are within 50
miles of Pawnee Fork.

    ° These entries for September 7 and 8 were crossed out, as Parkman had missed a
day, of which the record follows.—Ed.

[*Sept.*] *9th*. Picked up three more horses. Met at noon a train of trading waggons, and got information as to the road. Saw several Pawnee forts, and passed a large Indian trail. In the afternoon, we left the main road along Arkansas, and took the "Ridge Road"[197] —made ten miles and camped on Coon Creek. No wood. Severe gusts of rain at night.

[*Sept.*] *10th*. The traders yesterday told us that we should find plenty of water, but we rode some 25 miles without seeing a drop. Very warm. At length met a company of Price's regt. straggling along in their usual manner. We had just discovered some water, or rather mud, in a ravine two miles from the road. We told the soldiers of this, and they told us in return that there was good water three or four miles farther on. Capt. Garrison, the commissary, was of the party.

Rode on, and as we descended the hollow where the water lay, saw the opposite swell covered with waggons and footmen, and the water itself surrounded by white tents, cattle, and waggons drawn up in order. These were other companies of Price's regt., the Mormon battallion[198] commanded by Col. Smith, and waggons of Mormon emigrants. There is, it seems, a general movement of the Mormons to California. The battallion consists of 500 men, who have volunteered as soldiers, taking this method of emigrating. We encamped lower down the little stream, and were soon surrounded by the inquisitive throng.

Yesterday afternoon, all our American horses were reclaimed by the rightful owners, to the great dissatisfaction of the finders, especially Jim, who parted very reluctantly with his mare.

[*Sept.*] *11th*. Advanced 15 miles to a creek three miles from Pawnee Fork, where we spent the day to recruit the animals. Here we began to see signs of the settlements. There were fine ash and elm trees along the creek.

[*Sept.*] *12th*. Crossed Pawnee Fork—a stream running in a deep channel—plenty of trees—prickly-pear fruit.

Picked up three stray mules. Crossed towards Walnut Creek—made about half way, and turned aside to encamp on Arkansas. About dark, 28 gov'nt waggons came up and formed their *coral* on the road. Hodgman, as usual, rode out on a begging expedition, but upon his hailing the waggons from afar off with "Camp, ahoy!" he was frightened almost to death at seeing the whole force turn out and level their guns at him. They thought he was a band of Inds. raising the war-whoop—were as frightened as he—and came very near shooting him. He behaves on all occasions very foolishly and childishly.

[*Sept.*] *13th*. Met this morning another train of waggons. Nooned on Walnut Creek, where we found grapes, and another trace of the settlements in the shape of walnut trees. Camped on the Big Bend of Arkansas, where the road leaves the river.[199] A train of Sutler's waggons came up.

[*Sept.*] *14th*. Moved across to Cow Creek—16 or 18 miles. H. and I left the line to hunt—chased several bands all in vain, on account of the perverse vigilance of the bulls. Very hot—no water—we were very thirsty, and drank mud-puddles. Approaching Cow Creek and in sight of our camp, saw a band of cows. I held the horses in a ravine—H. approached. He had just got within shot, when a tremendous rattle of musketry came from the bushes on the creek, and out rushed a dozen fellows, belonging to a train of gov'nt waggons that was approaching in the distance. Off ran the cows. We found on the creek plenty of plums and grapes, besides the welcome novelty of a spring of water.

The waggoners proved a very disorderly set, and quite set at defiance the authority of Brown, the master waggoner.

[*Sept.*] *15th*. Advanced to Owl Creek and nooned. Camped on Little Arkansas. Rain at night.

[*Sept.*] *16th*. My 23rd birthday. Nooned at a mudpuddle. Hodgman afflicted with a variety of complaints. Ellis impudent to S. and effectually silenced.

Munroe gives me an acct. of California. Tells a story of a Sioux medicine chief who, Decius-like, sacrificed himself in battle to secure victory to his followers.

[*Sept.*] *17ᵗʰ*. Last night camped on one of the Turkey Creeks. Ceased to keep guard. H. saw signs of Kanzas Inds. Met waggons. The usual questioning. Dead cattle and broken waggons along the road. Prairie hens. Camped on Cotton Wood Creek, where we arrived late. Character of the Prairie entirely changed—green and rich. The Creek a pretty and well timbered stream.

[*Sept.*] *18ᵗʰ*. Nooned, after a long morning, on Lost Spring, where, as last night, we enjoyed the novelty of good water. Moved only two miles in the afternoon, and camped on a mudpuddle. We had brought water to drink with us. Met waggons. Animals getting poor and weak. Rouge's [Hodgman's] feet very sore. Munroe, Jim, and Ellis went ahead, and we saw no more of them.

[*Sept.*] *19ᵗʰ*. Nooned at the beautiful Diamond Spring. Met waggons, *three weeks* from Fort Leavenworth.²⁰⁰ Camped at Rock Creek. A beautiful sunset. Made only 17 miles.

[*Sept.*] *20ᵗʰ*. Came at noon to Council Grove—beautiful meadows and woods. Here was a blacksmith's shop, and a train of waggons repairing. Passing through the luxuriant woods at this place was a foretaste of the settlements. Nooned two miles farther on at the excellent spring called Big John. More woods, and more waggons. The men, like the volunteers, well tired of their trip. Camped on one of the Beaver Creeks, and met another train, conducted by an old man of seventy.

[*Sept.*] *21ˢᵗ*. Camped at Dragoon Creek, after travelling 21 miles. Met waggons. "Whar are ye from? Californy?" "No." "Santy Fee?" "No, the Mountains." "What yer been doing thar? Tradin'?," "No." "Trappin'?" "No." "Huntin'?" "No." "Emigratin'?" "No." "What *have* ye been doing then, God damn ye?" (Very loud, as we were by this time almost out of hearing.)

[*Sept.*] *22ⁿᵈ*. Nooned at the Hundred and Ten. Made a late camp, having come nearly 30 miles with our jaded animals, at Rock Creek. Here we found Messrs. Folger, Lee, and Upton, connected with Bent & St. Vrain, whose waggons were encamped a few miles behind.[201]

[*Sept.*] *23ʳᵈ*. Met Bent's train this morning. St. Vrain was there, as also a brother of Catlin's friend, Joe Chadwick.[202] Nooned at a spring by the roadside. It rained at night. Camped near waggons.

[*Sept.*] *24ᵗʰ*. Hodgman left us. Nooned at a puddle. Met wagons. Camped at another puddle, 30 miles from Westport.

[*Sept.*] *25ᵗʰ*. Nooned at Elm Grove, where we met some men sent to hurry on the tardy waggoners. With them, were a Sac Ind. and a number of squaws—the round faces and flattish features of these Inds. were characteristic of the Algonkin stock, and quite different from the Sioux. Camped at a stream about 12 miles from Westport. Here was a party of traders with their waggons. A cold night.

[*Sept.*] *26ᵗʰ*. Met Maj. Doroughty[203] on his way to look after the waggons. Soon began to see Shawnee farms. A beautiful country; the foliage just touched with the hues of autumn. Neat houses—fields of corn and grain—pastures with cattle—and a glorious day after the dreary rain of yesterday—combined to make the ride agreeable. Saw the Shawnee mission—passed the borders of the forest country where in place of the blossoms of last spring was now hanging fruit hardly less fragrant—and at length saw Westport. Met Jim and Munroe. Sold off our outfit, and in the afternoon rode to Kanzas, Delorier on his gaunt yellow horse, in tip-top spirits. Pawpaws. Slept under Col. Chick's roof.

[*Sept.*] *27ᵗʰ*. Sunday—remained at the Col.'s.

[*Sept.*] *28ᵗʰ*. Went over to "Wyandot City"—the payment for improvements on their lands in Ohio was going on.[204] A throng of sickly faces about the building—very few full-blooded Inds. A few were adorned with plumes and gewgaws, and had their faces stained with pokeberries. There are men among them, it is said, of considerable education.

Oct. 1st. Stuck on a sandbar in the river. There is a gang of slaves below. Two of them are chained together. Another fellow, with an immense mouth, is beating the banjo, and a dance is going on with the utmost merriment. None are more gay and active then the two fellows chained together. They seem never to have known a care. Nothing is on their faces but careless, thoughtless enjoyment. Is it not safe to conclude them to be an inferior race?

> "The mind is its own place and of itself
> Can make a Heaven of Hell, a Hell of Heaven!"

Appendix: Account Book, Historical Notes, and Chronological Itinerary of Oregon Trail Trip

[St. Louis]

[J. B.] Clapp,[205] 62 St. Ch[arle]s north of ——

[M. S.] Cerré, 36 Pine St.

At Wiggins', Main St., near Market

[Cambridge]

Commons, up to Nov. 3 —— 5

1

[Philadelphia]

Feb. 15

[F. J.] Fisher—85 Front St.

Pine Ids Sch 8th

[J. S.] Hav[iland]—196 Spruce

White, Walnut St. bet. 4th & 5th

Mrs. Richard [Biddle?]

[St. Louis]

Campbell[206] & Fitzpatrick, Main St. 3rd House above Bank

Corner of Morgan and 7th, Waggon Murffit

[Baltimore]

Brantz L. Mayer[207]—82 St. Paul St., office at 10 o'clock

Burnap, 49 N. Calvert St.

Eliot & Swartout

10th Peters

[Law School]

Omit Estates Tail
do ——— after possibility
Copyholds
Statute Merchant, [staple?,] Elegit
Advowsons, Tithes, Commons
Offices, Dignities, Franchises
Escheat
Not read Vol. 5—except Private Acts and King's Grants & Recoveries

---

Sept. 28, '45

Preface to Pope's *Iliad*

Blackstone
Lieber on Property & Labor
Law of real property—3rd vol. of Kent.
Tenures—Wright on tenderers—Dalrymple on Feuds
Sullivan's Dig.—Lomax's Digest. Woodson
Estates for Life—Bisset's
Roper—Merchand & [?]
Bacon's Abridg.—Estates for years
Woodfalls on Landlord and tenant. Comyn, do.
Bacon on Statute of Uses—Chief Justice Gilbert, do.
Powell on morgages by ——— Cornish on morgages—Patch, do.
Gilbert on rents
Angell on adverse enjoyment
Angell on limitations
Alienation
Shepherd's precedent of a deed.
Shepherd's Touchstone—on conveyancing.
Barton—Preston—on conveyancing—Perkins, do.
Powell on divises. Wigram [?] on wills.
Feuds. Dalrymple on feuds—Cruise on Real properties
Leges Barbarorum
Executory Devises
Hawley v. Northampton, 8 Mass.
Forfeiture for treason abolished by U. S. statute—and by the statutes of *some* of the States.
International boundary by rivers—Dunlap v. Stetson—Mason's Rep. Maine and Mass. claim the marsh for 100 yds. from the shore.

Historical Notes

Arbuth. *John Bull;* Addison on Italy.

Read John Ledyard's remarks on different nations of savages—see his *Life* towards the end *passim.*[208]

Write for *Del[aware] Reg.*

For notice of Amherst see *Gent.'s Mag.,* Sept. 1797, "Annual Necrology 1797-98." Chalmer's *Biog. Dict.,* Collin's *Peerage.*

Burnap, Baltimore. Furness

Mr. P. A. Remsen's—two miles from B[altimore] on Hookstown road, a little beyond first gate (Draper's Address)

[New York]

Call on [J. R.] Brodhead[209]

Leave letters

Knickerbocker [Magazine].[210] Hist. Soc.

[Ramsay] Crooks[211]—Univ. Pl., between Eleventh & Twelfth

John R. Bartlett

[Law School]

Studies Parallel to Cruise

Law of Real Property—Wright on Tenures—Lomax's Dig.

Coke, Lit.; Life, Bisset

Parke on Dower

Comyn's Landlord and Tenant

Uses & T

Bacon

Cornish—Saunders

Fletcher

Mortgages

Patch—Coats—Rand's Powell

Remainders

Farn

Common

Abner—Woolwich

Gilbert

Prescription

Best on presumptive

Deeds

Shepherd's Touchstone

Watkins—Preston
Cornish—Perkins
Devises
Jarman- -Foxhead
Ram—Wigram
Art. on Consuls—*Hunt's Merchants' Mag.*—late no. (English Consuls)[212]

Historical Notes

"Young Bolton," a clergyman, who, says Morris, is writing a history of Westchester C'nt'y.

The extracts from E[nglish] newspapers down to 1800 mentioned by Brodhead as being in the N. Y. Hist. L'b'ry.

There is also there a set of *St. James' Cron[icle]* '63 '64.

Simms, *Schoharie County and Border Wars of N. Y.*, contains a sketch of Devil's Hole Fight, etc.

The Clinton Papers—in Mrs. Beekman's possession, N. Y.

The map in the Hist. Soc. L'b'y.—Sullivan's march.

Mrs. [W. L.] Stone has, says Moore, two trunks full of Johnson papers, belonging to an Eng. or Irish family—she proposes to write J's life.

Oneota

Whitehead's *History of N. Jersey*

Enquire of the Rutherford family.

    "   of Mr. King, co-editor of the *Courier*, N. Y.

Mrs. Stone is a sister of Dr. Wayland.

Gordon—Trenton

Fenno Hoffman, N. Y.

Write to R. Conyngham—Stevens—Shippen and Burd papers in possession of Mrs. Thompson.

Write to Chs. Miner about the Elder papers still in his hands.

The Armstrong papers now at Carlisle—to be sent to the Hist. Soc.

Write to Mr. Biddle of Pittsburg. J. W. Biddle.

Bouquet letters in the Fisher family.

Francis papers in the ——— family

Lee papers on the Inds.

Minutes of the Friendly Ass.

Peter's papers

Mr. Smith

J. W. Biddle, Pittsburgh.

St. John de Crèvecœur's work—Bouquet—Phil. Soc. Lib'y

Watson's *Annals of Phil[adelphia]* for acct. of Friendly. Ass.

C. A. Poulson, Jr. Philad[ia]

John Penington, Bookseller

St. Clair Papers in Philadel. mentioned by [L. H.] Draper

Foulke family—the son at Kittunning, father near Freeport. Bouquet MS.

J. N. Whiting, Bookseller, Columbus, write for Hist. Soc. *Coll.* of Ohio part Second, Vol. I.

Hist. of Indiana by John B. Dillon at Indianapolis

Brown's *Hist. Illinois* (F[rench] settlers, etc.)

Patterson's *Hist. of the Backwoods*

American Pioneer 2 vols.—John S. Williams, Cincinati (descrip. & plan of Ft. Pitt)

Ind. Wars of the United States by Moore. Philad[ia], Gorton, 56 N. 3rd St. 1843

Wm. Leaner & Son, Bookseller, Batavia, N. Y. (write for Mary Jennison)

Washington Papers in Congress—examine them carefully.

"Address delivered before the Vincennes Hist. Soc." By Judge Law. (Send for it.)

Hon. John Law, Vincennes (ask concerning the Hist. Coll. there).

Col. John Johnston, Piqua, Miami County, Ohio. (He has been Ind. agent, and can give traditions of Pontiac.)

Hon. Nathaniel Pope, Kaskaskia.

Rev. John M. Peck, 31 N. 6th St., Philad[ia] (till 1st May—then Rock Spring, Illinois) (Enquire of Pontiac War.)

Campbell's *Bushy Run?*

Get for Draper, Hutchins. Send Whiting's *Discourse.*

Cresap Papers mentioned by Mr. Brantz Mayer as to be sent to Baltimore Hist. Soc.

(Copy for Mr. Mayer the poem on Maryland in H[vd] L'b'y. For Fisher, copy Hamilton's letter.

Ask Mead where Hutchin's Papers are.

An old Seneca, named Blacksnake, 96 yrs old, living at Allegania settlement, 30 miles from Buffalo, was at the Devil's Hole massacre, and tells the story.

Notes

Jan. 15 [1846]. The Swiss on the Sound Steamer—he was from Splügen —had walked with his box of watches and trinkets on his shoulders, all over Germany, Austria, etc. What chiefly displeased him in America was the treatment of women, who in his country, he says, are served in the same way as men, and he could see no reason why it should not be so.

Jan. 17. The black barber at whose shop I waited on Sat. night. "Coffee" said that he was a conglomerate of Caffer [Kaffir] and Moorish blood on his father's side—and Indian, white, and Negro, on his mother's. He had been a traveller—had laid up a few dollars, and, instead of trying to multiply them, had taken the whim of seeing the world.

April 17. Tradition here (St. Louis) says that Pontiac was killed in a drunken fray *near Cahokia.*

Letter to Pliny Miles, care of Chs. A. Hough, Baltimore, Md.

Baptiste Vallée of St. Geneviève must have seen Pontiac.

Mr. Lignest P. Chouteau tells me, as coming from his father, that Pondiac had a high command over the Inds. in Montcalm's army—that the English hired an Indian to kill him at Cahokia—that the Spanish requested his body, and buried it at St. Louis.

Old Mr. Chouteau speaks of him as six feet high, of very commanding appearance, and when he saw him, very splendidly dressed.

Opium and Brandy (Diarrhea)
Ipecac—vomit
Sup. Carb. Soda—acidity
Rhubarb and aniseed (costiveness)

Sandford's *Hist. of the Indians.*

Hildreth of Marietta (says [N. B.] Craig) has the St. Clair papers. He is writing a history of Ohio or the Reserve, and has in press a Hist. of Va.

Blister once a week—in front of ear—behind—and on back of neck.
1st ointment for a month.
2nd do., six weeks, applied every other day.

Proceedings, N. Y. Hist. Soc., 1844—p. 77 Schoolcraft's *Indian Names of New York*

Consult Edwin James[213]

Dobson's *Annals of the War* (Old F[rench])

Some Acct. of the N. A[merican] Inds., their Genius, Character, Customs and, Disposition towards the F. and E. Nations, 8 vo. 1754.

The Country of the Confederate Inds. 1760 (Evans' Analysis of his Map).

Benjamin P. Poore, No. 5 Rue Chananielles, Faubourg St. Germain [Paris]

John F. Watson, Germantown

Rev. John F. Schermerhorn (from near Albany) has some of Johnson's letters.

For Wayland: No competent person would undertake it. Money or affection for the deceased would be the only motives.

[W. L.] Stone's plan could not be strictly carried out by me—I have not his resources of recollection, etc.—the work would be meagre.[214]

Notes on the North West & Pontiac

Alfred Elwyn, M.D., Walnut St., East Schuykil 8th, Philada.

Mem. of Heckewelder, just published

Edward Armstrong

John Jordan, Jr.

R. L. Dickson, No. 59 South 3rd St., Phil[a].

Miss Mary Heckewelder, Bethlehem, Northampton Co., P[a]. Inquire for the Heckewelder MS. relating to Bouquet's exped. *Jordan.*

Samuel Brenizer, Harrisburg

Richard Biddle, Esq. Pittsburg. (Mr. Reed)

Look up the C[n]. Pt. [Crown Point] orderly books and the Letters for J. Sonntag Havilland (copy)

Neville B. Craig, Pittsburg, (ed. of *Olden Time*)

John Jay Smith, Librarian, Philad[a]. L'by.

William B. Reed, Atty & Councillor, Philad[a].

Write to Watson (See *Annals,* V. 2, p. —) F. appreciation.

Write to Robert (?) Clark, son of the late Gen. W[m]. Clark, St. Louis, enquiring of his father's papers.

Keep an eye on McKenney's lost trunk of papers, deposited at the Washington House—it contained the original papers of his accts. in the *Tour,* etc.

Write to Trowbridge, Detroit.

Shawnese = Chasuanous (*Am. State Papers*)

Jouett's "Report, containing the Descrip. of Detroit," is in *Am. St. Papers,* Vol. V.

Indian Affairs, Vol. I, 758, also, *Public Lands,* Vol. I, p. 190.

Cagnawagas = Kaughnawaugas = Caunawagas

"Conferences at Burlington and Easton 1758." Appendix to Smith's N. Jersey

Franklin's *Hist. Review of the Govn't of P*ª.

Gordon's *Gazetteer of P*ª.

Barton's *Views*
Volney's *View*
Douglass's *Summary*
Chalmer's *Collection of Treaties* } Inds.

Geo. H. Moore, Historical Rooms, University, N. York

Giles F. Yates, ask Schoolcraft, Schenectady

N. Y.: [G. H.] Moore—Allen—Crooks—flask—cotton.

Phil.: Elwyn—Fisher (Peters, McMurtrie), Poulson, Reed, Jordan (Bird [Burd] papers)—Frémont—ticket—map.

Harrisburg: Craig—Brenizer—return papers.

Hildreth of Marietta (says Craig) has the St. Clair papers.

Oregon Trail Accounts
Travelling Expenses March 28, 1846

March 28:	Fare to N. Y.	$ 5.
	Tea on board	.50
M. 29:	Sundries	1.00
31:	Bill at Astor	4.75
"	Porter, etc.	.75
"	Fare to Phil.	4.00
"	Copying MSS.	4.50
Apr. 1st:	Fare to Pittsburg	11.00
"	Book from Penington	.75
"	Bill at Jones	2.25
"	Porter, etc.	.50
"	Drinking flask	1.25
"	Porter	.12½
Ap. 2:	Brenizer, copying	25.00
Ap. 6:	Meals on road	2.00
"	*Olden Time*	2.00
"	Dinner, etc.	.66
"	Map of R[iver] Ohio	.25
Ap. 7:	Hotel Bill—Pittsburg	4.81
"	*Am. Pioneer*	4.00
"	Fare to Cincinnati	5.00

Ap. 7:	Sundries	.25
9:	Boots cleaned	.12½
"	Hotel at Cin.	.75
"	Porter	.25
"	Johnston's *Articles*	1.00
10:	Fare to St. Louis	6.00
"	Writing apparatus	1.00
"	Sundries	.25
13:	"	.25
" 13[14?]:	Porter	.25
"	*Desc. of St. Louis*	.50
"	Bath	.25
"	Hunting knife	2.25
"	Swab-stick	.50
15:	Concert	1.00
"	Postage	.10
"	Horse & Ferry, etc.	1.40
17:	Vest	5.20
"	Sundries	.30
20:	Hat	1.25
"	Suspenders	.25
"	Goggles	1.75
"	Pistols	14.00
"	Bath	.25
"	Cape	.20
22:	Horse hire	.50
"	Gun repaired	1.57½
"	Collar	.20
"	Sundries	.20
24:	Shirts	3.00
"	Saddle bag	2.50
"	Spurs	.75
25:	Bullets, etc.	.75
"	Pistols repaired	1.00
"	Pencil for F.	3.00
	Cr. Shaw to Holster & Guncase	5.00
26:	Exchange	1.50
"	Veil, etc.	.82
"	Horse	40.00
27:	Sundries	1.75

May :   Horse Prov., etc.   3.00
  ,,   Carriage of horse   5.00
  ,,   Moccasins, etc.   1.10
  4:        Horse   60.00

Accts. in Common with Shaw

	Paid by	
	S[haw]	P[arkman]
Powder (¼ keg)		1.75
Hooks & lines, Caps, etc.	2.85	
Powder horns	1.50	
Tobacco	6.25	
Shot, Caps, etc.		
Water-proof cloth	3.15	
Blankets & powder	20.50	
Bread	7.42	
Tent equipments	5.00	
Shot	.62	
Ind. presents	*75.11	
Harness		65.48
Groceries	16.75	
	139.15	67.23
Spy Glass		7.00
Patent pencils		.50
Porter		.50
Basins		.50
Cart	43.00	
Tent	20.23	
Drayage	1.50	
Ribbons, needles, etc.	2.85	
Fare etc. to Westp[ort]		32.00
Sundries		2.00
Waggon hire, etc.		4.00
Buckskin		.80
*Henry	10.00	
De Lorier		20.00
Sundries		4.25
Sundries		5.00
	77.58	76.55

	S.	P.
Horse for Henry	38.00	
Col. Chick's Bill		8.00
Lead	.50	
Henry's Saddle		2.75
Horses shod		1.87½
Pots & pans		6.12½
Mule—to Henry's Acct.	15.00	20.00
Sundries		2.25
Bacon, etc.		9.92
Delaware Ferry		2.00
Mules		75.00

    *Paid Henry on joint acct.
     Ind. presents—23.82 (Shaw)
     Advance wages— $10.00 (Shaw)
     Mule—30 (check on C[houteau] & V[allée])
       "   5 (P.)

| | 53.50 | 127.92 |

Paid Delorier advance wages 20.00 (P.)
Engaged Raymond June—on leaving Ft. Laramie for Chugwater Camp.
Advanced Raymond $3.00 price of shirt at Laramie (pd. from draft on Fur comp'y)

Advanced Raymond, Taylor's work	.75
Exchange for rifle	10.00
Bill at Planters'	25.00

Bought on Credit at Fort Laramie, June 28

Sundries	29.95
12 lb. Flour (.25 pr. lb.)	3.00
1 Shirt for Raymond	3.00
42 lb. Bacon (.13½ cts.)	5.25

    Henry bought on our acct. July 2nd of Richard and Bissonnette:

70 lbs. flour (.15 pr. lb.)	10.50
(he bought also 25 lbs. for himself)	
10 lbs. coffee & sugar—1.00 per lb.	10.00
8 lbs. bacon (.10 pr. lb.)	.80

Bt. [Bought]—Ft. Laramie
$105.50

| Common ac. | 49.50 |

Q.A.S.	49.50
F. P.	$ 6.50
Q.A.S.	10.00

Ft. Bent

Common Acct.	43.00
F. P.	6.00
Raimond's wages	38.00

Receipts

P.	$47.00
S.	35.00
Common	66.00
P.	

Historical Notes

Armstrong family: The Col. had two sons—of the[m] the youngest, Genl. A., has a son living near Baltimore—others, one of them called Koskiusko, in N. Y.

Dr. A., of Carlisle, thinks the family papers in their hands.

Baird of Reading (formerly of Carlisle) has collected materials for a history of Cumberland Cnty.

Expenses

Jan. 16, 1846:	Fare to N. Y.	$5.00
	Dinner	.50
	Carriage	.25
	N. B. Always take a driver's card.	
	Supper	.25
17:	Breakfast	.25
	Omnibus, etc.	.16¾
	"	.12½
18:	Breakfast	.25
	Din[n]er—Astor House	1.00
	Tea	.25
19:	Breakfast	.25
	Dinner (at Florence's)	.67½
	Tea	.25
	Omnibus	.25

Jan. 20:	Lodging: (at the Globe—room without fare—3 days and one night—three shirts washed)	3.00
	Breakfast (Globe restaurant)	.37½
	Porters and boots	.37½
	(N.B. employ a porter in preference to a carriage for baggage)	
	Fare to Trenton	2.50
	Porter at T.	.25
	Dinner & Tea	1.00
	Fare to Phil.	.75
	Porter	.25
	Ale	.06½
	Roger's *N. America*	1.25
22:	Bill at Sanderson's: ($2. per day—every fire .50!— candle .12—lunch for two .50)	4.83
	Waiter	.25
	Beggar	.18
	Museum	.25
	Ale	.12½
26:	Bill at Washington House: $2 pr. day	10.00
	Waiter and porter	.50
	Fare to Baltimore	4.00
	Sundries	.12½
27:	Chaise to Draper's	2.00
	Hist. of Backwoods	1.00
28:	Breakfast: (Tea, eggs, rolls, & toast—at lunch room under hotel)	.25
	Bootblack	.10
	Ale	.12
29:	Breakfast, etc.	.37
	Umbrella	.75
	Chocolate, etc.	.18
	Ale	.12
30:	Breakfast	.25
	Dinner	.75
	Copying	1.50
	Tea	.25
31:	Breakfast	.25
	Dinner	.75
	Chocolate	.12½

Feb. 3:   Bill at Barnum's   14.83
            Waiters, porters, etc.   .75
            Fare to Harrisburg   .03
            Bill at Buchler's   1.25
            Fare to Philada.   4.00
            Omnibuses   .42
    4:      Books   1.50
    5:      Copying   5.00
    7:      Bill at W. House   6.75
            Waiter   .25
            Carriage   .50
            Fare to N. Y.   4.00
            (Always ask for a porter's card—see your baggage
            ticketed in person and get the number of the car
            that contains it)
    10:     Omnibuses   .30
            Ale   .12½
    11:     *Oneota*   1.25
            Omnibus   .30
            Museum   .25
    12:     Omnibus   .18

HENRY CHATILLON

FRANCIS PARKMAN

Howland & Aspenwall, South St. [N. Y.]

Crooks, 30 Ann St. [N. Y.]

Hayes & Barber, Market St.

Comstock, Main St.

Tow—cooking implements

Flour?—Bacon—tongues—cups and plates—spoons—tea—matches—flint & steel—patches—salt and pepper: 5 lbs., 2 lbs.—axe—bullets for gun.

R—— Powder, 17 Levee Smith & B., Enfield, Conn.

Paid Henry on joint account by Q. A. S.: $33.82—(paid along with Ind. present acct.)

Baird, Reading, Penna.

Miss Lyons, Lancaster

Mr. G. Lyons,   Cross corner of —— and Paine St.

Mr. T. Green[?]

Genl. J. A. Armstrong, eminently notable general, for patriotism, valour, and piety, departed this life 9th March 1795, aged 77

[The following appear to be catch lines to material dealing with the Paxton Boys and the Carlisle massacre—Ed.]

In my last
Besides this tribe
Whilst these precautions
Whether this butchery
Whilst they were upon their march
In the morning
Notwithstanding
The day passing over
Before I proceed
The persons in arms
About 11 o'clock
In the afternoon
Night
The weather now clear
The following day
It was now hoped
The Paxton chiefs
think it is now
P. S. I should take it
Struck the Dog
Aug. 19th

CHRONOLOGICAL ITINERARY OF OREGON TRAIL TRIP

March 28.	Left Boston.
March 29.	In New York City, consulting authorities.
March 30.	In New York City, consulting authorities.
March 31.	To Philadelphia.
April 1.	Left Philadelphia for Pittsburgh. Reached Harrisburg.
April 2.	Carlisle.
April 3.	Chambersburg.
April 6.	Pittsburgh.
April 7.	Visited Braddock's Field and site of Fort Pitt.
April 8.	Took steamboat down Ohio.
April 9.	Cincinnati.
April 10.	Louisville.
April 11.	Fort Massiac. Paducah.
April 13.	St. Louis. Shaw did not join Parkman here until after the 16th.
April 15.	Cahokia. Visited Madame Jarrot. Met Midshipman Woodworth.
April 19.	Cahokia. Visited P. L. Cerré. Quotes Thomas Fitzpatrick's letter to Lt. Abert.
April 22.	Jefferson Barracks. Reports meeting with Fitzpatrick.
April 25.	St. Louis. Met Dixon, Ewing, and Jacob.
April 27.	Met Pierre Chouteau, Sr., and Lignest P. Chouteau. Parkman, Shaw, and guide Chatillon took steamer *Radnor* for Kansas Landing [Westport].
April 29.	Entered Missouri River.
April 31 [May 1?]	Jefferson City.
May 2.	Reached Independence Landing at sunset. Walked about camp of Santa Fe traders and Oregon emigrants.
May [3].	Reached Kansas Landing. Put up at Colonel Chick's.
May 5 [4].	Rode to Westport and to Sauk encampment on prairie. Joined Chandler's party and bought horse.
May 5.	Rode across the Kansas to visit the Wyandots.
May 6.	Bought two mules at Westport, and led them to Kansas Landing.

May 7.   Rode to Independence. Emigrant party from western states setting out for rendezvous on prairie. Rode back to Westport with Woodworth. Emigrant train to be organized on 9th or 10th and set out on 11th. Met Shawnee Chief Parks at McGee's in Westport and visited Boone's store.

May 8.   Chandler's party set off. Parkman's delayed by balky mule.

May 9.   Parkman, Shaw, Chatillon, and *engagé* Delorier left Westport. Passed Shawnee Mission. Camped on the Kansas.

May 10.   Crossed Kansas on ferry [Lower Delaware Crossing]. Camped 8 miles beyond, on Delaware reservation.

May 11.   Joined Chandler's party [Captain Chandler, Jack Chandler, Romaine, Sorel, Boisvert, and Wright] at Fort Leavenworth.

May 12.   Visited Colonel Kearny at fort, and Kickapoo village. Lunched with trader and returned to fort. Entertained by Kearny.

May 13.   Left Leavenworth with Britishers and lost trail within a few miles. Ended up at Kickapoo trader's and then followed fresh dragoon trail. Thunderstorm at night.

May 14.   Wagon stuck in creek after nooning. Pontiac ran off on back trail in afternoon.

May 15.   Nooned on Clough Creek (?). Met four dragoons, who told them that they had missed last year's dragoon trail a day and a half back, and were on way to Iowa Village and St. Joseph's Trail. Decided to keep on.

May 16.   Nooned on deep creek. Struck St. Joseph's Trail. Camped on week-old camp site of "Mormons." 30 miles in last three days.

May 17.   Twenty miles before nooning. Bath in pool full of snakes and insects. Dorbugs infested camp.

May 18.   Horses ran off before start. Nooned on old "Mormon" campsite. Trail better and prairie treeless.

May 19.   Crossed Little Nemaha (?) and nooned after 10 miles. Trouble with Britishers last night and today about camping and nooning pláces. Camped together that night, having done 20 miles in day. Violent thunderstorm.

May 20.   Camped in shelter of line of trees as bad storm broke.

"On the Mormon trail and probably within ten days of the Platte."

May 21.   Set out at noon, after storm had ended. Passed recent grave. Picked up stray cow.

May 22.   Trouble with wagons on muddy prairie. Picked up another cow at nooning. Camped on Little Vermillion (?). Made 18 or 20 miles.

May 23.   Reached Big Blue. Rafted across. Camped on creek, 5 miles beyond. Emigrant wagons in sight. Captain visited them in evening.

May 24.   Struck Oregon Trail beyond Big Blue, seven days from Platte. Kearsley, captain of emigrant train, came to their camp in morning. Passed 20 wagons of advance guard of train in morning. Romaine invited Kearsley and 4 wagons to join Parkman's party, after break-up of train. Advanced 25 miles to Turkey Creek. More wagons in sight.

May 25.   Broke axle of wagon at Elm Creek and emigrants went on ahead.

May 26.   Nooned on Black Walnut Creek. Camped on Wyeth's Creek, after 20 miles.

May 27.   Nooned on nameless creek and camped on Little Blue (?).

May 28.   Grave of 4 year-old child, "May 1845." Nooned on Little Blue. Camped on same stream after doing 12 miles in afternoon. First night-guard. Two Delawares.

May 29.   Kept along Little Blue, and camped on it.

May 30.   Thirty miles from Little Blue to Platte. Met Turner and another emigrant, just stopped by 6 Pawnees. At camp, emigrant from Robinson's party came in looking for Turner. Large party of Pawnees ahead. Parkman had crossed large Pawnee trail in afternoon.

May 31.   Met hunting party of Pawnees in morning. Overtook Robinson's party of 40 wagons bound for Oregon. Camped after 12 miles. Emigrants went on.

June 1.   Passed Robinson's party again. Caught up with Kearsley's wagons, passed them, and camped on Plum Creek after 25 miles.

June 2.   Pawnee horse grave. In company with Kearsley. Shaw wanted to separate from Chandler's party. Camped on flat by Platte.

June 3.   Ten miles in morning over plain. First buffalo hunting in afternoon.

June 4.   Met Papin and boats from Laramie. Saw Woodworth, with party close behind. Buffalo hunt in morning, 10 miles in afternoon. Camped amid hills.

June 5.   Buffalo hunt. Emigrants' cattle driven off by wolves that night.

June 6.   Thus detained, went buffalo hunting. Parkman got lost. Camped near Side Fork [South Platte].

June 7.   Followed South Fork. Parkman and Shaw decided to part company with emigrants and Chandler's party after crossing South Fork. Four emigrants from party ahead, in search of 123 cattle and horses run off by large Indian party. Sorel, Romain, and two emigrants did not return at night from buffalo hunt.

June 8.   Crossed South Fork. Stranded emigrant party on north side. Romaine and others returned.

June 9.   Advanced 16 miles.

June 10.   Parted with Chandler's party. Passed around head of Ash Hollow and camped on North Fork [North Platte]. Camped by emigrant corral [Missouri party].

June 11.   Ten miles in morning. Overtaken by emigrants at nooning, pushed on, and camped by clear, swift stream. No wood for several days.

June 12.   Nooned on Lawrence Fork. Saw Frédéric's wintering place. Chimney Rock in sight. Overtook emigrant party of Americans and foreigners, with whom 5 east-bound men from Laramie were encamped. Camped by Robidoux' party, a mile or two ahead.

June 13.   Joined by Robidoux. Nooned after 8 miles on Platte. Camped by spring at Scott's Bluff after 15 or 16 miles. Joined by western emigrant at camp.

June 14.   Met Smoke's village in morning. Passed two emigrant parties from Missouri. Nooned on Horse Creek with Smoke's village. Camped ten miles farther on.

June 15.   Visited Richard at Fort Bernard. Met Reynal. Nooned by Platte, entertaining Richard. Passed Sabille and Adam's deserted fort. Received at gate of Fort Laramie by Bordeaux. Vasquez, Simoneau, Monthalon, Knight, etc., at fort.

June 16.	Fort Laramie. Smoke's village arrived in morning. Visited Indian camp in evening. Emigrants arrived.
June 17.	Fort Laramie. Emigrants gave feast for Indians. Chandler's party arrived.
June 18.	Fort Laramie. Shaw treated sore eyes of Smoke's squaw and daughter.
June 19.	Fort Laramie. Indian begging dance.
June 20.	Fort Laramie. Smoke gave Parkman puppy feast at noon. Chatillon sent for his squaw Bear Robe to join party. Parkman swapped Pontiac for Paul Dorion's mare Pauline. Parkman, Shaw, Chatillon, Delorier, Raymond, and Reynal, his squaw, and her two nephews set out for Chugwater. Camped seven miles from fort on "wild and beautiful bottoms of the Laramie."
June 21.	Rode 10 miles to Chugwater, camped by its mouth.
June 23.	Chugwater. One of Reynal's nephews, His Horses, sent to find Bear Robe's lodge and get news of war-party rendezvous at La Bonté's Creek.
June 24.	Chugwater.
June 25.	Chugwater. Rode to Fort Laramie. Smoke's village gone north of Platte. Illinois and Michigan emigrants at fort. His Horses returned with son of Bull Bear. Tunica's [Whirlwind's] village 4 days off and Bear Robe due on 27th.
June 26.	Chugwater. Rode to Fort Laramie for supplies. Part of Russell's company arriving there. Tunica arrived. Minniconjous a day or two away. Recent emigrant ball at fort.
June 27.	Chugwater. Rode to Fort Bernard with Paul Dorion. Found Russell's or Bogg's party, the Boones, Ewing, Jacob. Sent letter east by Tucker. Returned to camp and found Shaw and Chatillon gone to bury Bear Robe. Reynal in alarm about Indian raid.
June 28.	Chugwater. Shaw and Chatillon return. Indian at camp, on way to leave squaw with Bissonnette while on war party.
June 29.	Chugwater. Indian left for Fort Laramie.
June 30.	Chugwater. Trappers from fort arrived, and reported arrival of Bissonnette.

July 1.   Chugwater. Henry went to see him. Tunica talked out of war by Bordeaux.

July 2.   Chugwater. Shaw, Parkman, and Reynal rode out in search of Tunica. Met Indian who tells them plans changed and returns to camp with them. Young Bull Bear, his brother, and several others came to camp.

July 3.   Chugwater. Tunica's village arrived and camped near by. Parkman visited camp and was given a pipe by Tunica. Met Old Borgne and Mad Wolf. Mourning for Bear Robe. Given dog feast. Tunica's village abandoned rendezvous at La Bonté's and planned hunt beyond Laramie Mountains and then war party.

July 4.   Chugwater. Three Indians arrived, with rescued Negro Jack.

July (5).   Moved camp to Forks [of Laramie]. Strong Heart Dance. War parade.

July 6.   Shot a war eagle. Left Indian village with trappers for Bitter Cottonwood Creek to meet Bissonnette and accompany him to La Bonté's. Emigrants feast Indians.

July 7.   Waited at Bitter Cottonwood for Bissonnette. Rouleau and Séraphin set out to trap in mountains. Chatron and party arrived from fort with news that Bissonnette will arrive on 8th.

July 8.   Rode to Horseshoe Creek, since Bissonnette did not arrive.

July 9.   Rode to La Bonté's on Platte. No Indians or buffalo. Morin, his squaw, and her brother in camp, as well as her father, a medicine man. Gingras also.

July 10.   Abandoned hope of Indian rendezvous at La Bonté's. Shaw went to Horseshoe Creek in search of Bissonnette.

July 11.   Shaw returned near daybreak, having lost his horse. Parkman and Raymond set out in pursuit of Tunica's village; Chatillon in search of Shaw's horse. Shaw to accompany Delorier and the cart to Horseshoe Creek. Parkman headed south, nooned on Horseshoe Creek, and followed Oregon Trail to Bitter Cottonwood Creek.

July 12.   Animals ran off ten or twelve miles to Side Fork of Laramie [North Laramie]. Camped there.

July 13.   Headed for Laramie Creek. Found tracks on tributary southern creek [Sibille?]. Nooned and headed for mountains. Laramie Peak in sight. Camped where Laramie comes out of hills.

July 14.   Followed southern tributary of Laramie. Then on Indian trail up into "bare and scorching valley" of mountains. Descended into grassy parks amid hills. Crossed bare prairie and followed defiles, like Dixville Notch, beneath bare cliffs. Nooned after 12 miles. Indian forts. Climbed narrow pass and camped beyond its head. Buffalo in sight on distant butte as they emerged from hills.

July 15.   Stony Prairie. Medicine Bow Mts. in distance. Trail led towards head of Laramie Creek. Little lakes. Approaching Snake and Arapaho country, according to Raymond. Found Reynal and Indian village on banks of Laramie.

July 16.   Feasted Indians.

July 17.   Moved camp westward. Camped on fine spring, 10 miles off.

July 18.   Made two moves westward in search of buffalo. First buffalo killed.

July 19.   Meat cached and camp moved 12 miles westward to unknown stream [Rock Creek?].

July 20.   Moved short distance higher up creek. Buffalo surround. Sioux on guard against Snakes and Utes.

July 21.   Robe-making.

July 22.   Parkman and Raymond went out hunting antelope. Séraphin and Rouleau arrived from Laramie Hills, headed for Rockies [Medicine Bow]. Indians out on another surround, though in great fear of Snakes.

July 23.   White Shield uncertain about war party because of sore throat.

July 24.   Squaws still making robes and lodge covers. Rouleau and Séraphin left. White Shield did war dance.

July 25.   War party abandoned. Moved to last camp on creek to collect cached meat, and then to cut lodge poles in Laramie Mountains. Indian quarrel. Squaws mourned dead of last year.

July 26.   Moved nearer mountains [Laramie Hills]. Ceremony in lodge.

July 27.   Moved to mountains. Camped in valley of "clear, cool creek." Shongsha cut. Parkman wandered among mountains like those of New England, while Indians cut lodge poles. Much game, pine and spruce forest,

rocky and precipitous mountains. Mourning for warriors last seen at this spot last summer.

July 28.   Parkman went hunting with Raymond in mountains.
Descended to prairie and saw buffalo. Circled back to
village over mountains.

July 29.   Climbed high, rocky mountain a few miles from camp,
crossing wooded ravines with small, icy streams. Heap
of Hail killed elk.

July 30.   Broke camp and moved "round" to the pass through the
mountains, about 12 miles. Passed campsite of last
year's war party. Hunted mountain sheep near camp.

July 31.   Parkman and Raymond went hunting in hills and rejoined
Indians at camp near crystal spring amid great basin
of rocks.

August 1.   In mountains, following grassy valley amid pine-covered
hills. Camped in grassy nook.

August 2.   Left Indians and set out for fort, with Heap of Hail as
guide. Delayed by butchering black-tailed deer and
rejoined Indians as they descended rocky gorge.
Mountains in front on fire. Descended into milder
region of valleys and streams, and emerged on prairie.
Left Indians and camped on Chugwater.

August 3.   Reached Fort Laramie in morning. Rejoined Shaw,
Chatillon, and Delorier.

August 4.   Parkman's party of five set out for Bent's Fort, accompanied by Rouville and his Ute squaw, bound for
Bissonnette's camp. Camped after ten miles.

August 5.   Nooned on dry stream. Crossed Goshen's Hole and
camped late.

August 6.   Nooned on Little Horse Creek. In afternoon reached
Horse Creek, where Bissonnette, N. Sabille, and party,
and 40 lodges of Tunica's Sioux village and several
Cheyennes were encamped. Horse races, with Paul
Dorion, Rouville, Antoine, and other French Canadians.
Bissonnette feasted Indians.

August 7.   At camp.
August 8.   At camp. Dance of Strong Hearts. The Stabber arrived
with news of Army of the West on the Arkansas and of
victory of Matamoras. Young Bull Bear took Parkman's
party under his protection.

August 9. Indians and Bissonnette moved. Parkman and party continued to Spring Creek.

August 10. Nooned on Pole Creek and camped on little stream beyond.

August 11. Delayed by horses running back to Pole Creek. Nooned on Crow Creek and camped on tributary.

August 12. Nooned low down on Crow Creek, and camped at 9 P.M. at mouth of the Cache à la Poudre. Saw Vasquez [Longs?] Peak.

August 13. Crossed South Fork [of Platte] and nooned near St. Vrain's Fort, after 10 or 12 miles. Rode on 5 or 6 miles and camped near Vasquez' Fort. Fresh Indian trail.

August 14. Passed Fort Lupton, 6 or 7 miles on. Nooned on the Fork. Camped on it, where trail left it to cross over to Cherry Creek.

August 15. Nooned and camped on Cherry Creek. Campsite of Mormons guided by Richard.

August 16. Nooned on Cherry Creek and camped on it where trail left to cross over to the Arkansas.

August 17. Pikes Peak in sight. Rode 12 miles and nooned at head of Kiowa Creek. Camped there because of sick horses.

August 18. Nooned on Black Squirrel Creek. Storm over Pikes Peak. Camped at Jamie's [James'?] Camp.

August 19. Nooned on Fontaine Qui Bouille and camped lower down it.

August 20. Made 12 miles in morning, nooned on Fontaine Qui Bouille. In afternoon saw Arkansas Valley and reached Lower Pueblo. Richard there. News of Matamoras, Kearny's march to Santa Fe, and of troops on Santa Fe Trial.

August 21. Rode across Arkansas to see Mormons. Met Bonney.

August 22-24. From Pueblo to Bent's Fort along Arkansas.

August 25. Nooned a few miles from Bent's, grass being exhausted about fort by Mormons and troops. Visited fort in afternoon. Received by Holt. Invalid soldiers. Simpson, Lt. Abbott of 1st Dragoons, Forrest. Rumor of capitulation of Santa Fe.

August 26. Delorier sent on with cart to camp a few miles below fort, while Parkman dined there. Hodgman, Munroe, Ben the sailor [Jim Gurney], and homesick emigrant [Ellis] join party; Raymond paid off. Both Bents absent. Forty supply wagons arrived. Cheyenne lodges near fort, but most of nation on Dry Creek after buffalo.

August 27. Left camp and nooned after 12 miles. Camped after eight miles more. Three stray dragoon horses caught.

August 28. Fifteen miles in morning. Camped on Arkansas, after "good march."

August 29. Nooned on Arkansas. Met Magoffin's wagons. Buffalo reported a day and a half below, with Arapahos this side of them. Also Pawnees on trail, who had killed Swan, whom Magoffin reburied.

August 30. Met government wagon train under Coates. Trail reported dangerous. Ewing's brush with Pawnees, who tried to steal his horses. Parkman urged to hurry between the Caches and Pawnee Fork.

August 31. Saw Arapahos on south bank and crossed over to visit them in afternoon. Camped on north bank at night. Many wolves.

September 1. Plenty of buffalo bulls. Nooned on Arkansas and afterwards saw Arapahos pursuing band of cows across the river. Rode across and found prairie black with buffalo. Parkman got caught in stampeded herd.

September 2. Advanced a dozen miles among buffalo and camped. Met traders' wagons and two companies of Munroe and Platte City mounted volunteers. Hunted buffalo for supplies for homeward journey.

September 3. More hunting and meat-drying.

September 4. Still at camp, meat-drying.

September 5. Still at camp, meat-drying.

September 6. Set out and made half a day's journey. Encountered companies of Price's volunteers.

September 7. Ran and shot buffalo as they traveled.

September 8. Nooned on Arkansas. More of Price's regiment. Picked up three stray volunteer horses. Fifty miles from Pawnee Fork.

September 9. Picked up three more stray horses. At noon met trading wagons. Saw Pawnee forts and passed large Indian trail. In afternoon left the Arkansas and took Ridge Road. Camped after ten miles on Coon Creek.

September 10. Twenty-five miles without water. Met company of Price's, with Captain Garrison, the commissary. Camped on little stream near more of Price's and the Mormon Battalion. Horses reclaimed by soldiers.

September 11. Advanced 15 miles to creek three miles from Pawnee Fork and camped. First ash and elm trees.

September 12. Crossed Pawnee Fork and camped on Arkansas, halfway to Walnut Creek. Train of 28 army wagons.

September 13. Met another train in morning. Nooned on Walnut Creek. Camped on Big Bend of Arkansas where trail left river. Train of Sutler's wagons.

September 14. To Cow Creek, 16 or 18 miles. Buffalo hunting. Plums and grapes. Army wagon train under Brown.

September 15. Nooned on Owl Creek and camped on little Arkansas.

September 16. Camped on one of the Turkey Creeks. Stopped keeping guard.

September 17. Camped late on Cottonwood Creek, after entering true prairies. Trail littered with dead cattle and broken wagons.

September 18. Nooned on Lost Spring, and camped 2 miles beyond. Met wagons. Munroe, Jim (Gurney), and Ellis went on ahead.

September 19. Nooned at Diamond Spring. Met wagon train three weeks from Leavenworth. Camped on Rock Creek after doing 17 miles.

September 20: Reached Council Grove at noon. Nooned at Big John Spring, two miles beyond. Camped on one of Beaver Creeks, after meeting many wagons.

September 21. Camped on Dragoon Creek after 21 miles.

September 22. Nooned at the 110, and camped at Rock Creek, after doing 30 miles, with Folger, Lee, and Upton of Bent & St. Vrain.

September 23. Met Bent's train, with [Marcellin] St. Vrain and Chadwick.

September 24. Hodgman left for Ft. Leavenworth. Camped 30 miles from Westport.

September 25. Nooned at Elm Grove. Met Sauk Indians. Camped on stream 12 miles from Westport, with party of traders.

September 26. Met Major Dougherty. Passed Shawnee settlements and mission, and entered forest country. Met Jim [Gurney] and Munroe in Westport, where Parkman and Shaw sold their outfit. In afternoon rode to Kansas Landing and put up at Col. Chick's. Delorier lived at Kansas.

September 27. Spent this Sunday at the Colonel's.

September 28. Went over to Wyandot City to seek payment for the Ohio lands.

October 1.   Stuck on sandbar in river.

October ?   Reached St. Louis, where Parkman and Shaw said farewell to Chatillon.

1856 & 1866 Notebook

French Colonization

Introduction

THIS apparently rather uninteresting record of references to authorities, books, and documents, relieved by thumbnail sketches of historic places in Canada, is far more important than it looks, for here is an early measure of Parkman's thoroughness as a historian and of the wide range of his research. Nine years before he published the first volume of *France and England in North America*, he knew most of the sources and many of the pioneers of the history of New France. Barred by illness from travel, after the publication in 1851 of *Pontiac*, his first historical work, he put in five years of concentrated study and carried on a vast correspondence with workers in the field that preoccupied him. Finally, in October and November 1856, during a brief interlude of comparative good health in the long period of physical and mental suffering which plagued Parkman from 1852 to 1862, he was able to make a brief excursion to Quebec, Montreal, and the Ottawa Valley to consult books, authorities, and the scenes of the great history which he had undertaken after publishing *The Conspiracy of Pontiac*.

The task was difficult enough in itself—"Go to work at consulting fifteen hundred books in five different languages with the help of a schoolgirl who hardly knows English, and you will find it a bore," Parkman wrote to his friend E. G. Squier on September 17, 1851—but the young historian was also beset by difficulties quite apart from the task. His eyes were so sensitive that they could not support sunlight, so that his work had to be carried on largely with the aid of others. But still worse was the mental disorder which he thus describes:

"Between 1852 and 1860 this cerebral rebellion passed through great and seemingly capricious fluctuations. It had its ebbs and floods. Slight and sometimes imperceptible causes would produce an access which sometimes lasted with little respite for months. When it was in its milder moods, I used the opportunity to collect material and prepare ground for the future work, should work ever become practicable. When it was at its worst, the condition was not enviable. I could neither listen to reading nor engage in conversation, even of the lightest. Sleep was difficult, and was often banished entirely for one or two nights during which the brain was apt to be in a state of abnormal activity which had to be repressed at any cost, since thought produced the intensest torture. The effort required to keep the irritated organ quiet was so fatiguing that I occasionally rose and spent hours in the open air, where I found distraction and relief in watching the policemen and the tramps on the Malls of Boston Common, at the risk of passing for a tramp myself. Towards the end of the night this cerebral excitation would seem to tire itself out, and give place to a condition of weight and oppression much easier to bear."—Letter to Martin Brimmer, 1886.

Under such handicaps Parkman ransacked the libraries of the Boston Athenaeum and Harvard College, and through correspondence sought the advice and help of other historical workers. The necessary books were rare and hard to come by; the essential documents were scattered among the disordered archives of Paris and public and private collections in France, England, and Canada. The collection of materials proved "abundantly irksome and laborious," but Parkman was considerably aided by the little group of historical pioneers in this neglected field. Among the most helpful was George Bancroft, then the dean of American historians. Another friendly fellow-worker was Dr. Edmund Bailey O'Callaghan, the Irish physician and politician, who made a new career for himself as the state archivist of New York after being exiled from Canada for his part in the Papineau Rebellion of 1837. His *Documentary History of New York* was of great value to Parkman, and probably Parkman owed the idea of visiting Papineau at Montebello to the latter's old lieutenant. John Gilmary Shea, the first American Catholic historian of note, also proved a most useful correspondent, since he was in close touch with the clerical historians in Canada, where he had spent some years in the Jesuit novitiate. Through Shea or others, Parkman was soon in correspondence with Abbé Ferland of Laval University, Père Félix Martin of St. Mary's College, Montreal, and other Canadian historians, and with Jacques Viger of Montreal and Georges-Barthélemi Faribault of Quebec, among the antiquarians. From this nucleus his circle of correspondents broadened out as his researches opened up new paths of enquiry. This correspondence is singularly rich in historical interest, for the field was almost untouched; and here are the eager reports of pioneers working from many different points of view. Through the exchange of letters, Parkman's correspondents became his friends; and when a brief interlude of good health enabled him to go to Canada, they showed him their treasures of books and documents and offered advice with the freedom of old acquaintances.

After his return home, the work went on as health permitted. In 1862 illness was banished for a period, and by 1864 Parkman was able to complete the first volume in his proposed series, *The Pioneers of New France*, as well as to report the following progress on the great task he had set himself:

"At present the work, or rather the series of separate works, stands as follows. Most of the material is collected or within reach. Another volume, on the Jesuits in North America, is one-third written. Another on the French explorers of the Great West is half written, while a third, devoted to the checkered career of Louis de Buade, Comte de Frontenac, is partially arranged for composition. Each work is designed to be a unit in itself, independent of the rest, but the whole, taken as a series, will form a connected history of France in the New World.

"How far, by a process combining the slowness of the tortoise with the uncertainty of the hare, an undertaking of close and extended research can be advanced, is a question to solve which there is no aid from precedent, since it does not appear that an attempt, under similar circumstances, has hitherto been made."—Letter to George Ellis, 1864.

In 1866 Parkman revisited Quebec and Montreal, renewing his friendships of ten years before and making new ones. His circle of acquaintance was soon to become larger in Quebec than in Boston; and in Montreal his favorite sister Caroline, now married to the Reverend John Cordner of the Unitarian Church of the Messiah, made him welcome in her home. Some of the following notes were clearly made on this later visit, although this notebook has previously been dated 1856. The references to *La Revue Canadienne* (founded 1863) and *Le Foyer Canadien* (founded 1866) are sufficient to indicate that there were later entries.

The present notebook is largely a collection of references to books, papers, and works in progress. These are not without interest, since the value of many Canadian primary sources depends upon the edition used. There are also some revealing stories about historians, and some accounts of the religious institutions so foreign to Parkman and so important in his history. The vivid shorthand notes on the localities visited form the basis of the famous descriptions in the later histories. Parkman was adept at catching in a few words a striking likeness of the scene before him, and sometimes these rough sketches are more effective than the more labored purple patches of which they were the source.

This notebook, which contains both the record of the 1856 journey and notes made as late as ten years after, is bound in brown pigskin and measures $3\frac{3}{4}$ by 6 inches. The writing is in ink and very legible. The front cover bears the inscription "French Colonization" in ink.

1856 & 1866

[On the inside front cover and flyleaf are written three tentative titles: "France in the New World: a history of French Dominion (Power) in N. America; its rise, growth & fall," "France in the New World: a history of French Colonisation in North America," and "French Colonial Empire in North America: its Rise, Progress and Fall."[1]]

M. Faillon is preparing an account at length of the settlement of Montreal[2]—consult his previous books.

Catalogue of the Bibliothèque Impériale (Royale) now being prepared.[3]

Papers Collected by Hon. L. J. Papineau[4]

Cass's Papers on Detroit[5]

Gayarré's Papers[6]

French's   "   [7]

In hands of J. G. Shea: Chaumonot's Autobiography—Perrot's Memoirs—Dablon's Relations 1672-3, 1673-9—Chronicle of the New Orleans Ursulines.[8]

MSS. at Rome—see Bancroft's note Aug. 9, '56.[9]

Biddle papers—Bancroft.[10]

Garneau examined the notarial registers of some 600 marriages at Quebec, where the place of birth of both parties is given. The result was that the emigrants came from many provinces, Normandy & the Isle of France (chiefly Paris) predominating. Many from Poitou, many from Brittany, a few from Burgundy—but chiefly the coast provinces from Flanders to Spain.[11]

Perrot, *Moeurs des Sauvages* is to be published.[12]

Montcalm—saw his skull at the Ursulines, where he was buried in their chapel—(see the Ursuline nun)—a chapel with plain white

517

walls, now hung with good pictures—a very handsome altar with ancient tapestry-work, gilded oak carvings, etc.—a large grating on one side, a pulpit on the other.[13]

Lorette—near the foot of a range of hills. Here the St. Charles foams over a broad rock, and rages along a wooded ravine. Below, stretches a vast level towards Quebec, once carpeted with forest. Lorette was once the advanced station of civilization. Saw Chaumonot's virgin.[14]

Cap Rouge. The shores of the St. Lawrence fall away gradually as one sails up. Near Montreal, a broad watery expanse—low lines of shore studded with habitans' cottages and trees, chiefly poplar.

C. P. Drolet,[15] Admiralty Court, Court House, Quebec.

Charles Panet, Jr.,[16] Student at Law, care Messrs. Lelièvre & Angers, Advocates, Quebec.

N. Fages,[17] Notary, Quebec.

Th. Sterry Hunt,[18] Esq., Montreal.

Very Rev. C. F. Cazeau,[19] Grand Vicar of Quebec.

Hon. Henry Black,[20] Quebec.

G. B. Faribault,[21] Esq., Quebec.

Rev. F. Martin,[22] S. J., Prest. [President], St. Mary's College, Montreal.

M. le Commandeur J. Viger,[23] 24 Notre-Dame St., Montreal.

Hon. L. J. Papineau,[24] Monte Bello, Petite Nation, River Ottawa. See a few pages farther

---

St. Anne [*-de-Bellevue*].   A narrow & swift current between the Point & Isle Perrot—then widens to the lake of 2 Mountains.

The Mission[a]—small houses & hovels along the shore—above, among the spruce & other trees, a great tract of sand.

The Calvary with its stations.

The river is a broad expanse as far as the Long Sault, where it narrows. A portage of 14 miles. Above, steamboat again to Petite Nation. Hilly picturesque shores.

Passed the night at the inn—the day at M. Papineau's. Above, to Ottawa. The shores rather low & tame. A little above Mr. P.'s,

ᵃ At Oka, on the Lake of Two Mountains.—Ed.

View of Montreal, 1830
Engraving by W. L. Leney after drawing by R. A. Sproule
(Coverdale Collection No. 112)

View of Quebec, 1850
Lithograph by T. Picken after a drawing by Captain B. Beaufoy
(Coverdale Collection No. 179)

is the spot where a detachment of soldiers was stationed to intercept traders going up without license.

At the Chaudière, the river foams over vast sheets & ledges of rock in horizontal strata, and falls boiling into two great chasms—then rushes down, on the left bank, between a rocky island and the shore.

Tanner[25] is of little acct. Alegambe[26] is valuable (a copy in N. Y. Hist. Soc.). (No.)

At M. Viger's is a portrait of Champlain[27] & of Mme. C. in his "Album"[28] (doubtful).

Also of Charlevoix[29]—a fine manly face.
    "   of Lafit[e]au[30]—young & good-looking.
    "   of Piquet[31]—lively—vivacious—full of health & vigor.
    "   of Crespel[32]—a sullen-looking monk.
    "   of La Corne,[33] uncle or great-uncle to M. Viger.

Also an illuminated drawing of a banner on which were embroidered the articles of covenant between a band of Iroq.—joining Picquet's mission of La Présentation—and the French. The banner itself is still in existence at Montreal. The cross, the emblems of the Virgin & the Savior, the *fleurs de Lys*, and the Iroq. totems, are all embroidered, and linked together by strings of wampum-beads wrought into the silk—the whole edged with a gold fringe; and on the reverse the covenant is written in French.

Notre Dame des Neiges was on the site of the Priests' farm. Some of the bastions still stand.

At Caughnawaga are the remains of a stone fort,[34] on the river.

At St. Anne's, a strong current. Five or six wooded islands just above.

At the Mission of 2 Mts.[35] is the original portrait of Picquet—very good pictures in the church.

I heard the squaws, wrapped in blankets like so many blue spectres, sing in the church. Their voices were strangely high-pitched.

Hospital Genl. at Quebec[36]—St. Vallier's[37] tomb, & picture.

Soeurs de la Congrégation,[38] & their school.

Visited the Soeurs de la Congrégation—teachers of children of all ages.

The Soeurs de la Charité[39] (Madame Youville). They receive the aged, infirm, & disabled.

The Bon Pasteur,[40] a new sisterhood, in part a Magdalen asylum.

The Hôtel Dieu,[41] a hospital.

The Ursulines,[42] a school.

At Charle[s]bourg, the farms were laid out in wedge-form, diverging from a common centre.[b] Each man built his house near the centre, and the houses, being contiguous, together formed a polygonal fort, with a common area in the middle. The farms still retain the wedge form, and the point of junction is called the *fort*, though the building has disappeared.[43]

Marie de l'Incarnation's *Lettres*[44] are in [the] Bishop's Library, Quebec.

Hon. J. Fraser, Quebec, has a copy.

Also, Rev. Mr. Plante,[45] Hospital Genl.

Charlevoix's *Life of Marie de l'Incarnation*[46] is in possession of the priest of Lorette (ask Mr. Black) and of Mr. Plante. Said to be now reprinting at Paris.

Mr. Faribault, Mr. Plante & Mr. Viger have La Tour [Latour].[47]

Juchereau,[48] 2 copies, in Seminary Library, Quebec.

Mr. Plante has Ragueneau's Life of Mère Augustin[49] (said to be only a leaf or two, and valueless).

On crossing the bridge of the St. Charles, one finds a level country, and shores easy of access but for the shallow extending out to the channel, where the water deepens very suddenly. The shore rises & grows abrupt as you approach Montmorenci.

Above Quebec, Cape Diamond forms a bold, precipitous height shouldering out into the river. As you go towards Wolfe's Cove, there are places where it is perfectly easy to walk down to the river, and which, except for the forces of the current, would have offered but slight natural obstacles to landing.

---

[b] A rough pencil sketch has been omitted here.—Ed.

The list of docs. on Louisiana which Margry offered me at $500. is in the hands of Govnt. at New Orleans—a copy.[50]

In the Bibliothèque Impériale, a MS. vol. of *Alphonse de Saintonge* [*Alfonce Santongeois*],[51] said to contain details of the first exploration of the Saguenay (note in "Catalogue of Library of M. Puibusque,[52] sold 1864"). (No.)[53]

Monsieur Pierre Margry,[54] Conservateur-adjoint des Archives de la Marine, Ministère de la Marine, Paris.

Penecaut, MS.[55] alluded to by Charlevoix. There is a copy in Canada. Shea will perhaps get a copy from it.

Hon. P. J. O. Chauveau,[56] etc., etc., etc., Montreal.

Canada, Documents Divers,[57] MS. in fol[io] in Bibliothèque Provinciale Canadienne (Faillon).

La Bibliothèque Canadienne (a collection, historical, literary & scientific).[58]

La Revue Canadienne (begun in 1863).[59]

Owen, *Exploration of Iowa & Wisconsin* (govt.)[60]

Munsell Series—Explorations of the Mississippi, St. Cosme, Guigues, etc.[61]

M. l'abbé H. R. Casgrain,[62] Quebec, has letters of Baby[63] ([concerning] Pontiac), his great-grandfather—also can point out various docs. on Canadian Hist. Offers aid. He is now President of the *Foyer Canadien*[64] (Mar. 1866).

Johnstone, *A Dialogue in Hades*[65] (Wolfe, Montcalm). (Montreal, Dawson, 1866)

De Gaspé, Philippe-A., *Mémoires*[66] (Ottawa, 1866, Desbarats). (Manners in Canada in the writer's youth.)

Vétromile, *The Abenakis & their History* (N. Y., 1866).[67]

M. Maurault has now (Oct. 1866) in press a history of the Abenakis.[68] He is missionary at Lake St. Francis.

First Paris Notebook
1869

Introduction

IN OCTOBER 1868, after enjoying reasonably good health for some seven years, Parkman suffered a return of what he called "The Enemy"—the cerebral confusion which made work impossible, except for the briefest periods. Since the attack, which was the worst since 1858, showed little sign of ceasing in the following month, he decided to spend the winter in Paris, hoping that the change of scene would benefit him and that the French doctors, then the leading specialists in nervous disorders, might be able to offer him some aid. It was not only the pursuit of health that took him to Paris. He was then engaged upon the volume which was called *The Discovery of the Great West* when it first appeared in the fall of 1869, and was published after 1879 as *La Salle and the Discovery of the Great West*. For this work he needed the use of the great collection of La Salle material which M. Pierre Margry, director of the Archives de la Marine et des Colonies, had amassed during a quarter-century of research. After surveying the Paris archives, Abbé Casgrain had reported to Parkman that Margry was "*très avare de ces richesses, qui sont grandes*"; and Parkman went to France prepared to offer Margry a large sum for the use of his collection.

But Pierre Margry was a jealous guardian of the riches entrusted to his care, if not a wholly scrupulous one. His years in the archives had given him an unsurpassed knowledge of their contents. He knew them not only as a curator but as a researcher, for General Lewis Cass had employed him to collect documents on the old Northwest; John Romeyn Brodhead had found him helpful in selecting material dealing with the early history of New York; and the Canadian government had commissioned him to select and arrange two series of colonial papers. This work, in addition to his official duties, had given him what he viewed as a vested right to the public documents entrusted to his care; and he kept his collection inaccessible to other scholars until he achieved his aim of publishing the results of his researches. In 1869 Parkman succeeded in winning Margry's friendship, but not the use of his great collection. This notebook contains the record of Parkman's conversations with Margry in January, February, and March 1869, in which the latter offers a few hints and urges his own theory that the Jesuits sabotaged La Salle's expedition to the mouth of the Mississippi. For the rest Parkman had to dig for himself in the Bibliothèque Impériale (formerly Royale, and soon to be Nationale), the Archives de la Guerre, and the Depôt des Cartes de la Guerre. At Margry's suggestion, he also hunted out the current Marquis de Montcalm, who proved most helpful and put him on the track of the Montcalm Papers purchased by Sir Thomas Phillips a few years before and of relevant material in the British Museum, which Parkman inspected in March before returning home. But Margry himself remained deaf to Parkman's pleas for the use of the La Salle material, and held up the latter's work for ten years by doing so. Nevertheless Parkman did not question Margry's private right to public documents; he became his friend and lifelong correspondent; and eventually he made it possible for Margry to reap a second crop from his labor by arranging for the publication of the collection under an appropriation by Congress as *Découvertes et Etablissements des Français dans l'Ouest et dans le Sud de l'Amérique Septentrionale, 1614-1754* (Paris, 1879-1888). Before leaving Paris, Parkman also commissioned Margry to supervise the copying of a vast mass of documents which formed the raw material of later books in his epic of New France.

Paris helped to rout "The Enemy," and Parkman led anything but an invalid's life during his stay. In addition to the historical investigations noted in the journal, he formed friendships with Count Adolph de Circourt, who was a friend of the George Ticknors; Count Jules Marcou, the translator of Bancroft; and General Dix, the American Minister. He wrote his sister: "If I accepted invitations, which I do not, I should have the run of the Faubourg St. Germain. I have just declined an invitation from the Prince de Broglie to dine." He saw the sights of Paris from Versailles to the sewers, and took pleasure in random walks about the city when his mental state prevented him from working in the archives.

Margry's influence on Parkman is historically important. After the publication, late in 1869, of *The Discovery of the Great West*, John Gilmary Shea protested that his friend "had been led too far by Margry, who is of the modern French school continually yelping at the Jesuits." The Puritan Parkman, amusingly enough, assured the Catholic Shea that Margry was "a most zealous Catholic." But Margry's letter to Sainte-Beuve (for text, see note 39), in reply to the latter's request for information about Parkman's *Jesuits*, supports Shea's opinion. Margry was so zealous a Catholic that he thought the militantly Protestant Parkman had been led up the historical garden path by the clerical historians of Canada. The book which raised the ultramontane storm against Parkman in Quebec was too Catholic for Margry's taste. The truth of the matter seems to be that Parkman was affected for the rest of his life by the growing anti-clericalism of France through his correspondence with Margry, and on the other hand was subject to the Catholic influence of his other great historical correspondent, Abbé Casgrain.

The record of this historian's holiday in the Paris archives is contained in a small black leather notebook, $5\frac{1}{2}$ inches by $3\frac{1}{4}$, which opens at the end. The text is largely in ink, with some passages in pencil.

1869

Paris, Jan[uary] 1869. 21 Boulevard St. Michel.[1] Portrait of Mad[ame] de Frontenac (Versailles 3508), young, blooming, handsome, with helmet, plume & shield; see catalogue of Versailles (apparently as Minerva).[2]

Plaster bust of Montcalm, Galerie des Batailles, Versailles. Better than any other representation of him I have seen.[3]

Picture of La Salle's exped. 1684, "La Salle découvre La Louisiane," Salles des Marins, Versailles. A deep bay—low shores, all lighted by a warm sunset—on the right, marshes with rank tropical vegetation and trunks of fallen trees—Indians gazing at the ships or pushing canoes into the water. The *Joly* in the foreground—a boat's crew about to land—on the left, more distant, another vessel—in the distance the *Aimable*, stranded.

Margry, 23 Jan. La Salle was the name of an estate near Rouen, belonging to the Caveliers.

Joutel was the son of a gardener of La Salle's uncle.

Margry says that his book was composed by Michel who accompanied La Salle on his first exped., the material being furnished by Joutel (see Joutel's title page).[4]

Acte de naissance de La Salle,[5] *registres de l'état civil, Paroisse Saint-Herbland, Rouen.*

"*Le vingt-deuxième jour de novembre, 1643, a été baptisé, Robert Cavelier, fils de honorable homme Jean Cavelier, et de Catherine Geest; ses parrain et marraine, honorables personnes Nicolas Geest et Marguerite Morice,*" discovered by Margry in 1847.

Margry in *Revue de Rouen*, 1847: "Réné-Robert Cavelier, sieur de La Salle."

"*La Salle partit pour le Canada en 1666 âgé d'environ 22 ans*"—baptised

22 Nov., 1643 in the church of Saint-Herbland—"*ses parents étaient merciers-grossiers.*"

26 Jan. Margry says that he has the letters of La Salle on which the *Relation des Découvertes* is founded.[6] That this is the official account but that the letters are full of La Salle's personality—complaints against Jesuits—his troubles from his rivals—pecuniary distress—the embarassments caused him by the weakness of his brother (who at one time tried to persuade him to marry). He alludes to the charges of harshness brought against him and defends himself, but adds that indeed *he will have no blasphemers in his camp: "Je suis Chrétien.*"

Margry insists that it was N. Perrot the voyageur who tried to poison La Salle.[7]

He says that he has positive proof of the treachery of Beaujeu, and that he was in league with the Jesuits.[8]

Margry says that all the papers of Frontenac's time, and sometime later, have been sent (copies) to New York or Canada, with the exception of those of La Motte Cadillac and the foundation of Detroit, wh[ich] are retained for publication. There must be also other exceptions—certainly the La Salle papers.[9]

Jan. 27. Margry says to-day that though the papers on Detroit are not in the government collection of Canada, they are among those copied for Cass and also for Papineau.[10]

He says that the Montcalm letters, found in Quebec after the capture, are at the Depôt de la Guerre [War Office] of England. These, he says, have been chiefly published by Dussieux.[11]

There is another collection in England in the hands of a person whose name he does not remember, but thinks he can find it out.[12]

Perhaps, he adds, there are papers in the hands of the Marquis de Montcalm at Montpellier.[13]

Frontenac's dispatch, 1672. The part about the Jesuits is written in cipher (figures) with the explanation interlined in another hand.[14]

30 Jan. Margry read a paper from his collection by which it appears that the father of Joutel received from Henri Cavelier, La Salle's uncle, who employed him as a gardener, 50 francs a year, equivalent perhaps to 300 now.

Young Cavelier, La Salle's nephew, who was with him on his last voyage, died a few years after, an officer in a regiment.

The La Salle who wrote the letter preserved in Thomassy[15] was no relation to the Caveliers, but the son of a naval official at Toulon.

The concluding part of La Salle's letter to the Minister from St. Bernard's Bay, 4 mars, 1685,[16] partly printed in Thomassy, accuses the *"capitaine"* of the *Aimable* of having purposely wrecked her & says that he (La Salle) was convinced of his treachery before leaving St. Domingo. He adds that it is his purpose to retire within the mouth of the river (supposed[ly] the western mouth of the Mississippi) to avoid the notice of the Spaniards—that he proposes a journey to the Illinois—that if he does not hear when there that peace has been published in Canada, he will proceed to the mines of St. Barbe— that though his soldiers are wretched, he can still succeed, his chief reliance being on Inds., who only want to feel that they are supported by F[rench] soldiers, and will never know whether the soldiers are good or not.

_____

A map (Margry), bearing the name *"Minuty del."* & entitled: *"Plan de l'Entrée du Lac où on a laissé M^r. de la Salle."*[17]

minuty del.

A Camp of La Salle
B C Indian huts
D Aimable wrecked   The Joly is represented not far
E La Belle   from shore.

Margry: A map (a mere sketch) of Raudin on which is laid down *"Rivière de la Divine ou l'Outrelaise."*[18]

On another map of Raudin, the Mississippi is called "Buade" (1688?)[19]

A very curious map of Le Sueur of the Upper Mississippi.[20] Great detail—names of all the Sioux nations.

Several curious maps of La Verandrye [Vérendrye], one of them made up from Indian maps.[21]

Margry: By a letter from a Jesuit to Margry, it appears that La Salle must have been 16 years old before he could enter the novitiate. Then 2 years, and afterwards teaching in the schools.

Map, MS: "Route que firent les Espagnols pour venir enlever les François restés à la Baye St. Bernard ou St. Louis après la perte du vaisseau de M.ʳ de la Salle, en 1689."[22]

By this it appears that they passed from C[o]ahuila by the [Rio Grande] del Norte, the upper Nueces, the "Hendo" [Hondo, or Rio Frio], the de Leon [San Antonio], the Guadalupe. After crossing the del Norte their line of march west marked out.

La Hontan's *"Rivière longue"*[23]

Route marked east & west from *"Chacagou"* down *"R[ivière] à la Roche"* to the Mississippi.

"Tabula Novae Franciae Anno 1660" (Creuxius)[24]

Bib[liothèque] Imp[ériale]: Duval, 1677: *"Village avec palissades attaqué par Champlain"*[25]—about midway between the Oswego and the Genessee. This map is very much behind its time and is founded partly on Champlain. The Lakes all wrong.

Cornelli, *"Partie occidentale du Canada ou de la Nouvelle France 1688."*[26] Lakes laid down with great accuracy (like Fran(c)quelin). Upper Mississippi after Hennepin. As far south as 34°.

Bib. Imp.: Vaugondy, Canada (1756?) (Argenson, secretaire d'Etat)[27]

Nolin, *"Canada et La Louisiane, 1756*[28]

"Canada et La Louisiane." Le Rouge, 1755[29]

Bellin, 1745[30]

"Partie de la N. France." Jaillot, 1685.[31] Hudson's Bay & forts on it, etc.

Bib. Imp.: Ms. map of Pierre Raffeix, S.J.[32] Indicates voyage of La Salle 1679, who, he says, writes that he went to the sea in 1681. A better way, says the Jesuit, would be from L. Erie by the Ohio. Marks out Du Luth's course & says he rescued Hennepin.

"Canada, Louisiane et Terres Angloises," D'Anville, 1755 (very large).[33]

"*Amérique Septentrionale,*" D'Anville, 1746.[34]

"*L'Amérique Septentrionale,*" Bellin, 1755.[35]

Popple's Map, (old F[rench] war)[36]

Le Marquis de Montcalm, 27 Rue Casimir-Périer, Paris. He has a fine portrait of his ancestor, also a miniature taken at an earlier age, and an old engraving, not very good, from the portrait.

For genealogy of Montcalm see *Armorial de la Noblesse de Languedoc,* par La Roque, Firmin Didot, 1860.

M. de Montcalm says that the Marquis his ancestor was of short stature and rather fat. He kept aloof from court intrigue. His mother, Mad. de St. Véran, a *femme maîtresse,* urged him to go to America, & it was her influence that induced him to take the command.[37]

Feb. 25. Margry says that Sir Thomas Phillips is the person in England who has the Montcalm Papers; and that a catalogue of the Phillips collections exists, and is probably to be seen at the British Museum.[38]

Margry read me his letter to Ste.-Beuve about the "Jesuits."[39] He insists that I have not exposed their political character—that they controlled the Co. of the Hundred Associates, and held the colony in a subjection so irksome that it could not long be tolerated—that they constantly tried to make the governor their instrument—in short, to absorb everything. He says that he has a document, of date subsequent to 1660 (1663?) "very damaging for them." I do not find that he has anything earlier, though he says that this doc. refers back as far as 1642.

It might be added to the text that the "Northern Paraguay" could not long have endured, as the growth of political and commercial interests must sooner or later have subverted the Jesuit empire.

Feb. 27. Several small *bouches à feu* of the 14th century at the Musée d'Artillerie, in general principle of construction like that found at Ottawa,[40] but the tube is of 3 or more staves, instead of one piece lapped and welded. Made of wrought iron, and not much larger than the Ottawa piece. See cat. of Museum, No. 1-5.

The Marquis de Montcalm says that, soon before the battle of the plains of Abraham, Montcalm heard of the death of one of his daughters—which one he could not learn—and that his distress almost overcame him.[41]

Archives de la Guerre. The papers here on America do not antedate Louis XV. Abundance on the war of 1755-63.[42]

I was shown only 1 letter—"Talon au Ministre, 19 Oct. 1667"—of the reign of Louis XIV.

Légende de la carte:[a] *"Canada (carte des limites du) avec les colonies anglaises depuis les montagnes de la Virginie jusqu'à la ville des 3 Rivières sur le fleuve S^t. Laurent. Echelle d'environ 4,5 lignes pour une lieue."*[43]

Cette carte est un essai fait sur les limites en 1758—elle n'est nullement curieuse. MS.

La carte est classée aux Archives des Cartes du Dépôt de la Guerre, à Paris, sous le classement 7—b. 59. La carte est manuscrite.

"Le port de Louisbourg, dans l'isle Royale, représenté de basse mer."[44]

L'Isle royale, au Sud de laquelle est ce port, forme avec l'Isle de terre neuve l'entrée du golfe de S^t. Laurent, d'où les vaisseaux montent le fleuve jusqu'à Québec dans le Canada. Carte dessinée avec soin. MS. Classé à 7-B-64.

A large MS. map of Detroit (1796?), colored, with a picture of the fort and town of Detroit.[45] This map is in great detail, very large, and well executed.

The above are in the Dépôt des Cartes de la Guerre, which contains little else besides printed maps which may be found elsewhere.

Several maps of Vaugondy, time of Old French War.[46]

The following is the title of the Detroit Map: *"Plan topographique*

[a] This and the following entry are in the handwriting of Pierre Margry.—Ed.

du Détroit et des eaux qui forment la jonction du lac Erié avec le lac St. Clair, dressé pour l'intelligence des voyages du Général Callot dans cette partie du continent en 1796." Carte MS. classée à 7-6, 61. (Dépôt de la Guerre— Archives des Cartes.) Settlements extended as far up as Lake St. Clair on west side, and as far down as middle of Turkey Island on east side.

The MS. maps are in the Dépôt des Cartes de la Marine, 13, Rue de l'Université.

Mar. 7. Margry says that Beaujeu had an understanding with the Jesuits to defeat La Salle's plans, as, he thinks, may be inferred from the following:

1st. Beaujeu says in a letter to Seignelay, that since La Salle *knew that his wife was devoted to the Jesuits*, he has been very cold and reserved. Hence Beaujeu was in relations with the Jesuits.

2nd. Beaujeu's separations from La S. in the Gulf was clearly intentional, and his refusal to return in search of the river was grounded on false pretences, for M. says that he has evidence that, after leaving La Salle, he *did* return, find the Mississippi, and take its latitude & longitude, after wh[ich] he sailed for France, leaving the colonists and La Salle to their fate. La Salle, as M. thinks, had given him the latitude of the river.

3rd. That there was a plot on the part of the Jesuits was shown by the behavior of Allöuez when Joutel saw him at St. Louis, and his agitation when told that La Salle was approaching

4th. The Jesuits, after La Salle's death, hastened to enter upon the field which he had occupied, and undertook to discover and possess the Mississippi, completing the work of La Salle (see the memoir in my possession).[47]

P. S., Mar. 8. The evidence alluded to by M. as to Beaujeu's return to find the Mississippi is that of a manuscript map wh[ich] he showed me. Here is laid down the mouth of the Mississippi "as described by M. de La Salle," but on the *back of the map*, immediately under this part of it, is another representation of the mouth of the Missisippi, with the words, "*Embouchure du Mississippi telle que nous l'avons trouvée.*"[48]

La Salle had a triple aim, the discovery of the western passage to

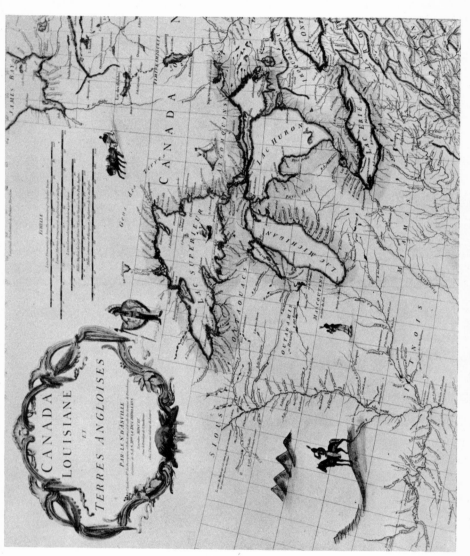

D'Anville's Canada, Louisiane et Terres Angloises, 1755
(Coverdale Collection No. 592)

China—the opening of an interior commerce—and action against the Spaniards by war in time of war and by *contraband trade* (Margry) in time of peace.

Frontenac was needy. La S., to gain his aid in his schemes, approached him on this weak side. F. had no money to give—therefore, unlike all others whom La S. induced to aid him, he lost nothing—but he gave his influence and authority as capital. La S., a man of broad views and not mercenary, was forced to use the greed of others as a means of success. His associates hoped for large profits. Thus alone he could raise money.

Early in his career La S., having no money, was forced to look to his brother for supplies. Hence his enemies were always trying to discredit him with the priest. La S. complains much of him for trying to direct him & meddling in his affairs. Once, when he wished to marry a young demoiselle of Canada, his brother annoyed him greatly by his interference.[49]

The Marquis de Montcalm says that Montcalm was so abandoned in Canada that he was forced to make great outlays on his own credit—that his family paid after his death a hundred thousand francs to his creditors, for debts contracted in Canada, and that the family was so reduced in means that his three surviving daughters had only 1,000 francs a year.[50]

9 March. The Marquis de Montcalm says that 5 or 6 years ago a collection of papers on the Canadian war and his family (autographs) was sold in Paris & bought by an Englishman.

Q. Sir Thomas Phillips?

Sir Thomas Phillips, Bart., Thirlestane House, Cheltenham

11 March. British Museum: *Lettres de Monsieur le Marquis de Montcalm Gouverneur Général en Canada à Messieurs de Berryer & de la Molé écrites dans les années 1757, 1758, 1759, avec une version Anglaise. (Londres, J. Almon, 1777)* 8 vo. Title of translation: Letters from the Marquis de Montcalm & Messieurs, etc. (1777). 28 pp. of the French, each opposite a page of the version bearing the same number.[51]

There are but 3 letters of Montcalm:

1st to Berryer, 4 April 1757, enclosing a long letter from S. J., dated Boston, 4 Jan. 1757.

2nd to Montreal, 1 Oct. 1758.

3rd Quebec, 24 Aug. 1759. This is the famous letter of wh. I have a copy.

All relate to political affairs of Eng. colonies.

Mt. Desert Notebook
1870

Introduction

THIS notebook stands alone among the later journals, for it is the commonplace book of Parkman the poet rather than of Parkman the historian. Parkman was first drawn as a young man to poetry, but after a few ventures in the ballad form on themes from colonial history, he decided, in his own words, to "confine his homage to the Muse of History, as being less apt than her wayward sisters to requite his devotion with a mortifying rebuff." But like many another literary man he wrote better prose for having once written verse, and many pages of the great history are almost lyrical. Nature always evoked the poetic mood in Parkman, and when at forty-seven he spent a few weeks with a college friend, Judge Horace Gray, at Mount Desert and Grand Manan Island, off the Maine coast, the glories of September called forth these vivid prose poems devoted to sea and shore, which rank among his best pictures of the nature which he loved so well. Evidently he could not resist paying a visit to his old haunts in New Hampshire on his way back to Boston; for the final entry in the notebook is a description of the scene about Center Harbor on Lake Winnipesaukee, when the frosts of early October had set the forest afire with scarlet and crimson and gold.

Since this 1870 notebook is devoted to literary sketches, it will not be amiss to consider here Parkman's style. He was trained by William Russell at the Chauncy Hall School and by Edward Tyrrel Channing at Harvard in the old rhetoric based upon classical models; and he never lost his fondness for the periodic sentence, with one clause balanced against another and the whole piling up to a formal conclusion, reminiscent of the great classical orations. Byron, Cooper, and Scott, his favorite authors, taught him how to describe action in words, and also gave him a certain tendency to wordiness and to formal rather than familiar language. Byron encouraged his native romanticism and lyricism. His wide reading for professional purposes among the early chroniclers—Hakluyt and Purchas and the authors of the *Jesuit Relations* were among his favorites—clearly affected his stylistic development, and he gained from them an appreciation of the rhetorical force of simplicity, which was a valuable antidote to the early Augustan influences upon his writing. From them, too, he probably learned the great Elizabethan trick of using the well-worn word in such a way that it took on all the vigor and force that it had held at first; and also acquired the habit of using a slightly archaic idiom, appropriate to accounts of an almost forgotten past.

Parkman's great weaknesses as a writer were to strain too hard for rhetorical effects and to allow his sentences to become of unwieldy length and congested with unnecessary words, with a consequent loss of the simplicity and vigor so necessary to good narrative. It is difficult to explain the first tendency entirely: his early training had much to do with it, but there seems to have been a natural instinct for the phrase that is just a shade too high, just as his ear was naturally faulty. The second weakness undoubtedly can be explained by the methods of mental composition that were forced upon him by the condition of his sight: the writer who is unable to revise a dictated draft with pencil or pen habitually falls into this fault. In later years the improved condition of Parkman's eyes allowed him to edit his own work carefully, to its notable benefit. In the earlier period, when this process was not possible, there is an interesting difference in style between the advance chapters of *The Pioneers* which appeared in the *Atlantic* and the final version in book form: a great gain in clarity and simplicity has been achieved by the pruning away of unnecessary epithets. This revision seems to have been the work of Charles Folsom, a friend of Jared Sparks, who served as librarian of both Harvard and the Boston Athenaeum, and who is thanked by Parkman in the preface to the book for his "skillful and friendly criticism."

In the present notebook (in printing which all variants have been preserved) there is abundant evidence of Parkman's talent for self-criticism, as well as of his methods of composition. First he struggled for perfection of phrase, and when that was attained, he had little difficulty in constructing sentences which have something of the finality and inevitability of the classics. He relied too much upon adjectives for the modern taste, but this was perhaps unavoidable in descriptive writing. But there can be no question of his flair for language and of his literary power; he was no mere phrasemaker, unable to sustain a theme for more than a few notes, but rather the capable composer of historical operas, who could carry an epic drama along on a high level, punctuated by brilliant arias which are the purple patches of the anthologies. He is certainly the greatest writer among American historians, and consequently these sketches which illustrate his methods of composition are of major interest.* They are also more perfect poems than any he wrote in his poetic youth.

These notes are written in pencil on the pages of an orange paper-covered account book, $3\frac{5}{8}$ by $5\frac{3}{4}$ inches.

* Similar sketches of Acadia occur in the 1871 & 1873 Notebook, pp. 551-53.—Ed.

1870

Mt. Desert,[1] *Sept[ember] 1870.* ~~The lifeless water~~
~~—The forest, black in sunset shadow,~~

The pale dull blue of the lifeless waters; the forest black in sunset shadow, tracing its ridgy line against the sky, and, above, one small cloud-speck, bathed by the vanished sun in opalescent fire, floating in the rosy crystal of the west.

The forest, where sunbeams stream aslant among the deep-green verdure of the hemlocks, and athwart the white gleaming stems of the slender birch trees; and the tall spruces rear aloft thin tall and tapering spires, high in the illumined air.

~~—where breakers surge and pound against the adamantine granite~~

Under a leaden sky, the island rocks rest sombre and cold upon the leaden water, as strong men, under the clouds of an inexorable dreary destiny, bide their hour in still and stern endurance.

~~Betwixt. The~~
Towering, and ledge above ledge, half seen ~~athwart~~ betwixt the restless plumage of the birches—dark sheets of sun-scorched rock, where in rift or crevice, and every point of vantage, clings a hardy population of storm-defying trees.

Cliff and ~~rock~~ crag and long black reef, where ~~in crested~~ ~~ranks~~ the ~~fierce~~ crested breakers charge headlong against the adamantine granite, to be dashed ~~back~~ to a chaos of creamy foam, tossed on high in clouds of shining spray, and poured back in snowy cascades from the impassive rock.

The low hanging clouds—the streaked and mottled surface of the gray torpid sea pitted ~~with~~ by restless rain drops—the dark coast line of islands whose tops are veiled in ~~mist~~ fog—the wet rocks & the spectral host of fir-trees half wrapped in fleeing mists.

~~Under the keen wind sunlight and the keener wind,~~ The white topped waves flash and foam under the keen sunlight and the keener wind; the island rocks are dim with ~~bounding~~ silvery spray, ~~and~~ all the vast reach of iron-bound coast is edged with creamy foam, and breakers leap madly aloft as if to scale their craggy barrier.

Where vast crags cast their shadows on the deep blue sea that surges at their base.

The cliffs of the Grand Menan[2] are much higher than those of Great Head, and extend for miles with scarcely a break. Cape Split & Cape Blomidon (Bay of Fundy) are also greatly superior.

Pemaquid[3] may be easily reached from Bath.

Katahdin[4] is now very accessible.

~~The breathless water is like a sea of glass~~
~~The quivering mirror of the (breathless) glassy water.~~
~~Pale sunbeams chase each other along the rocks.~~

Soame's Sound. Reflected from the quivering mirror of the glassy water, pale sunbeams chase each other along the bordering rocks, carpeted with ~~juni~~ trailing juniper and plumed with ferns. The leaves of the poplar and the birch hang ~~unstirred~~ motionless in the breathless air, and in the dry top ~~arms~~ of the dead pine an eagle sits basking, his white head gleaming in the sunlight.

Sunrise, Sept. 10. The low murmuring of the tranquil sea; shores and islands painted in shadow against the ~~glowing~~ rosy east; the light that glistens on the wet black ledges, the brown waste of lank seaweeds, and ~~the~~ pools left by the receding tide; the moon that pales from gold to pallid silver before the advancing dawn, and the mountains that, dusky and cool, ~~lie~~ sit waiting for the sunrise.

Deep mountain gorges where brooks plunge and gurgle in the damp and silence; where ~~the~~ firs and ~~the~~ hemlocks, anchored in the rifted rocks, cast funereal shadows, and corpses of fallen trees lie mouldering, swathed in green winding sheets of moss.

~~Where~~ The mountain rears its bluff bold front, where knarled spruce trees, ~~stretch their shaggy~~ grisly with pendant mosses, stretch thin shaggy arms against the storms.

————

Senter [*Center*] *Harbor*,[5] *Oct. 7.* The ~~rocky~~ verge of some sunny cliff, where birch trees shake thin gilded leaves, and ~~the~~ crickets chirp from among the crisp mosses—~~far~~ below the forest ~~stretches~~ lies outspread for many a league, a carpet of red & russet, green & gold, with far mountain ranges dark with evergreen, and lakes of lustrous blue, ~~and~~ where islands float in hazy light.

Acadian Notebook
1871 & 1873

Introduction

IN THE summer of 1871 Parkman first visited Acadia, which he saw again in 1873 and in 1879, and whose history he chronicled in *Montcalm and Wolfe* (1884), *A Half-Century of Conflict* (1892), and the revised edition of *The Old Regime* (1893). A note to this last edition, sent to press only a few months before Parkman's death, indicates that his original intention had been to take up the subject in the first edition (1874): "I was unable to gain access to certain indispensable papers relating to the rival claimants to Acadia— Latour and D'Aulnay—and therefore deferred all attempts to treat that subject." Twenty-two years having passed and the papers having come to hand, Parkman supplied the three missing chapters by adding a new first section, "The Feudal Chiefs of Acadia," which covered Acadian history from 1604 to 1710 and was chiefly devoted to the struggle between the rival seigneurs Latour and D'Aulnay for control of the rich fur trade of the region.

Parkman's Acadian history was written backwards; for he discussed the final phase in *Montcalm and Wolfe,* and the middle period in *A Half-Century,* the last volume of the series to be written, though not the last in chronological order. This odd procedure was demanded by the fact that the necessary source materials were long lacking. The ancient bitterness over the deportation of the Acadians in 1755 was fanned up once more in the 1880's by a controversy among the historians concerned with the question, and by Longfellow's sentimentalization of the matter in *Evangeline.* Parkman's two Acadian chapters in *Montcalm and Wolfe* involved him in a long feud with Abbé Casgrain and Philip Smith, who were backed by Rameau de St. Père and Edouard Richard, as Parkman was backed by Sir Adams Archibald, William Kingsford, and George Stewart, Jr. Parkman had based his work upon documents edited by Thomas

Akins of the Nova Scotia Archives. Casgrain demonstrated that Akins had tampered with the evidence, and expounded his case at length in *Un Pèlerinage au Pays d'Evangéline* (1889), and in three volumes of new documents, *Collection des documents inédits* (1888-90). Parkman reviewed *Un Pèlerinage* condescendingly for the *Nation* (March 14, 1889—XLVIII, 232-3), remarking that the Abbé "has chosen to make the question a national and religious one." Of course the question *was* essentially a national and religious one, which accounts for the bitterness which its discussion evokes. In such circumstances Casgrain's emotional temperament was apt to lead him astray, but so was Parkman's growing bias in his closing years against Catholicism and its clergy. It is unfortunate that Parkman came to treat one of the most difficult problems of his subject only when his zest for research and his passion for objectivity had been somewhat dulled by a lifetime of unrewarded labor. Casgrain really had the better of the controversy, and Parkman was doubtless glad to bury the hatchet in his last few years. The modern view is that Parkman was led astray by insufficient and altered evidence.

On his trip to Acadia in July and August 1871, Parkman went first to Annapolis, Nova Scotia, then north to the Minas Basin, and then across the Bay of Fundy to St. John, New Brunswick. After going up the river to Fredericton, he returned home by way of Bar Harbor. In November of the same year he paid a flying visit to Quebec. In August 1873, after visiting Abbé Casgrain's old family home at Rivière-Ouelle on the lower St. Lawrence, opposite the mouth of the Saguenay, Parkman returned to Nova Scotia, visiting Annapolis, and then crossed the Bay of Fundy to St. John, returning home by way of Eastport and Portland, Maine.

The record of these early visits to Acadia is contained in a maroon leather notebook, $6\frac{3}{4}$ inches by $3\frac{7}{8}$, which opens at the end rather than the side, and from which seven pages, either cut or torn out, are missing. Parkman sometimes removed such field notes to insert them in books which concerned the subject. Three loose pages from another notebook, $6\frac{5}{8}$ inches by 4, held together in a blue paper wrapper marked "Acadia, local notes, 1873," contain the record of the 1873 journey.

1871 & 1873

[Two pages have been cut out.—Ed.]

Annapolis, 26ᵗʰ July. The site of the fort perfectly apparent on approaching the shore from the direction of Digby Gut[1]—a rising ground between Annapolis River on the left & Allen's River, also called Lequille River, on the right.[2] A blockhouse to guard the bridge across the ditch at the entrance, a range of barracks, a magazine, & two wells are the principal remains besides the earthworks, which are very strong, though almost exclusively directed to defend the water side, the rear being made very difficult of access by the two rivers.[a] There is also an arched covered way from the body of the work to a strong exterior work, facing the basin and showing the remains of a battery. Other exterior works command the meadows bordering the Lequille. There are remains of *chevaux de frize*[b] all along the water. The magazine seems to be French. The cream-colored limestone with which it is arched is said by Judge C.[3] of this place to have been brought from France.

Remains of French occupancy are said by Judge C. to have been found about 3 miles up the Lequille.[4] There seems to be none near the town.

There is a Micmac town on Bear River,[5] towards Digby, and a F[rench] Acadian settlement at Clare near St. Mary's Bay.[6] There are none here or in the direction of Minas Basin.[7]

[A page torn out here—Ed.]

Lyon's Cove, near Cape Blomidon,[8] 28 July. Large rich meadows along

[a] "There was a garrison here within 18 or 20 years."—F.P.
[b] Sharp-pointed stake barricade.—Ed.

549

Annapolis River, separated from the Bay by North Mt., which extends from Digby Gut to this place, and forms the heights at the Gut, wh[ich] is less than half a mile wide. Current extremely swift, Annapolis Basin being like a great mill-pond. Tide rises 36 feet. Goat Island in the basin said to be the site of Sir Wm. Alexander's settlement.[9] Heights about the Gut covered with forests, except some cliffs on the outside.

The part of North Mt. about Blomidon, and apparently the rest also, is a red sandstone, which forms cliffs along all this part of Minas Basin. It is very friable & rapidly disintegrated by wet & frost, changing into a rich red soil which is washed by the tide over the meadows, and, when the salt water is diked out, makes them extremely fertile.[c] This is the character of the meadows of Grand Pré and the neighborhood, which is reclaimed by dikes. Several streams, as the Avon, Habitant, Perreau [Perrot],[10] etc., run up into the country, with fertile diked lands about them, all formed of this red soil. No French left about here. The river Gaspereau,[11] which enters the basin between this place & Grand Pré, is full of mill privileges: the F. are said to have had more than 20 mills on it.

Sunrise at Lyon's Cove. Tide out, leaving a broad expanse of red beach between the steep red cliffs & the water. Blomidon is of this red rock,[12] but the upper part is covered with wood.

Last evening the North Mt. was covered with sea fog from the Bay.

On the way from Lyon's Cove to Canning, a fine view of the country between the N[orth] Mt. & the South Mt., extending from Minas Basin towards Annapolis.

From Blomidon one sees Grand Pré and the Minas Basin from a height said to be about 450 ft. Could not get down to edge of cliffs, which are said to be 150 ft. perpendicular.

Grand Pré is described as a vast expanse of rich grass land, reclaimed by dikes.

[Page headed "Digby Gut, Sat. 29 July" cut out.—Ed.]

[c] "Every spring, the rock, as far as the frost penetrates, falls from the face of these red cliffs and is quickly changed to soil."—F.P.

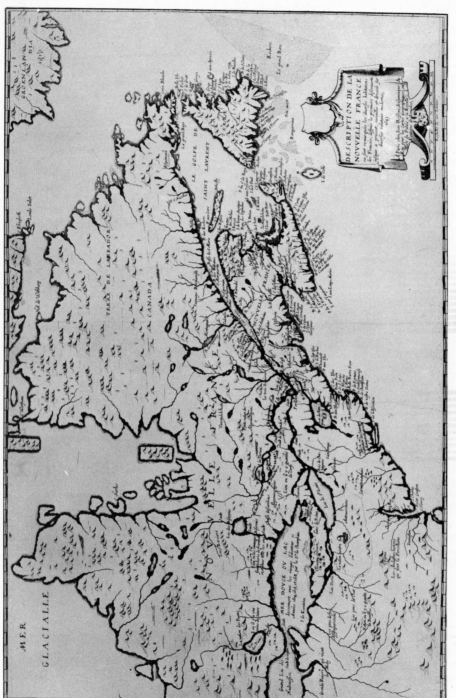

Boisseau's Description de la Nouvelle France, 1643
One of the oldest and rarest maps of Canada
(Coverdale Collection No. 1675)

The country around Grand Lake, from wh. the Jemsec [Jemseg][13] flows, is said to be hilly.

Nashwaak River, the site of the fort attacked by Church,[14] is just opposite Fredericton. Somewhat low flat shores here.

River St. John, below Fredericton, 31 July, morning. Warm drizzling rain.

The distant hills lie pale & faint, & along the dim shores, the elm trees loom like dark phantoms through the dull grey mists.

St. John, 1 Aug. "Fort La Tour" is on the site of Carleton, just opposite Navy Island. A few traces of earth works visible among the mean houses which occupy the ground. It is generally known as the "Old Fort."[15]

The rapids are a short distance above. Below them, the tide rises *27 feet*—above them, *18 inches.* Hence there is a fall of 25½ feet. At high water the rapid is effaced and vessels go up & down with ease! Steep limestone rocks, forming a narrow passage, spanned by the suspension bridge.

Above are the narrows where the river runs between rocky heights, feathered with evergreens, then expands into Grand Bay, to which the Long Reach succeeds. The steep rocks here turn to undulating hills. Nerepis River, where is said to have been a F. Fort,[16] enters on the left as you ascend. Above the Long Reach, a rich farm country—at first upland, but above the Jemsec it takes the character of broad meadows of the richest kind, which continue above Fredericton.

2 Aug. Sea, off St. John. The dull grey sky, the dull grey sea; the dark waste of ridgy forests; the mists that float around the brows of cold stern cliffs; the reefs & rocks that lie in sullen slumber on the leaden waters. Now the fog rolls in and all is veiled from sight, till the seamed & scarred front of some grisly headland, crowned with bristling firs, looms grimly through the mists.[d]

[Two pages missing; the second headed "Bar Harbor."—Ed.]

[d] Last sentence was crossed out.—Ed.

Quebec, Nov., 1871. Height of citadel 350 feet (P. L. Morin)[17]
Rock an argillaceous limestone (Sterry Hunt)[18]

Quebec, Nov. 4, [18]71.

[Page and a half missing.—Ed.]

St. Lawrence, near Saguenay, after a shower. The setting sun, half sunk behind the hills of Tadoussac, bathes with soft golden fire the fleecy clouds that hang above the west, pours floods of level radiance athwart the falling drops, and paints a mighty rainbow against the grey eastern sky.

Acadia
Local Notes, 1873

Aug. 9, 1873. Approaching entrance of Annapolis Basin.
Dark mountain ridges rise above the faint blue haze that slumbers on the sparkling sea.
The entrance. Where the fierce tide surges between opposing walls of verdent forest and weather-beaten rock.
Annapolis Basin, tide out, shores near Goat Island. Vast beds of oozy mud, studded with brown rocks and patched with stranded seaweeds, where the blue heron stalks in the shallow pools, and flocks of crows feed on the countless shell-fish.
The tide rises about 40 feet at Digby. Rode in a wagon thence to Annapolis. Views of Basin & shores very fine. There is a small Indian settlement on Bear River. The French in Digby [Annapolis] county[19] are said to form more than a third of the population— descendants of the Acadians.
As Gray[20] and I smoked our cigars on the rampart of the old fort at Annapolis, the moon rose full, among small dense clouds drifting before a strong wind. They took strange reptile-like forms, with silvered edges and black bodies, and seemed to devour & disgorge the moon by turns. The effect was so weird that the legal mind of Gray was moved to wonder and admiration.

Aug. 11. Sea, near the coast between St. John & Eastport. The north is thick with mustering clouds whose fleecy mists hang lowering above the shadowed forests and the sombre sea.

Aug. 12. Morning, entrance of Portland Harbor. Under the flush of dawn, dark reefs & islands slumbering on the glazed and quivering sea.

Second Paris Notebook
1872

Introduction

IN THE autmn of 1872 Parkman returned once more to Paris, to resume the research he had begun in 1869. During the troubled years of the Franco-Prussian War and the Commune, he had worried over the fate of the archives so necessary to his work; but the tides of war and revolution had washed over them without harm. Once more he laid siege to Pierre Margry, who proved somewhat more helpful and listed references to La Salle material in his own cramped hand in Parkman's notebook. Parkman also met Gabriel Gravier, the great Rouen authority on La Salle, and Henry Harrisse, whose knowledge of Canadiana and Americana was unmatched. Harrisse—whose *Notes pour servir à l'histoire, à la bibliographie et à la cartographie de la Nouvelle-France et des pays adjacents, 1545-1700* (Paris, 1872) remains a standard work today—had formed a collection of manuscripts and printed maps of Canada, which passed into the hands of Samuel L. M. Barlow of New York soon after Parkman was in Paris. This notebook is devoted mainly to references to maps, plans, and documents inspected by Parkman under the guidance of Margry and Harrisse.

Parkman's acquaintance with Margry had ripened into friendship through correspondence, and the latter produced a long birthday ode in honor of the American historian who had hymned *"les beaux actes de notre histoire."* But Margry was still unwilling to let Parkman use his La Salle collection; and Parkman found that many essential documents had been withdrawn from the archives by the collector-curator. The best that Parkman could obtain from Margry was authorization to offer the rights of publication to the former's Boston publishers. But when Parkman returned home, he found Boston in flames; and since the business section of the city was nearly wiped out by the great fire of November 17, no Boston firm was inclined to undertake what at best would be a bit of philanthropic publishing. Parkman went to work creating a lobby for a Congressional appropriation for the publication of Margry's documents, with the help of O. H. Marshall and Charles Whittlesey. Eventually the lobby included Senator George Frisbie Hoar, General James Garfield, and William Dean Howells among its members; and its efforts were crowned with success and the publication in 1878 of the first three volumes of the *Découvertes et établissements des Français*.

Only in one respect was Parkman's Paris stay wholly unrewarding. He had hoped to find materials of interest in the archives of St. Sulpice and among the papers of Abbé Etienne Michel Faillon, who had died in 1870 soon after publishing his *Histoire de la colonie française en Canada* (Montreal, 1865-66). Abbé Casgrain had arranged with Abbé Villeneuve, the superior of the Montreal Sulpicians, that his friend should be well received when he visited St. Sulpice in Paris, but Parkman found "nothing of much account" in their archives and little to his purpose in Faillon's papers, which are now preserved in Montreal.

The terse record of this September and October stay in Paris is found in a black cloth clasped notebook, opening at the end and measuring 5¾ inches by 3. The notes are in pencil.

1872

Paris, Sept. 19, 1872. "*Epures de De Lisle*"[1] 13 (17) Rue de l'Université, Archives du 4me étage

Alcan, Rue St. André des Arts, no. 53, is about to publish an *étude* on the Cramoisys in 2 vols.[2]

Papers on La Roche [Le Rocher], containing testimony of the returned colonists, at Rouen. Ask Gravier (Harrisse).[3]

------

17 Rue de l'Université, "Grandes Archives," No. 122-143 (Amérique Septentrionale): Le Gardeur, La Verandrye, Carton 5, No. 18.[4]

Bibliothèque du Depôt des Cartes, Recueil A. Du L'hut? 33e.[5]

Amérique Septentr[ionale], Canada No. 35. Franquelin?[6]

Amérique Septentr., Cartes anciennes, Recueil B. Franklin [Franquelin] Maps.[7]

9 a.b.c.d.e. Picture of Quebec.[8]

10. Quebec (earlier).[9]

D. Joliet–Franklin map.[10]

14. Beautiful Map[11]—Varennes de la Veranderie

Carton 5, No. 17

" " No. 19[a]

" " No. 18[12]

Joliet, *Labrador*. Carton 5, No. 15.[13]

Quebec, picture[14b] (1695-9?). Chateau St. Louis: 2 *étages*, gallery below. Redoubt on Cap Diamond. Recollets', Jesuits', Cathedral (tall steeples), Ursulines', seminary, where now they stand. *Evê(s)ché*, top of Mountain St. Projecting battery in river just below chateau. In river, Algonquin, Abenaquis, & Ottawa canoes, the two former

[a] "Oldest 1716."—F.P.

[b] "La Potherie's picture is founded on this."—F.P.

559

thus: [with rounded bow and stern]; the latter thus: [with pointed bow and stern].° A map of the river attached. Nearly all the settlements above 3 Rivers have small forts. Those below rarely have them (marked 9a by Harrisse).

Another drawing (10a Harrisse) (No. 240)[15] evidently earlier,[d] gives only a platform in place of the battery, a *buste du Roy* a little below, near the shore. Cemetery below *evêché*. No redoubt on Cape Diamond. A windmill above the town. Steeple of cathedral unfinished.

Another drawing of Quebec is attached to the great map of Franquelin 1699 (12 Harrisse, No. 259 of his catalogue).[16] Vol. no. 4042, Am[érique] Sept[entrionalle], cartes anciennes. P.S. The picture marked 9a by Harrisse is that used by La Potherie as the foundation of his engraving of Quebec.

Names of the Great-West:
Mamtoumie (Jesuits)
Frontenacie (Raudin)
Colbertie
La Louisiane° (La Salle)

A great number of maps and sketches of Franquelin are preserved in the Dep[ôt] des Cartes de la Marine. Nearly all bear, distinctly and more or less completely, the features of the great map of 1684, which is more complete and elaborate than any. That of 1683 (Harrisse No. 219)[17] is very handsomely executed but lacks the lower parts of the Mississippi.

Document in wh[ich] the Recollets demand the expulsion of protestants from Canada (Harrisse No. 421).[18]

Depêche de Richelieu urging restitution of Canada, 1629. (Harrisse No. 443).[19]

Jesuit fur-trade. *Ibid.*, No. 501.[20]

The name of Louisiane is mentioned in the act of concession of Bellisle to La Forest, *10 Juin 1679.* (Harrisse No. 150)[21]

° Two very rough sketches in the text have been omitted.—Ed.

d "Harrisse gives date 1689."—F.P.

° "See Harrisse [p.] 201."—F.P.

The *MS. Joutel* is probably at the Depôt des Cartes, though "mislaid."[22]

Expédition contre les Iroquois en 1695. M. De Frontenac représenté porté dans un canot.[†]

Bibliot[hèque] Nat.? Lorsque j'ai consulté, il y avoit un Portefeuille, Intitulé "Amérique Septentrionale Canada, Etats Unis, Mexique"[†]

La Pièce indiquée plus Haut peut Etre dans un autre portefeuille, je ne m'en souviens plus.[†] Not found (Sept. 24).

Brienne papers, Brit[ish] Museum, contain, says Faillon, a great deal on Canadian Missions (Har[r]isse).[23]

Jesuit collections, Rue des Postes.
Ask Father Tailhan, Missions étrangères, rue de Sèvres.[24]

Engraving of Frontenac, at *Bib. Nat.?* (Margry)

Archives, Dep. des Cartes Marines.
"A correct Plan of the Environs of Quebec, 1759" (engraved) detail of fortifications. Archives, Dep. des Cartes[25]

"*Carte des Environs de Québec, par Villeneuve 1688*"[26] (great detail), lines of settlements, more or less continuous, radiate from Quebec along the St. Louis & St. John's roads to Cap Rouge & Ganderville; up the St. Chs. [Charles] to Old Lorette, and down the shore to the church of Ange Gardien, where the map ends. Numerous houses at Charlesbourg, Bourg Royal (Talon), and Grand & Petit St. Bernard.

Others on Isle of Orleans, and about the church of Point Levi[s]. A few scattered along south shore. Beauport forms a considerable village. Between these lines spreads what seems to be forest. Near Charlesbourg are the Déserts Grand St. Joseph and Petit St. Antoine, the latter near the site of Jeune Lorette (falls of St. Chs.).

"*Carte des Environs of Quebec 1685.*" Villeneuve (5 feet square).[27]

Archives, Dep. des Cartes de la Marine: "Véritable plan de Québec fait in 1663."[28] 17 scattered houses extend along St. Louis St. The *maison* of Jesuits, thus:

† In Pierre Margry's handwriting.—Ed.

Lower town, scattered houses.

A plan of New York by Franquelin, 1693. Also coasts of N. E. [New England].[29]

An article on Canadian society, Frontenac, and *la comédie* by P. M. [Pierre Margry] in *Annales des Voyages*, Jan. 1844. P. M. has a paper about this affair by La Motte Cadillac.

P.S. Margry promises a copy of the passage from La Motte Cadillac. An extract is printed in the *Annales*, as above.

Dep. des Cartes de la Marine: "Partie de l'Amérique Sept., etc., etc.," par J. B. L. Franquelin, Geogr. du Roi 1699" (M.S.?)[30] Drawing of Quebec, cartouche. Extreme right, distant tower of hospital, mountains beyond. Nearer, towards the left, by the St. Chs., the tall, slender spire of the Hôtel-Dieu. On the rock, the Seminary, with its wall and trees of garden. Next, the Cathedral: tall square tower, surmounted by cross & weather cock. Close beyond, the more slender spire of the Jesuits. Then the trees of the garden of the Ursulines and their massive convent, with its short spire. Next, and nearer, the Recollets, a spire surmounted by cross & weather cock. In front, the Chateau, with its gallery resting on a solid wall & buttresses at edge of rock. One range of large windows above, & a double roof with windows, thus:

The magazine and garden on the left at foot of slope of Cape Diamond. A windmill beyond them. Lower town, many closely built houses—a straggling line up Mountain St. Short tapering spire of N. D. [Notre Dame] des Victoires. *Evê(s)ché* and burial ground near top of ascent. In the earlier drawing (10 Harrisse),[31] not only is the spire of the cathedral unfinished, but the garden of the chateau, and the line of palisades and towers or blockhouses wh[ich] border it in the map of 1699 are omitted. Neither does the Recollet church appear at all. The *Evêché* is different and much smaller. This map must be between 1680 & 1690.[g]

The map marked 9 by Harrise is also of 1699 (Fonville).[32]

Mad[ame] de Frontenac. De Lude [Luth] gave her rooms at the Arsenal. This does not imply, as has been said, that she was *entretenue* by him. He was governor of the Arsenal and apartments in it were granted, to a recent period, to such persons as had the influence to secure such a favor.[33] (P.M. [Pierre Margry])

Oct. 6. At St. Sulpice I was shown 4 Ms. vols., as all that Abbé Faillon had left. Notes from *greffe* of Montreal, etc., etc. Nothing of much account.[34]

Dep. des Cartes, *"Fortifications des Colonies,"* 359, 369.[35] Plans of Quebec.

Over library, Dep. des Cartes

D'Avezac,[36] 42 Rue de Bace

The publisher Teschner (?) has a MS., in a vol. of autographs, of a young man named, I think, La Salle, in one of the expeds. of Cavelier de la Salle. Margry has tried to get a copy of it, but says he has failed. About 40 pages.

Probably the author of the letter of 3 sept. 1698, cited by Thomassy.[37]

La Salle Docs. formerly in Dépôt de la Marine, 13 Rue de l'Université.

Archives scientifiques (Notes of Harrisse).

Canada, etc. Carton 64, no. 1: *"Mémoires, lettres et notes sur le Canada*

[g] 1689—Ed.

et sur quelques parties de l'Amérique Septentrionale (1541 à 1732)."—
"Délivré au Ministère."

Carton 67, No. 1: *"Cahier contenant relation du voyage de M. de la Salle dans le nord de l'Amérique Septentrionale pour y faire un établissement dans la partie qu'il en avait auparavant découverte (1684 à 1687).—Prêté le 26 juin '69 à M. Margry."*

Carton 67², no. 1: *"Cahier contenant lettres de M. M. Delasalle et de Tonty par lesquelles on donne la description de l'embouchure du fleuve Mississipy (1685-1686). Prêté le 26 juin '69 à M. Margry."*[38]

Dép. de la Marine, Archives scientifiques, Carton 67², no. 15: "Rapport que fait le Sᴿ de la Salle écrivain dans la Marine de ce qu'il sait de la découverte de la partie septentrionale de l'Amérique qui a esté faite par ordre du Roy sur le commandement du Sᴿ de la Salle depuis 1678 jusqu'en 1685."

Toulon, 3 sept., 1698. 6 pp.[39]

Mr. Saml. L. M. Barlow,[40] 1 Madison Avenue, N.Y.
Maps of M. Harrisse are to be sent to him; send to him for permission to see them.

Clerembault, Purse.
The *Fond[s] Clerembault*[41] at Bib. Nat. may contain papers on Frontenac.

Henry Harrisse, 30 Rue de Cambacérès. (Send *Pontiac & Oregon Trail*)
John Meredith Read Jr, Consul Gen. U.S., Rue de Chateaudun. Send *Pontiac & Oregon T.*
Pierre Margry: Send new ed. *Pontiac* and *Oregon Trail.*
D'Avesac, 42 Rue du Bac—send *Great West.*
Mrs. W. F. Wharton, Barningham Rectory, Barnard Castle— *Oregon Trail.*

1878 Notebook

Lake George, Ticonderoga & Quebec

Introduction

IN NOVEMBER 1878 Parkman visited Lake George, Ticonderoga, and Quebec, in order to re-examine the battlefields of the Seven Years' War, which he was to chronicle in *Montcalm and Wolfe*, published six years later. The ground was already familiar to him from many visits, but with typical thoroughness he covered it once more to fix the scenes of action firmly in his mind, jotting down notes on distances and the terrain about the ruins of the old forts. Such fieldwork as this accounts for much of the extraordinary vividness of Parkman's descriptions. At Quebec he sought out rare books and documents which could contribute to his purpose, benefiting as usual from the suggestions of his great Canadian friends and fellow workers, Sir James Macpherson Le Moine and Abbé Henri-Raymond Casgrain. And at the request of Le Moine, while at Montreal on his way home, he wrote a letter encouraging the Quebec Literary and Historical Society to continue its archival work of collecting and publishing historical documents. Until 1924 this society, of which Parkman became an honorary member, carried on the work now done by the Provincial Archives of Quebec, as well as functioning as a private library.

By 1878 Parkman was a familiar figure in Quebec, and shortly after this visit he attained unwelcome notoriety there. Le Moine announced his coming in a letter to the editor of *Le Journal de Québec*, comparing him to Garneau, Ferland, Faillon, and Laverdière as a great historian of the Canadian past, and proposing that he be honored by the Literary and Historical Society and the Institut Canadien. Jules-Paul Tardivel, no friend of Le Moine and an ultramontane journalist of the most intransigent type, replied with a bitter attack on Parkman as a Protestant American who had undertaken to write the history of a French and Catholic country, and, "not understanding the glorious destiny of the French-Canadian people," had failed to write a single page which might be dignified with the name of history. Tardivel thought that Parkman's writings insulted his race and his religion, and belittled them in the eyes of the world. This onslaught, and the storm of journalistic controversy which followed, prevented Laval University from awarding Parkman its honorary degree of *docteur-ès-lettres*, as planned at the instigation of Abbé Casgrain, Dr. La Rue, and other French-Canadian friends of Parkman in Quebec. McGill University, the stronghold of the Protestant English Canadians in Montreal, soon after gave Parkman its honorary doctorate; and by accepting this degree Parkman convinced the Quebec ultramontanes that he was on the side of the enemy. The incident doubtless served to strengthen his anti-Catholic basis.

This brief record of Parkman's 1878 journey is found in a small red leather notebook, 3⅜ by 5¼ inches. It is written in pencil, and the writing has become smudged. The notebook is marked "Lake George–Quebec 1878" in ink on the front cover.

1878

Ticonderoga. Tuesday. F[rench] lines[1] are 800 or 1,000 yards from fort.[a]

2 Redoubts near R.R. tunnel to protect heights in rear of F. left, which could easily be climbed at this point without exposure to cannons of fort.

In front of the works, the land slopes away gently like an immense glacis; opposite the flanks, it is more broken.[b]

Behind the lines, the ground slopes towards the fort.

A redou[b]t on left rear of F., opposite to the two on right rear, to protect the ascent from the valley of the stream, which, after passing a rocky promontory nearly opposite F. left, runs through marshes which make landing from boats very difficult or impossible. This side much less exposed than the other to flank attack.

Fort to Falls = 2 miles.

Rapids, 1 mile long.

Upper fall, head of rapids, to landing, 1 mile.

Between landing & mountain on left side, $\frac{1}{2}$ mile of rich meadow. This continues till near head of rapids, where the ground becomes broken & hilly, but rich & capable of bearing heavy forests. Upper fall very beautiful—a sheet of foam over steep sloping ledges.

An Ind. path led over back part of Mt. Defiance to L. Champlain.[2] The gap through wh[ich] it runs is visible from near landing place, i.e., old steamboat landing.

There is a path just below Rogers' Slide by wh. valley of Trout

[a] A very rough sketch by Parkman of the right front of the French lines has been omitted.—Ed.

[b] "Especially on the left flank of the F., where an enemy could in some places approach to within fifty yards without exposure to fire. The works here are very elaborate & strong."—F. P.

Brook, now called Lord Howe's Brook,[3] may be reached. It may also be reached by Hague.

Head of Lake George,[4] Friday, Oct. 3ᵈ. Johnson's position seems to have been about 300 yards from lake, between the hill & an extensive swampy hollow, full of young trees, on the right, his front being not more than 150 to 200 yards. A shallow ravine, running down to the lake, intersects the position and soon branches into two. The ground in front is broken, and slopes somewhat towards the camp. Bullets in abundance are found in the fields within musket shot of this supposed line.

The low rocky hill on the left is crowned by the ruins of Fort George,[5] chiefly stone laid in mortar. The work is small, but the walls are of very considerable height & thickness.

Some apparent remains of the old road, where it turns from the present road to Ft. Wᵐ. Henry are distinguishable, but are soon lost in ploughed fields. It might run about 100 to 200 yards in front of Johnson's supposed line, or perhaps much nearer, and even into the camp,[6] in wh. case, the F. must have left it and filed to the right as they approached.

The forked ravine wh. intersects J's camp, is prolonged into a hollow now filled with trees & bushes, and wh. seems to have been directly in his front, within easy range of shot. The general slope of the land in this direction is, however, upward.

From Artillery Cove a marshy ravine runs back from the lake, with good camping ground on the north side.

Levy's [Lévis'] camp was on a level plateau towards the west mountain.[7]

A small sluggish brook, running through a marshy hollow, enters the lake between Caldwell and grounds of Wᵐ. Henry.

Oct. 4. R. G. Bradley & Co., Hundred Island House, Lake George.

Whitehall is opposite Bolton. The head of South Bay may be reached over a low ridge of mountains, or a high gorge 10 or 12 miles from the head of the lake. The distance over is 5 or 6 miles. Why did not Johnson send a party this way to destroy Dieskau's

PLAN
du FORT
CARILLON
Echelle

ATTAQUES DES RETRANCHEMENS DEVANT LE FORT CARILLON
en Amérique
*par les anglais commandés par le général Aberozombie contre les français
aux ordres du Marquis de Montcalm le 8 Juillet 1758.*

RENVOIS.

A *Le fort Carillon.* B *Retranchemens, que les français ont commencé à faire le 7 Juillet,
au matin.* C *Camp de l'armée française, où elle se rendit le 6 & resta sous les armes pendant
la nuit du 7 au 8. Le 8 à la pointe du jour elle prit la position* D *en ordre de bataille derrière les
retranchemens.* E *Les grenadiers & les piquets pour reserve derrière chaque bataillon.* F *Colonnes des
anglais, qui attaquent les retranchemens à midi & demie.* G *Pelotons de troupes legeres & provincia-
les fusillant entre ces colonnes.* H *Les canadiens sortent du retranchement, & attaquent une colonne
anglaise en flanc.* I *Chaloupes des anglais, qui parurent pendant l'attaque, & furent repoussées par
l'artillerie du fort.* K *Retraite des colonnes anglaises dans leur premier camp près des moulins à scier
vers sept heures du soir; leur troupes legeres couvrirent cette retraite par leur feu prolongé jusques
dans la nuit.* L *Position des français après la retraite des anglais.* M *Batteries redoutes &
retranchemens, que les français établirent après le combat.*

C.P.S.CM.

*Plan du Fort Carillon (Ticonderoga), 1758
Line engraving by Contgen after Engineer Lieutenant Therbu
(Coverdale Collection No. 1796)*

boats & provisions? The stream that enters the head of South Bay is rapid and rocky—not navigable. The road thence to Brown's,[8] four miles from Caldwell, is about 15 miles, behind the mountains on east of L. George, and round the end of French Mt. At Brown's the road from South Bay & Fort Ann[e] joins the plank road to Caldwell.[c]

The principal cross street in the village of Caldwell [Lake George], nearly opposite the Lake House and in the midst of the ground covered by the siege lines, is called Montcalm Street.

Uncommon brilliancy of swamp maples in swamp by W[m]. Henry[9]—orange, claret, & gold.

7 Oct. W[m]. Henry to Brown's, 4 miles. *Ib*[*id*] to Bloody Pond, 2 miles. Height of land just south of the pond, which is a mere pool without outlet or inlet. Valley rugged & broken, between French Mt. & West Mt.

Drove to Fort Anne, 16 miles from W[m]. Henry[10]; 12 from Brown's. South Bay, 19 from W[m]. Henry, 15 from Brown's. Turned E[ast] round end of French Mt.; then N[orth] along E[ast] side. Sandy, hilly, country. Mountains in front & on left.

South Bay is surrounded by mountains. The stream[11] at its head is navigable for small boats for a little distance & then becomes rocky.

Fort Ann[e].[12] The fort stood on a knoll on Half Way Brook, near its junction with Wood Creek,[13] overlooking wide meadows, bordered by rocky hills.

Wood Creek writhes through meadows between low hills.

Oct. 8. Soon after leaving Whitehall, the entrance of S[outh] Bay appears on the left, and part of the bay is seen, with mountains sloping on all sides.

Lake Champlain is here, and for some distance below, only a few rods wide. The channel runs through inundated meadow, with rank grass growing in the water.[14] Rocky hills on each side. "The Two Rocks" are high cliffs, crowned with wood, between which the lake runs at one point. Then the marsh begins again. A few miles above

---

[c] A rough pencil sketch by Parkman of Fort William Henry has been omitted.—Ed.

[below] Ticonderoga, the lake widens to a gunshot across and sometimes more.

Quebec, 12 Nov. Memoirs of Laterrière[15] contains matters of interest on condition of Canada just after conquest.

Mère de Ste. Hélène wrote *Hist. de l'Hôtel-Dieu* from dictation of Mère Juchereau (Casgrain).[16]

Papers of Judge Ne[i]lson.[17]

Papers of Seminary.[18]

Maples Leaves: 1873,[19] "Fraser's Highlanders at Quebec," (good) p. 141.

Buttes à Neveu,[20] where the Martello towers stand.

Ruisseau St. Denis—the name of the stream in Wolfe's Ravine.[21]

Did Stobo or De Vitry guide Wolfe's men up the height?[22]

MSS. of Abbé Bois[23] of Maskinongé—probably a great deal about the war.

"*Siège de Québec en 1759, copié d'après un MS. apporté de Londres par l'hon. D.-B. Viger.*"[24]

1834-5 (Hartwell Lby [Library]) Have I got this? (Yes)

Hon. George Baby[25]—Ottawa—a great collector of autographs—has 10 or 12 original letters of Montcalm.

Send M. Bédard[d][26] the paper Mandement mentioned in *Frontenac,* p. 330, note.

Send Le Moyne [Le Moine][27] the pamphlet on the false letter of Montcalm.

Bédard's *table* of Reg[istres] du Conseil Souv[erain] will be printed in 3 months, up to 1700.

"*Résumé des Evénements les Plus Remarquables des Annales du Monastère des Dames Ursulines de Québec*" (in Beatson).[28] Montcalm died in Chateau St. Louis, 14 Sept. Buried same evening by torch light, not in hole made by a bomb, but in a grave.[29] Nobody could be found to make a bier, so M. was buried in a box made of old boards.[e]

Candiac is near Nîmes.

d "T. P. Bédard, Parlement, Q."—F.P.
e "From Beatson."—F. P.

Gleig, *Lives of Eminent British Military Commanders*[30] (Montcalm & Wolfe).

"Plan of the Town & Basin of Quebec and part of the adjacent country, shewing the principal encampments & works of the British army commanded by Maj. Gen. . . ."[31] (have it)

Write to J. M. Le Moine about importance of collecting maps & docs. relating to 1759—Quebec Hist. Soc.[32]

Ask J.M.L. about the pamphlet on Siege of Quebec wh. I have not got.

Send *Frontenac* to Mr. Marmette,[33] Treasury Dept., Quebec.

Rev. Thomas Hamel,[34] Rector of Laval University, Quebec.

Paul	3 yrs.
Marie Luce	6 "
Marie Louise	13 "

children of Dr. H. La Rue,[35] cor[ner] St. Ann[e] & St. Ursule sts.

Write to J. M. Le Moine about publication of Index to Registers, which Bedard is making.

Hon. F. G. Baby, Joliette, 10 autograph letters of Montcalm. Has a large coll[ection] of autographs.

The height of the plateau above Wolfe's Cove is about 200 feet, by measurements of Royal Engineers.

The Ruisseau St. Denis runs down to the cove through a huge ravine, & a few rods from its mouth leaps down a rock of considerable height; whence it runs to the St. Lawrence. The local tradition—probably correct—is that the grenadiers climbed into this ravine and then, turning to the right, scaled its side at two points to the plateau above. Vergor's[36] post was then but a few rods before them.

1879 & 1885 Notebook

Quebec & Acadia,
Carolina & Florida

Introduction

IN AUGUST 1879 Parkman returned once more to Quebec. Since the cover of his notebook lists the children of his good friend Dr. Hubert La Rue, it is probable that he stayed at the latter's home in St. Louis Street, where he was a welcome guest on his Canadian visits. Dr. La Rue was one of the leading members of the Laval faculty, whose manifold interests embraced medicine, the physical sciences, agriculture, and folklore. He found relief from his intellectual labors in managing the family farm on the Ile d'Orléans near Quebec. A farmer friend of his once called at his town house while he was entertaining Parkman and other distinguished guests; the farmer wished to go away when he found that his friend was engaged, but Dr. La Rue insisted on making him, as the best Canadian of them all, join the company.

This notebook also contains a long précis of the journal of Louis Franquet, a royal engineer who was set out from France to inspect the fortifications of Louisbourg, Acadia, and New France in 1750-51 and 1752-53. His *Voyages et mémoires sur le Canada*, published by the Institut Canadien of Quebec in 1889 from an Ottawa copy of the original in the Archives de la Ministère de la Guerre, Paris, (Bib. Can. 229) affords a richly detailed picture of New France in 1752. Parkman, with his mind already at work on the problems afforded by the tale he was to tell in *Montcalm and Wolfe* (1884), also examined the battlefields on the Plains of Abraham where the fate of New France was settled in 1759.

Equipped with letters to Acadian curés from his friends at the Séminaire de Québec, Parkman set out for Nova Scotia, Cape Breton Island, and New Brunswick, where he carefully examined once more the chief scenes of the long struggle between French and English for possession of this gateway to the New World. He visited

Louisbourg, Beauséjour, Fort Lawrence, Port Royal, and St. John's, in preparation for writing the Acadian chapters of *Montcalm and Wolfe* (IV, VIII, and XIX) and of the later *Half-Century of Conflict* (VI, VII, IX, X, XIX-XXII), which were to involve him in one of the greatest controversies of his career, the long feud with Philip Smith, Abbé Casgrain, and Edouard Richard over the thorny Acadian question, which Parkman finally summed up thus: "The truth is that the treatment of the Acadians was a scandal on both sides."

In March 1885 Parkman spent two weeks visiting the sites of the early French Huguenot settlements at Port Royal (Beaufort, South Carolina) and the River of May (the St. John's River, Florida), whose brief history he had chronicled in his first link in the chain of histories, *The Pioneers*. A revised edition of this book was in prospect, and with his conscience troubling him for having once written without going over the ground involved—that had been impossible at the time, because of the Civil War—Parkman took this opportunity to acquire "a more exact knowledge of the localities connected with the French occupation of that region," as he put it in his preface dated the following September. The New Englander reveled in his first taste of the tropics, and the lushness of the Floridian flora delighted the eye of Harvard's first professor of horticulture. Parkman was an impassioned amateur gardener, who devoted much of his leisure and means to the cultivation of rare plants, and this side of his nature finds here its sole expression in the journals.

The records of these two journeys, separated by six years in time, are found together in a small purple cloth notebook, 4 inches by $6\frac{1}{2}$, with a paper label marked 1879 (in ink) and 1885 (in pencil) in Parkman's hand. A loose page refers to his visit to Beaufort.

1879 & 1885

[The front end papers list the following names:[1] "Alphonsine La Rue, Marie Louise, Marie Luce, Paul, Luc, Joseph" and also this series of numbers: "200, 100, 200, 100, 100."—Ed.]

Quebec, 9 Aug., 1879. Journal de Franquet, 1752.[2] Church of Caughnawaga. No seats. Men *"sont assis, ou si mieux l'on aime dire, accroupis sur leur cul."* Women separated by a balustrade from men. (Copy p. 52-53, 72.)

At *Two Mountains,* was a post commanded by Benoist, and a fort belonging to Sulpitians, adjoining (containing ?) the church. A square, bastioned—with loopholed wall 12 ft. high—refuge for families. Iroq[uois], Algonkins, Nipissings, Iroq. live in log houses. About the *"jour des trépassés,"* they go hunting with wives & children —generally come back at Christmas. After Ash Wednesday they go again for furs. They raise beans etc.

Many F[rench] traders in the village.

At a dance, a widow was allowed to dance with an E[nglish] scalp on a pole to comfort her for the loss of her husband, who had been killed.

A very curious acct. of Two Mts. (pp. 64-75).

"Balises" of *"sapin"* [spruce] planted on ice of river to guide travellers.

Officers at Montreal engage greatly in trade.

Quarrels among officers at Ft. Frédéric [Crown Point], because Lusignan, the commander, traded with E. and would let nobody else trade—even in ginsing. Hence great dissatisfaction. Abuses like this ruin the service. Trade of officers should be prohibited.

Varin withdrew right to trade from Lusignan and gave it to the *"garde-magasin,"* who was thought to share profits with him— Lusignan extremely wroth.

Mentions Carillon [Ticonderoga].

The portage of St. Sacrement [Lake George] is the chief road by wh[ich] our Inds. carry on contreband trade with E.

Proposes a *"fort de pieux"* [stockade] at Carillon & another at R[ivière]-au-Chicot, with an Ind. settlement *"à titre de mission."*

Fort Frédéric is in a ruinous state.

Description of Ft. Fréd. (copy p. 112, 113).

12 houses near St. John [St. Jean]. There was a habitant named La Bonté some distance below I(s)le-aux-Noix.

Chambly impregnable without cannon. Land cleared all around it.

Description of Chambly (copy 127-129.).

The curé of St. Ours (133).

Sorel (copy 134, 135).

St. Francis (139-141). Becancourt, only 19 *"cabanes."* All Inds. had gone to trade in N. England or to gather ginsing. Cabins closed.

Lorette. (Copy 150-160.)

At St. Louis, Inds., set on, says F[ranquet], by Jesuits, opposed the establishment of a garrison. The village has now an imperfect palisade & is surrounded by trees & bushes. The fort is of *"pieux"* on 2 sides.

At 2 Mts. the Algonquins & Nipissings have 113 warriors, and the Iroq. 105: a total of 1,060 souls. There is a stone fort, enclosing church & presbetery, and an *"enceinte de pieux"* for the whole village except the part occupied by this fort.

Bigot (Copy 218.).

Country manners (221).

Two Mts. (220-224).

St. Francis—51 cabins of logs, *"carrés longs,"* covered with bark and planks.

Jean Langelier,[3] Bureau du Registraire
Hon. Luc Letellier de St. Just,[4] P.Q., Canada

---

11 Aug., Quebec. The high ground on which the prison stands is evidently that on wh. Wolfe took his stand before the battle.[5]

From this to the Buttes à Neveu is 600 paces.

Send to Abbé Bois:[6] *Book of Roses, Jesuits, La Salle.*
To Evanturel:[7] *La Salle,* etc.
["] Faucher de St. Maurice:[8] *La Salle.*
["] Jean Langelier: *La Salle.*
["] La Rue: entire set, except *old Regime.*

"Attack of July 31, [17]59," contemporary engraving from drawing made on the spot by Capt. Hervey Smith [Smyth] (shown me by Faucher de St. Maurice). This one of a set of contemporary engravings, including views of Quebec, Miramichi, Gaspé, etc.— large & well executed.[9]

Alfred Garneau[10] has collected many odds & ends in Canadian history. Says that in *Memoirs of Academy of Inscriptions*[11] is a curious incident, recorded by Bougainville, of the attack on Carillon, 1758.

Mr. & Mrs. William M. McPherson:[12] Steamer[a] *Dunara Castle,* Martin Orme & Co., leaves Glasgow every Thursday for outside Hebrides. *Deck cabin.*

John Henderson, (Tiree) Scotland; Woodlands, Maidenhead.

Dec. 29, 1757. In a letter of this date, Wolfe suggests to Pitt the capture of Quebec, as the true way to end the war. He became the victim of his own project. Grant's *Mem. of Wolfe.*[13]

---

morue[14] ⎰ Basque: *macaillaioua*
⎱ Esp.: *baccaliau*
⎩ Gascon: *mouru*[b]

---

23 Aug., Forts Lawrence [&] Beauséjour [Nova Scotia]. About 2 miles apart. Lawrence[15]—of which the traces are slight—stood on a rising ground, with marsh, of great extent on each side. On the side towards Beauséjour, wh. is plainly visible near the end of the long high ridge— beyond the marsh, runs the Missiguash [Misseguash], filled with water to the brim at high tides, but at low tides a great winding ditch of reddish mud. Tide rises at least 20 feet. Marshes covered

[a] Remainder of this entry is in another hand.—Ed.
[b] "The above from a semi-Basque Gascon, on the steamer from Sydney."—F.P.

with coarse grass. Low wooded hills in extreme distance—fir & spruce, as everywhere.

The view from Beauséjour[16] is of vast extent. On one side, Ft. Lawrence in full view, 2 miles off across the marsh. On the other, the great Tant(r)amar marsh, traversed by the Aulac, in character like the Missiguash. Westward, another vast tract of marsh, with Cumberland basin beyond, visible to a great distance—muddy shores, bare at low tide. *Aboiteaux*ᵉ everywhere (the word is still in use). Bricks are made of this red mud.

Ramparts of Beauséjour well preserved. Magazine—capacious casements, extremely well built of stone & brick. One curtain is of stone. In front of it, towards Cumberland Basin,[17] an immense stone structure, apparently a bomb-proof, in tolerable preservation. On this side the ground slopes towards the basin. Five bastions, with deep ditches and embrasures towards east or land side, where the ground is level. Foundations of 2 ranges of barracks. The fort is visible from a great distance, being much higher than Ft. Lawrence.

When at Pictou, visited Micmac village. Lazy beggars. Those on Cape Breton work well at farming and coopering. Near Truro, they make butter firkins. Though tolerably industrious here as at Cape Breton, they are said not to increase.

Mr. Gillies, Sydney

On Wed., 20 Aug., visited Louisbourg; 21 Aug., Sydney to Hawksbury; 22, Hawkesbury to Pictou, & thence to Truro and Amherst; 23, Visited Beauséjour & site of Ft. Lawrence. Thence to St. John.

The 42ᵈ [Highlanders] at Ticonderoga: "on the top of their breast-work, they had plenty of wall pieces. . . . They took care to cut down monstrous large oak trees which covered all the ground from the foot of their breastwork about the distance of a cannon shot every way in their front. . . . Even those who were mortally wounded

ᵉ A special dike, allowing the water to enter at the flood, and retaining it at the ebb.—Ed.

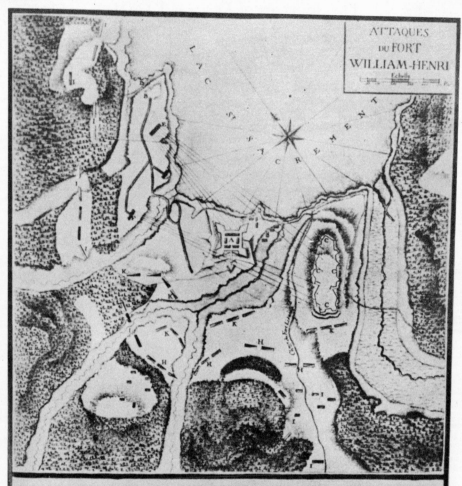

ATTAQUES DU FORT WILLIAM-HENRI
en Amérique
par les troupes françaises aux ordres du Marquis de Montcalm.
Prise de ce fort le 7 Aôut 1757

Renvois

A. Fort William-Henri B. Ouverture des tranchées la nuit du 4 au 5 Aôut
C. Camp retranché que les anglais allèrent occuper lors de l'arrivée des français
D. Baie où les français débarquèrent leur artillerie. E. Batterie de huit
canons & d'un mortier. F. Batterie de dix canons & d'un mortier G. Batterie
de six pieces dont on ne fit aucun usage H. Position de Mr. de Levi
pendant l'investissement du fort. I. Position des troupes durant le siège
K. Leur position après la prise pendant la démolition des retranchemens
faits par les anglais ▭ Troupes sauvages

C. P. S. C. M.

Attaques du Fort William-Henri, 1757
Line engraving after Engineer Lieutenant Therbu
(Coverdale Collection No. 1797)

cried to their companions not to mind or lose a thought upon them, but to follow their officers and to mind the honor of their country. Nay, their ardor was such that it was difficult to bring them off. When shall we have so fine a regt. again?" Letter from Lieut. Wᵐ. Grant, in Maclauchlan's *Highlands*, II, 340 (1875).

———

Plan of Ty[conderoga] in *The Scot's Mag.*, Aug. 1758.

———

Capt. John Campbell with a few men forced their way over the breastwork & were bayonnetted. (Maclauchlan, II, 339)

St. John, 24 Aug. Ulysse de Fabremont, Belgian, says that he saw a Mr. Wiggin(?) at Halifax who said he had doc[ument]s wh. he wanted to give me. F.B. Webster, Counsellor at Law, 121 Bank St., Cleveland, O., can probably give his address, as it was to him that he spoke about the docs.

St. John, 24 Aug. Tides not less than 30 feet. At slack water—that is, when the rising tide overcomes the downward current—vessels of considerable size go up over the falls. At this time, there are a few minutes of still water, after which the course of the current is reversed, and the tide rushes up with great force over what was before the fall. In spring freshets, however, the river keeps the mastery and the downward current maintains itself. Large ships are built above the falls.[18]

1885

South Carolina and Florida Notes

9 Mar. [*1885*], *Beaufort, S. C.* Wide entrance, low shores on each side, long strips of white sand with bushes and pine trees behind. Harbor forks not far from entrance, Beaufort River on right, Broad River on left. Port Royal a little above fork. Archer's Creek, close to Port Royal connects the two rivers, thus;

Sandy soil: live oak, cypress in flower, holly, myrtles, cherry, eleagnus, Spanish moss abundant. Peaches & wild cherry in flower. Also narcissus.

Harbor well given on a county map of Beaufort County pub[lished] in 1873 at Charleston.

A great marsh, covered with tall grass, and bordered by distant woods. At the spot marked *x* is a small coquina fort,[20] said to be older than St. Augustine. It is near the bank of the river.

10 Mar., 1885, Fernandina, Fla.[21] Harbor bordered by broad meadows of rank grass or rushes, intersected by creeks & inlets.

R.R. from Fernandina to Jacksonville. "Saw" palmetto in abundance—dwarf—said never much to exceed 6 feet, while the cabbage palm is a considerable tree. Sandy soil covered with pine, chiefly long-leaved. Little or no underbrush. Ground beneath covered with low, coarse grass. Occasional vast meadows, of rank grass or rushes, looking dark and dingy at this season, traversed by creeks and rivers; woods, chiefly pine, in the distance, sometimes dim and faint, sometimes nearer, like islands or promontories studded with the tall pines, sometimes massed together, sometimes apart, their irregular tops shaped something like the Italian pines. Cherries, oranges, roses in bloom at Jacksonville.

Jacksonville, 11 Mar. Red-bud maples in early seed. Yellow jasamine, rubia, wild cherry in flower. Magnolia—dark-green lustrous leaves—

bloom in June or a little earlier. Andromedas in bud. A delicious warm balmy morning. Mocking birds in many porches.

Fort George, 11 Mar., Evening. Came down this P.M. from Jacksonville —about 25 miles by course of steamer, 18 direct.

Drawn by the steamer captain

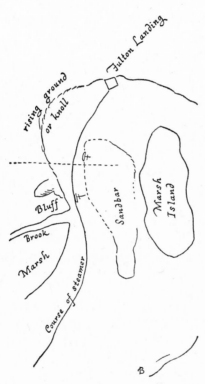

12 Mar. Returned to Jacksonville. River[22] nearly a mile wide at entrance, widening as you enter. Brimful of lazy, breathless water, quivering under the setting sun. Marshes of bulrushes or rank grass, almost level with the river, forming islands, or stretching to the lines of forest, faint in the haze, that bound the view to right & left. These are traversed by creeks or broad belts of torpid water.

Pelican Bank[23] is destroyed by the Eads system of jetties. It was in the entrance.

About 5 miles from the entrance, a long ridge of fine yellowish sand, covered thickly with pines & deciduous trees, rises on the farther side of a sedgy marsh, and abuts on the river, forming St. John's Bluff. The tide here is very strong and the bluff is constantly cut away, as are the sandy shores into which it slopes away above. About ¼ of a mile above is a sandy knoll, half cut away, and behind it a meadow extends back between woody slopes (Q. The vale of Laudonnière?).[24] The knoll seems the most likely site of the fort. (See the plan drawn by the steamer captain).

Opposite the bluff is a marsh island, and beyond this, across the river, vast marshes stretch to the dim line of woods of the north shore. For some miles above, the river is often bordered by marshes, inter-sected by creeks.

Towards Jacksonville the shores are sometimes ten feet or even more high. Fine yellow sand in which trees grow well. The main feature is tall, bare-stemmed pines with tufts of foliage at the top often mixed with deciduous trees. Palmetto (dwarf), occasionar magnolia, cabbage palm, & yucca, with live oak, etc.

Saw a golden eagle. Other birds are pelicans, white & grey, herons, egrets, cranes, cormorants. Spoonbills rare. Flamingoes are only seen above.

River a dark brown opposite Jacksonville. Profusion of animal and vegetable life. Shores at entrance low & sandy.[25]

Friday, [*March*] *13ᵗʰ*. Woods opposite Jacksonville. Tall, lank, bare-stemmed pines. Wire grass, etc., below. Sun easily penetrates. Palmetto thickets. Pools of stagnant water. Marshes of bulrushes. Masses of deciduous trees & magnolia—creepers, Spanish moss, sometimes choking the trees like tattered cobwebs, slowly killing them. Liquid amber, maples, live oak, etc.

Up the river to Palatka, 75 miles. 3, 4, or 6 miles wide—low, wooded shores, pine mixed with young foliage of deciduous trees. Thunder, heavy rain. Waves pitted with the great drops. Water coffee-color. Calm at sunset. Water suffused with red. Heat light-ning. Forest fires in distance.

The Entrance of Louisbourg Harbour, 1779
Aquatint by J. F. W. Des Barres, from the Atlantic Neptune
(Coverdale Collection No. 52)

Soft, pea-green, young foliage of deciduous cypress.

Sat., [*March*] *14ᵗʰ. From Palatka to mouth of Ocklawaha.* Forests on nearly same level as water. Chiefly deciduous. Many trees killed or nearly so by Spanish moss. A few intervals of sandy banks several feet high. The pine here reappears.

Entered Ocklawaha. A decided current. Water not so dark as main river. Swamps on either hand with pools of dead water. No pine. A tangled mixture of tropical & northern vegetation. Ash, maple, cabbage palm, cypress, sweet gum, "bay." Mistletoe (or something like it, clinging to ash & other trees) and two curious parasites, one like a tuft of bristly hair, the other like a pine-apple growing out of the trunks of trees. Palms taller & more numerous as we went southward. Evening. Grating of pine knots burning on pilot house. Effect very striking. Occasional yells of birds disturbed in the forest.

Not only the cypress but also the ash, & perhaps other trees growing in the water of the swamp, have their stems enlarged into a cone shape at the base. It is melancholy to see the effect of the Spanish moss. The tall trees, especially cypress, for mile upon mile, are covered with it, a few opening leaves alone visible above the dismal drapery. At rare intervals, sandy banks interrupt the swamp—always with a settlement. The yellow water lily and many other water weeds fill the coves & line long reaches of shore, and masses of floating vegetation collect among half sunk rotten logs.

Sun. [*March*] *15ᵗʰ, Daybreak.* The steamer—a little tug—makes her way through a solitude, varied by an occasional small alligator, large turtles, the large brown bird whose cries were heard so often in the night, a white heron, a blue heron, etc. Numerous leaping fish. The stream scarce wide enough at times for the tug to pass, brushing against the boughs. Strong current. Entered the stream from Silver Spring—20 or 30 yards wide, very deep, water of a pellucid, greenish blue, tinting the white sand & limestone of the bottom, where the waterweeds did not hide it. Black bass, cat-fish, garfish large & small, and many large turtles, plainly seen 20 feet below. Reached the spring at about $11\frac{1}{2}$. Extensive marshes for some miles below.

From Silver Spring to Ocala. The usual sand, covered with pine &

wiregrass. Then some shell limestone, and an undulating country, dry & uninteresting. Deciduous oaks.

Saw this A.M. many palms of from 40 to 60 or perhaps even 70 feet.

Mon., 16ᵗʰ Mar. Ocala to Palatka. Rolling or flat country. Sand, whitish or yellow. Pine, long bare stems, wire grass, with palmetto beneath. Occasional shell limestone. Hummock land at intervals with magnolias, bay, *cornus florida*, gum, maples, and sometimes numerous palms, rarely over 30 feet. Some *mag. glauca.* One or two cypress swamps. Orange lake, water & marsh interspersed. Many small lakes & ponds, sometimes covered with weeds. A heron & other game. Deciduous oaks. Marshy places choked with matted vegetation.

Tues., [March] 17ᵗʰ, Daybreak, St. John's below Sanford. Narrow stream, between marshes, and woody islands. Tall, reedy grass, 8 or 10 feet high along banks. Willows. Extensive grassy meadows, backed with woods and interspersed with tufts or bushes, trees, & rank vegetation. Morning mists. Fish leaping. White cranes abundant; blue & white herons also. Large hawks. A bushy point alive with singing birds, like blackbirds. Maple, ash, gum, cypress, laurel, etc. Banks low & swampy almost everywhere. Palms numerous, sometimes large tracts of them—hundreds together. Water covered in in coves and along banks with bright green glistening leaves of yellow water lily.

Back to Palatka. Stream very tortuous. Strange floating water plant, drifting with the current. Alligator 8 or 10 feet long, lying in the mud. Continuous swamp, with intervals of sandy banks, in every instance occupied by settlers. Lake George—wide, low banks. Ducks of several kinds. Stream wider below. Swamp, with a few intervals of dry banks. Strange climbing plants, one with a fruit like a gourd, hanging through winter. Mistletoe. Palms numerous in some places below L. George.

18 Mar., Palatka to Jacksonville by rail. Pine, with hummock land. The decidous or hummock growth alway[s] in wet places, usually with water visible. The water indeed seems even in the pine lands to be near the surface.

From Jacksonville to St. Augustine. Pine, bare lank stems in innumerable multitude. Beneath, tufted wiregrass, palmetto in extensive tracts, pools of water. Frequent wet hummock land, often forming an impervious jungle of dense matted bushes & trees, creepers etc. Occasional cabbage palms. Extensive meadows of rank grass near St. Augustine.[26]

Thursday, Mar. 19. Anastatia [Anastasia] Island.[27] Bordered by extensive marshes, deep mud, and rank grasses on the side opposite St. Augustine. The island is of sand over coquina, covered in most parts with a jungle of low bushes, bay, myrtle, etc., with tracts of large yucca and palmetto, occasional prickly pear; sometimes mere wire grass, in ragged patches. On eastern side a wide beach formed of fragments of shell from the disintegrated coquina. Waves breaking in the sand shallows across the channel, which follows the shore.

Menagerie. Rattlesnake—*alive, 7 feet long.* Water mocassin, 4 to 5 feet. Hooping or sandhill crane. Black vulture. Darter or snake bird (*Plotus*). American barn owl. Opossum. Red tailed hawk. Gray fox. Lynx. Gopher. Gopher-snake. Ground rattlesnake.

Anastasia Island extends about 13 miles to inlet wh. is narrow.

———

Dr. DeWitt Webb, St. Augustine.

———

21 Mar. From St. Augustine to Jacksonville. Near St. A., marshes of bulrushes. Then higher levels covered with palmetto, then pine woods with palmetto, wire grass, & stunted bushes beneath. Gopher holes. Frequent hummock tracts of great extent, always low & wet— deciduous trees, palms, bushes, tangled vines, fallen logs, black mud, water-weeds. Almost impervious.

1889 - 1892 Notebook

Introduction

THIS last notebook summarizes aptly enough the closing years of Parkman's life. The opening pages (here printed as an appendix) are devoted to a careful account of his battle against insomnia: the date, the amount of sleeping draught taken, and the number of hours of sleep thus gained, from December 1889 to November 1892. The historical notes consist largely of references and queries for *A Half-Century of Conflict*, the last link in the chain of his history, and one which he feared might not be completed before death came or his strength gave out. Then there are lists of people who were to receive his new book or the revised editions of earlier works; the roll reads like a *Who's Who in America* in the 1890's, with an international supplement. As he neared the end of his lifelong task, his work was at last receiving the popular recognition it deserved. And, to the end, he kept on revising the books which had already appeared and sifting the sources for new material, for at sixty-nine Parkman's passion for history was as consuming as in his youth. The next-to-last summer of his life was devoted to preparing the new chapters on Acadia which he added to the revised edition of *The Old Regime*, published a few months before his death. It is appropriate that the very last note that he made in his journals concerned the correction of a slip in one of his early books.

Parkman's last years were a race against time. After 1884 his powers of work were sharply reduced by the insomnia from which he could get little relief, despite the aid of such eminent physicians as Dr. S. Weir Mitchell of Philadelphia. In a letter written to Abbé Casgrain in the spring of 1889, Parkman revealed his plight: "Two or three hours of sleep in the 24—which have been until lately my average allowance for long periods together—are not enough to wind up the human machine. . . . Though I have slept better in the last year, it is still an open question whether I shall manage to supply the missing link between that objectionable work [*Montcalm and Wolfe*] and its predecessor, *Count Frontenac*." He had written the more important *Montcalm and Wolfe*, the last in chronological order of the series and its crowning piece, before tackling the period from 1700 to 1750, in the fear that he might not be able to complete his life-work; but he struggled doggedly on as best he could, harboring his slender resources of energy, and in March 1892 he finished the book and with it the great historical epic he had planned in his youth. The great history of *France and England in North America* had been written, in the face of all the misfortunes and setbacks which had beset his path. It had taken nearly half a century, but Parkman permitted himself only a brief comment in his last preface:

The manuscript material collected for the preparation of the series now comprises about seventy volumes, most of them folios. . . . The collection was begun forty-five years ago, and its formation has been exceedingly slow, having been retarded by difficulties which seemed insurmountable, and for years were so in fact. Hence the completion of the series has required twice the time that would have sufficed under less unfavorable conditions.

Few others had traveled the same path far enough and grown sufficiently weary in the same service to appreciate what Parkman felt at the completion of the task and what a great triumph its achievement was. But one of the few, his cousin Henry Adams, wrote to assure him that "You have had the singular good fortune to complete successfully a great work which puts you at the head of our living historians; and I leave the dead ones out of account only because we cold-blooded Yanks detest the appearance of exaggeration so much more than we love what the French call *mesure*." Such a letter, among the flood of congratulations which poured in upon Parkman, surely offered some reward for his long struggle.

This last record is written in pencil and ink on the pages of a black leather-covered notebook, $4\frac{1}{4}$ by $7\frac{1}{8}$ inches.

1889 - 1892

Send some book to: Hon. John George Bourinot,[1] etc., etc., etc., Ottawa; also T. Roosevelt[2].

Change statement about Vetch[3] being relieved from fine in consequence of his scheme against *Canada*.
Benoni Stebbins[4]—his character *as a boy* (Miss C. A. Baker).[5]
"No trained soldier in Mass."? Vetch might be called one.[6]

The growth in Jamaica Pond is *oscillaria roseata*, a *European* species (Faxon).

Smith's, *Hist. N.Y.*,[7] 194
Juchereau,[8] 458, 473, 491
"The Four Kings of Canada,"[9] *Mag. Am. Hist.*, Mar. 1878
Articles [on] Vetch and Nicholson[10] in Appleton's *Cyc[lopedia of American Biography]*.

Consult *Mém. des Commissaires*,[11] II, *338*, 340, 642 (Capture of Annapolis).
Also Poore MSS.,[12] III, 25, 29 (*ibid*).
"Journal of the Voyage of the Sloop Mary, 1701," (O'Callaghan, 1866).
"Journals of Mad. Knight and Rev. Mr. Buckingham" (H. C. 6374,12)
N. H. [New Hampshire] *Provincial Papers*, II, 504-513 (Attack on P[ort] Royal, 1707)
Brymner, *Report 1887*, for Acadian matters about 1705.[13]
Acadians (after conquest), Poore Mss., III, 19, 20, 37, 40.
1708. "The *coup* struck by the Canadians *où Mars, plus féroce qu'en*

Europe, a donné carrière à sa rage ([at] Haverhill) makes me fear reprisals." *De Goutin au Min[istre], 29 Dec., 1708.*[14]

Send book to:

Theodore Roosevelt(ans.)	S. Weir Mitchell
Mrs. French	Col. Dodge(ans.)
Pres. Eliot	Barrett Wendell(ans.)
Mrs. H. Parkman	Capt. J. G. Bourke(ans.)
B. A. Gould(ans.)	Geo. Sheldon(ans.)
Justin Winsor(ans.)	Miss C. Alice Baker
C. S. Sargent(ans.)	James Grant Wilson(ans.)
G. E. Ellis(ans.)	Prof. A. L. Perry, Williams-town(ans.)
St. Botolph Club	
Chauncy Hall(ans.)	E. Rameau de St. Père
Hon. Geo. Bournot,(ans.) Ottawa	B. D.(ans.)
Mr. Brice	Mrs. Fiske(ans.)
Casgrain(ans.)	Dr. Oliver(ans.)
Henry Adams(ans.)	D. D. Slade(ans.)
Jas. F. Hunnewell	

E. Rameau[15] is preparing a new and enlarged edition of his book on Acadians & Canadians.

Modify statement about character of Nicholson.[16]

Read the following in [*Le*] *Canada-Français* I, 1re livraison, docs.:[17] 28 Nov. 1730, "*Estat de l'Acadie*"; 1735-1739, "*Lettres de Maillard.*"

On Dudley's meeting with Inds. at Casco in 1703, compare Rale's acct. (see Francis, *Life of Rale*,[18] 231).

Tanguay,[19] 1871, contains a list of English persons taken in the 17th century and baptized in Canada.

Examine: "Remarks out of the Fryar Sebastian Rale's Letters from Narridgwock, Feb. 7, 1720" in the *Common Place Book* of Rev. Henry Flynt[20] (Mass. Hist. Soc.).

Examine: Letter of Rev. Joseph Baxter to Rale (April, 1719).[21]
(Given to Mass. Hist. Soc. by Mr. Daniel Adams of Medfield)
    "Journal of Baxter," in N. E. *Hist. & Gen. Reg.*, 1867, p. 45.
Flynt's *Common Place Book*, in Mass. Hist. Soc.
"Strong box" of Rale, Mass. Hist. Soc.?[22]
Rale's *Abenaki Dictionary*[23] (H.C.)

Frye, see if his name is in *Quinquennial Cat[alogue]*, *H[arvard] C[ollege]*.
Bouton, *Lovewell's Great Fight*.
Fox, *History of Dunstable*.
Corr[espondence] Officielle, 3me Série, Vol. VIII, *Vaudreuil et Begon au Min[istre]*, *14 oct., 1723*, pp. 51-59 (see Calendar, 125).

Louisbourg:
    Mass. Hist. [Soc.] *Coll[ections]*, 2 ser., III, 192.
    Hist. Mag., 2 ser., VIII, 23, 25, 97.
    Mass. Hist. *Coll.*, 4 ser., V, 398 (Niles)[24]
    Coll. Essex Institute VI, 182 (Craft's "Journal"[25])
    "   "   "   III, 186.
    Mass. Hist. *Coll.*, 1 ser., VI, 108-112, 117.
    Hist. Mag., IX, V, 63; 2 ser., V, 396.
    Wm. Vaughan[26] in Harvard *Quinquennial*.
    Raynal, VII, 106.
    Gents. Mag., 1758, 102-XV, 649; XVIII, 105.
    Pepperell's journal, *Journal or Minutes of an Expedition made against Louisbourg*,[27] (Am. Ant. Soc., Worcester).
    N. E. *Hist. Gen. Reg.*, XXIV, 367; XXV, 249.
    New France, I, II (F. P[arkman] [Papers], Mass. Hist. Soc.).

1890, July.
    Examine Douglass's *Summary*.[28]
    "   Viscount Bing[Byng]'s account of the capture of Louisbourg in "Exodus of the Western Nations."
    Examine *Alloa* [Père Alloüez, S. J.?] often cited by Brown.

Robert Bancroft, descended from Col. Hale, told E.S.P.[a] of the

---

[a] Parkman's sister Eliza, who served as his amanuensis.—Ed.

diary of a soldier named Benjamin Cleves, in N. E. Historic-Genealogy Society—said to be good. Also of a curious letter to Col. Hale from a friend in Boston, written after the siege, and expressing anxiety as to the consequences of the excessive consumption of punch. Bancroft[29] has a copy of it. (Bancroft promises me a copy, Sept. 1.) (I have it.)

———

Stephen Williams[30]—look him up in Appleton's *Cyc.*

———

Jesuits, 257, correct "*evening* mass."

———

Appendix

Accounts

E. W. S. P.[b] ½		10.25
" "		6.48
E. W. S. P. ½		22.16
E. W. S. [P.] ½		37.25

3 July	recd. per F. C. Welch, B. & L. R.R.	175	returned to
	B. & A. " "	80	Welch for deposit
10 "	Welch, bal. of acct.	1,532.16	del. by post.
		625	Mass. Bk.

3 July	Paid S. S. Pierce	23.00
9 July	M. W. Quinlan	111.58
	Craffey, shoing	20.50
	Fenno, fodder	12.96
	Clough & Stuckley	13.60
	Balkam & Co.	9.25
	Dr. Williams	5.00
	Dr. Richardson	5.00
	Grant, saddler	4.15
31 July	Rowe, wood & hay	44.33
4 Aug	M. D. Ayers, carpenter	30.25
	S. S. Pierce	28
5 Aug	H. W. Beckwith	5
8 "	Bickford's Exp.	4.85
" "	Burnham & Co.	74.50
1 Sept.	Henry Lee	20
4 Sept.	S. S. Pierce	22
"	Saltonstall Portrait	10
	Journ. of Archaeology	5

[b] Parkman's sister Eliza, who ran his household and often acted as his secretary. —Ed.

1891

Receipts:

sent to Welch for deposit } June, Thompson-Houston   43.75
10 July, F. C. Welch,   1,622.78

11 July
1 Sept. Boston & Maine, R. I. (sent to F. C. W. for deposit, 2 Sept.)   30

E. S. P.

Pratt, butcher,	28.72½	14.36
Fodder	16.69½	8.34
Horse shoer	10½	5.00
Quinlan, sundries	82.50	12.
Burnham, coal	17.25½	8.62
Beckwith, carriage	5½	2.50
Rowe, wood	$7.½	3.50
Fallon, fish	½	3.44

1891

27 June, check to D. Foy, clothes   45.
9 July D.D. Lee, veterinarian   2.

10 Dec. Pulford & Son, 65 St. James st., S.W.
£ 15.17.

Look after:
Hansas Bonds (Jeffries)
10 New Sh[are]s B. & A. R.R.
Thompson-Houston shares (30 June, 1892 notice rcd. of readiness to exchange for N. Y. Electric shares—sent to Welch for execution this day). (Receipts are in Lee's vaults—of wh. I have key, 7 July.)
Books on La Tour [Latour][31] to go to Portsmouth:

Hutchinson 1.	Rameau, *Colonie Féodale*, I
Mém. des Commissaires	Moreau, *Acadie*, I
4 Mass. Hist. Coll. IV	Winthrop, *N. England*
„ „ „ VII	2 Mass. Hist. Coll VI (Hubbard)

Notes made on:

Mar. [18] '92 *Corr. Officielle*, Copy	Sir Wᵐ Alexander (Prince Soc.)
1857 Vol. I	Hazard, *State Papers*, I, II.
Poore MSS. (Quebec	Bradford, *Hist. Plymouth*
ed.) I, II	Williamson
Hutchinson Papers	Palfrey
Memorial Hist. Boston.	*N. Y. Col. Docs.* IV, IX

29 Sept., 1892.

Guarantee fund of *Good Government*[32] published by Civil Service Reform League yearly for 3 years from 1 July 1892— $15.

Oregon Trail

(ans.)	X B.Derby—Lit. & Brown 16 Oct.	(ans.)	XC. H. Cordner
"	Mrs. H. Parkman	(ans.)	J. T. Coolidge—L. & B. 16 Oct.
	Col. Dodge	(ans.)	G. P. Coffin
(ans.)	Casgrain—L. & B. 16 Oct.	(ans.)	Bijorby
given (ans.)	X Mrs Fiske	(ans.)	M. A. B.—L. & B. 25 Oct.
	X Mrs. C. S. Sargent	(ans.)	Mrs. J. Q. Adams 25 Oct.
" (ack.)	" Q[uincy] A. S[haw]		
(ans.)	John Bartlett—L. & B. 16 Oct.	(ans.)	Mrs. John Lowell, 30 Dec. 1893
" (ack.)	" Julius H. Ward	(ack.)	Mrs. Mary B. Hall, 25 Dec. 1893
" (ack.)	" E. S. P.		

Medicine and Sleep

	1889						
12 Dec. Sulph.	30	6 hrs	30 Ap.	30	7		
		6	4 May	30	7		
	1890		13 "	30	5½		
8 Jan.	30	7	16 "	30	6½		
17 "	30	6	20 "	30	6½		
1 Feb.	30	8	28 "	30	6½		
15 "	28	5½	4 June	30	5		
18 "	30	6	7 "	30	7		
25 "	30	6½	14 "	30	6½		
4 Mar.	30	8	21 "	30	5½		
14 "	45	6	24 "	30	6½		
21 "	30	6½	26 "	30	6		
25 "	30	6	1 July	30	7		
29 "	30	6	7 "	30	5		
4 Ap.	30	7	9 July	30	6		
7 "	15	6½	16 "	30	7		
9 "	20	10 4	22 "	30	5		
14 "	30	6	24 "	30	6		
16 "	30	6	31 "	30	6		
			17 Aug.	30	7		

27 Aug.		30	6
1 Sept.		”	6
6 ”		”	7
12 ”		”	5
17 ”		”	7
19 ”		”	8
26 ”		”	6½
2 Oct.		”	5
7 ”		”	3½
13 ”		37	5
29 ”		37	6½
1 Nov.	New Drug		6½
5 Nov.	Sulph.	37	6
7 ”	Ch^ld.		6
14 ”	Sul.	37	6
18 ”	Ch^ld.		5
26 ”	Sul.	37	6
29 ”	Nit. Soda		5
1 Dec.	Ch^ld		5½
3 ”	Sul.	30	6½
8 ”	Ch^ld		4
12 ”	Sul.	37	7½
22 ”	Sul.	37	6½
29 ”	Sul.	30	5

1891

10 Jan.	Sul.	37	6
18 Jan.	Sul.	37	6
27 Jan.	”	37	6
6 Feb.	Sul.	37	7
15 ”	”	37	7
6 Mar.	”	37	7
17 ”	”	37	7
22 ”	”	37	5
2 April	”	37	6
8 ”	”	37	5½
17 ”	”	37	7
27 ”	”	37	7
4 May	”	37	7
10 ”	”	37	5

17 May	Sul.	37	7½
25 ”	”	37	8
30	”(3D)”	37	5¼
2 June	”	37	6
4 ”	”	37	6½
12 ”	”	37	5½
18 ”	”	36	5
21 June	”	37	6
25 ”	”	37	6½
3 July	”	37	4
9 ”	”	37	6
19 ”	”	37	7½
25 ”	”	37	6
31 July	”	37	7 hrs.
6 Aug.	”	37	7 ”
13 ”	”	37	7 ”
17 Aug.	”	37	6½
21 ”	”	30	6½
28 ”	”	30	6½
3 Sept.	”	37	6½
7 ”	”	37	8 hrs.
11 ”	”	30	6 ”
15 ”	”	30	6½
19 ”	”	30	5
21 ”	”	37	5½
25 ”	”	37	6
29 ”	”	37	6
7 Oct.	”	37	5½
11 ”	”	37	5
15 ”	”	37	6½
20 ”	”	37	6½
23 ”	”	30	5½
27 ”	”	30	6
31 ”	”	30	6
4 Nov.	”	30	6
8 ”	”	30	7
17 ”	”	30	5½
21 ”	”	30	5
25 ”	”	30	5
30 ”	”	37 grs.	6

8 Dec.	Sul.	37	$4\frac{1}{2}$	14 May	Sul.	30	6
14 "	"	30	$5\frac{1}{2}$	21 "	"	30	6
20 "	"	30	5	27 "	"	30	$6\frac{1}{2}$
27 "	"	30	$6\frac{1}{4}$	5 June	"	30	6
				14 "	"	30	6
		1892		21 "	"	30	$3\frac{1}{2}$
5 Jan.	"	30	5	24 "	"	37	5
9 "	"	30	5	1 July	"	37	$6\frac{1}{2}$
13 "	"	37	7	9 "	"	30	5
23 "	"	37	5	20 "	"	30	7
1 Feb.	"	37	6	26 "	"	30	6
7 "	"	37	$6\frac{1}{2}$	10 Aug.	"	30	6
11 "	"	37	7	5 Sept.	"	30	$6\frac{1}{2}$
18 "	"	37	7	12 "	"	30	7
27 "	"	30	7	19 "	"	30	$6\frac{1}{2}$
5 Mar.	"	30	6	25 "	"	30	4
10 "	"	30	$6\frac{1}{2}$	5 Oct.	"	30	6
15 "	"	30	7	9 "	"	30	6
22 "	"	30	$6\frac{1}{2}$	16 "	"	30	7
30 "	"	30	$3\frac{1}{2}$	22 "	"	30	6
6 April	"	30	6	22 "	"	30	5
12 "	"	30	$5\frac{1}{2}$	2 Nov.	"	37	7
19 "	"	30	$5\frac{1}{2}$	9 "	"	30	5
24 "	"	30	$3\frac{1}{2}$	16 "	"	36	4
30 "	"	30	$5\frac{1}{2}$				

NOTES

VII. THE OREGON TRAIL
VOLUME I

[1] During his three days in New York, Parkman saw Ramsay Crooks, head of the northern department of the American Fur Company, who gave him letters of recommendation to the principals of the western department: George H. Moore, author of *The Indian Wars of the United States* (*Philadelphia, 1843*) and one Allen. (*1846 Account Book.*)

[2] Henry Whitney Bellows (1814-82), a graduate of Harvard College and the Divinity School, became pastor in 1839 of the first Unitarian church in New York City. Parkman probably had an introduction from his father, one of the leading Boston Unitarians. Bellows was a famous preacher and lyceum lecturer, and an editor of *The Christian Inquirer* and *The Christian Examiner*. During the Civil War he founded and directed the U. S. Sanitary Commission, the forerunner of the Red Cross.

[3] Mr. Kay, like most bookish Easterners of the period, was interested in the social theories of Charles Fourier and in the attempt to put them into practice at Brook Farm. Parkman had no use for the Transcendentalists, whom he called the "she-philosophers of West Roxbury."

[4] Henry Rowe Schoolcraft (1793-1864), explorer and ethnologist, first visited the Indian country on a geological trip through Missouri and Arkansas in 1817-18. He served as geologist on Governor Lewis Cass's expedition to the Lake Superior copper country in the summer of 1820, and described it in his *Narrative Journal of Travels Through the North-Western Regions of the United States* (1821). Two years later he was appointed Indian agent for the tribes of Lake Superior. He married the grand-daughter of an Ojibwa chief, and negotiated many treaties with the Indians. From 1836 to 1841 he was Superintendent of Indian Affairs for Michigan, and devoted much of his time to studying and writing about the Indians. His best known works are *Algic Researches* (1839), *Oneota* (1844-45), *Notes on the Iroquois* (1846), and his tremendous compilation, *Indian Tribes of the United States* (1851-57). In the *North American Review* for July, 1866 (CIII, 1-18) Parkman critized this last work savagely, for Schoolcraft was guilty of many inaccuracies and some deliberate fudging.

[5] In Philadelphia, Parkman consulted on historical matters William B. Reed, a lawyer; Dr. Alfred Elwyn; John Jordan, Jr.; C. A. Poulson, Jr.; and Francis J. Fisher, Jr.—many of whom are mentioned in his acknowledgments in the preface to *Pontiac*.

[6] In Harrisburg, Parkman saw Samuel Brenizer, to whom he returned some borrowed papers; and Neville B. Craig, editor of *Olden Time*, who told him that S. P. Hildreth had the St. Clair papers. (*1846 Account Book.*)

[7] [Carlisle] "Armstrong family. The Col. had two sons—[one] of the [*sic*] youngest, Genl. A., has a son living near Baltimore—others, one of them called Koskiusko, in N. Y. Dr. A. of Carlisle thinks the family papers in their hands." (*1846 Account Book.*)

"Baird of Reading (formerly of Carlisle) has collected materials for a history of Cumberland Cnty." (*1846 Account Book.*)

[8] Colonel Henry Bouquet (1719-66), a Swiss professional soldier, came to America with his compatriot Frederick Haldimand of the Royal Americans in 1754, after joining the British service. Bouquet took a leading part in the French and Indian War. In 1758 he marched with General Forbes against Fort Duquesne and commanded there, after it had been renamed Fort Pitt, until 1762. In the following year he returned and broke up the Indian siege, in the "dangerous enterprise" of which Parkman speaks (cf. *Pontiac*, II, 61-78). In the winter of 1763-64 Bouquet organized and led an expedition against the Ohio Indians, which resulted in the signing of a treaty of peace. Parkman wrote an introduction for William Smith's *Historical Account of Bouquet's Expedition* (Cincinnati, 1868), and revised the translation of Dumas' biographical account of Bouquet which prefaces it.

[9] "Colonel" James Smith led the Pennsylvania rangers in 1763 and 1765. In the latter year he waylaid a government pack train at Bloody Run (see *Pontiac*, II, 292-96). His narrative may be found in Samuel G. Drake's *Tragedies of the Wilderness*.

[10] General Edward Braddock cut a road from Fort Cumberland to Fort Pitt in the course of the expedition of 1755 against what was then Fort Duquesne, which ended in his defeat and death at the Monongahela. Bouquet's road from Fort Loudon to Fort Pitt was to the north of Braddock's road, along the course Parkman followed.

[11] The battle of Bushy Run in 1763 is described in *Pontiac*, II, 67-8.

[12] Jared Sparks (1789-1866), the first professor of history in an American university, began teaching at Harvard in 1839, after an earlier career as a Unitarian clergyman. He edited the *North American Review* (1824-30); published a *Life and Writings of Washington* (1834-37) and the *Works and Life of Franklin* (1836-40); and studied the history of the American Revolu-

tion in European sources (1840-41). He also edited the *Library of American Biography*, to which he made many contributions. He was Parkman's historical mentor, and later his guide and critic. He was president of Harvard from 1849 to 1853.

[13] Two Mr. Biddles of Pittsburg are mentioned in Parkman's notes: Richard, to whom he was referred by William B. Reed of Philadelphia, and John W.

[14] Fort Pitt was built by General Stanwix in 1759 on the ruins of Fort Duquesne, after the capture of the latter by Bouquet in 1758. It was named after the elder William Pitt.

[15] A fortification was first built at the junction of the Alleghany and Monongahela rivers, on the present site of Pittsburgh, by Virginians under Captain Trent in 1754. After the Great Meadows fight, the place was newly fortified and named Fort Duquesne by the French. In 1755, under Contrecoeur, it served as a base for the Indians with whom Beaujeu defeated Braddock. It was captured by Bouquet in 1758 and renamed Fort Pitt.

[16] "*La Belle Rivière*" was the old French name for the Ohio.

[17] Francis Fauvel-Gouraud published his *Phreno-Mnemotechny or the Art of Memory* (New York, 1845) after lecturing on his system, which he claimed was "founded on a purely philosophical basis and operates through the intellectual and not the mechanical action of the mind."

[18] Fort Massiac, or Massac, on the Ohio River in southern Illinois, was built by the French as Fort Ascension in 1757, and renamed after the Marquis de Massiac in the following year. It was abandoned in 1759, but another fort was built on the same site in 1794 by the Americans, on the orders of Anthony Wayne.

[19] The Planters' House in St. Louis, opened in 1841, was the best-known hostelry of the metropolis of the old West.

[20] Henry Clay (1777-1852), the "Great Pacificator," author of the Missouri Compromise, had been the Whig candidate for the presidency in 1844. Parkman admired him as the white hope of the Whigs, whom the New England Federalists supported against the Jacksonian Democrats.

[21] Quincy Adams Shaw, Parkman's cousin and companion on the Oregon Trail trip, was a lover of sport and travel, but not of history; and hence only joined the expedition at St. Louis, where they outfitted. He later acted as Parkman's amanuensis for the composition of *The Oregon Trail*, and helped to shape it into a record of holiday adventure rather than a history.

[22] Madame Julia Jarrot of Cahokia, a native of Ste. Geneviève and the

daughter of the wealthy Vital Ste. Gem of Kaskaskia, was the widow of Nicolas Jarrot, one of the principal inhabitants of the place in 1809. The Jarrot mansion was a center of hospitality, and according to local legend Lafayette was entertained there in 1825.

[23] Passed Midshipman Selim E. Woodworth, U.S.N., was the son of Samuel Woodworth, editor of the New York *Mirror* and author of "The Old Oaken Bucket." From Oregon young Woodworth made his way to California, where he was put in charge of the relief expeditions which sought to rescue the Donner Party early in 1847. He himself never ventured farther into the mountains than Summit Valley, and his conduct has been severely criticized. He was characterized by the milder-mouthed Californians as a martinet, a drunkard, and an egotist. During the Civil War he returned to the Navy and rose to the rank of Commodore.

[24] Pascal Louis Cerré, whose sister Marie Thérèse married Auguste Chouteau, the older half-brother of Pierre. A son, Michel Sylvestre Cerré, a veteran of the Upper Missouri fur trade, entered the mountain trade while supplying Captain Bonneville, and later was with the American Fur Company and Pierre Chouteau, Jr. & Company. The Cerrés ranked close to the Chouteaus among the first families of the St. Louis fur trade.

[25] Pontiac (1720-69), head of the Ottowa, Ojibwa, and Pottowatomie confederation, was perhaps the greatest leader the North American Indians ever produced. In 1746 he helped the French at Detroit to repel an attack by the northern tribes, and in 1755 he led the Ottawas at Braddock's defeat. After the fall of New France in 1760, he organized a great Indian uprising against the new masters of the continent. In 1763 he destroyed many of the British forts on the Great Lakes and massacred their garrisons. No less than eight of the twelve frontier posts were captured by Pontiac, and only in 1766 did Sir William Johnson succeed in subduing the Indians and making a treaty of peace. Pontiac was assassinated by a Kaskaskia Indian three years later. Parkman's first historical work, *The Conspiracy of Pontiac* (1851), was devoted to this period of American history; and it is interesting to see from this and earlier notes, and the later use of Pontiac's name for Parkman's horse, that the young historian's mind was already full of his subject.

[26] "*April 17.* Tradition here [St. Louis] says that Pontiac was killed in a drunken fray near Cahokia." (1846 Account Book.)

"Baptiste Vallée of St. Geneviève must have seen Pontiac." (1846 Account Book.)

[27] Thomas Fitzpatrick (1798-1854), "Broken Hand" or "White

Head," was perhaps the greatest of the mountain men, and played a notable part in the opening of the West. He was with W. H. Ashley's fur brigade on the second voyage up the Missouri in 1823, and in March 1824 was among the first white men to use South Pass. He was once Jed Smith's partner and Kit Carson's tutor in the ways of the wilderness. In 1834 he headed the Rocky Mountain Fur Company, with Jim Bridger and Milton Sublette as partners, and later joined the American Fur Company, which became Pratte, Chouteau & Company. He twice guided the misnamed "Pathfinder" Frémont along the routes long known to the mountain men, and led the first emigrant trains to set out for the West Coast by the Oregon Trail. He guided Father De Smet, S.J. and his fellow missionaries all the way into the Flathead country. In 1845 he showed Colonel Kearny and his dragoons the road to South Pass, and led Lieutenant Abert safely through the hostile country from Bent's Fort along the Purgatoire and the Canadian to Fort Gibson. In this summer of 1846 he was to guide the Army of the West to Santa Fe, and the California expedition as far as Socorro, returning to St. Louis with dispatches for Washington in November. With an unmatched experience as a trapper, explorer, Indian fighter, and trader, he was named as the first Indian agent for the Plains tribes, a post which he held until his death. Parkman could have had no better informant. Cf. L. R. Hafen & W. J. Ghent, *Broken Hand* (Denver, 1931).

[28] Lieutenant James William Abert, Topographical Engineers, U. S. A., mapped much of the West. He was the son of Colonel J. J. Abert, the Chief of Engineers, who sent Frémont on his expedition of 1842. Young Abert accompanied Frémont in 1845, and on his orders made a survey of the Purgatoire. His first report, dated 1845, deals with the Bent's Fort–St. Louis route; his second, in Major W. H. Emory's *Notes on the Topographical Survey*, App. 6 & 7, covers the Fort Leavenworth–Bent's Fort route and New Mexico.

[29] Fitzpatrick's picture of the Western tribes is strikingly modern on the whole, though faulty in some respects. Of the tribes which Fitzpatrick left out of his two main divisions, the Pawnees and Arikaras belong to the Caddoan linguistic group, the Mandans to the Siouan, the Cheyennes to the Algonkin, and the Kiowas to the Kiowan. The first great group of which Fitzpatrick speaks was the Siouan, which was second in numbers only to the Algonkin among the Indians north of Mexico. To this group belong all the tribes which Fitzpatrick includes, save the Sauks and Foxes, which are Algonkin. Other Western tribes also included in this Siouan group are the Crows and Assiniboins. Fitzpatrick lumps the

Iroquoian group, including the Mohawks and Tuscaroras, with the Algonkin, which includes the Shawnees, Delawares, Chippewas, and most of
the Indians of the Northeast and the Great Lakes, as well as the Blackfeet,
Arapahos, and Cheyennes of the West. Properly speaking, the Iroquoian
group includes only the Hurons, the Tobacco Nation, Neutrals, Iroquois,
Conestogas, the Tuscarora Confederation, and the Cherokees.

Owing to the peculiar geographical position of the Crows, their Siouan
dialect was known by such linguistically different tribes as the Nez
Percés, Blackfeet, and Gros Ventres, as well as by the Siouan Dakotas
and Mandans. It was often used by traders as an intertribal language,
instead of sign talk.

The Comanches, Utes, Bannocks, and Shoshonies all belong to the
Shoshonean group, as Fitzpatrick has it. But the Nez Percés and Chinooks
belong to the Penutian family, while the Flatheads and Spokans were
Salishan tribes, usually considered to be Algonkin. The Salish, who were
known as Flatheads from the tribal designation in sign language (which
referred to their ancient practice of deforming the heads of their children),
and as Diggers for their digging up of wild roots for food, differed very
widely from the Plains Indians.

[30] Jefferson Barracks, an army cantonment near St. Louis, was an
important military center during the Mexican and Civil wars.

[31] *"Vide Poche"* ("Empty Pocket") was the nickname of Carondelet,
the poor French suburb of St. Louis.

[32] The Crows, a Siouan tribe closely related to the Hidatsa or Gros
Ventres of the Missouri, were divided into two main bands, the River
Crows of the Yellowstone and the Mountain Crows of the Rockies. The
latter, with whom Fitzpatrick and Parkman were concerned, were much
more important than the Dakotas to the mountain fur trade, because of
their strategic position. They produced better buffalo robes than any other
tribe, and their language was used as a common medium of communica-
tion in the trade which centered about their territory in the valley of the
Big Horn. After the Crows separated from the Hidatsa in the eighteenth
century, their chief enemies were the Dakotas, Sioux, Blackfeet, Pawnees,
and Arapahos. They were nomadic hunters, living on the buffalo and
planting only a little tobacco for use in their religious ritual. Prince
Maximilian of Wied considered them the proudest of the Indians, and
pointed out that they more often plundered than killed the whites. The
Crows were expert horse thieves and robbers, but professed friendship
with the whites, many of whom resided among them at various times.
Two mulattoes, Edward Rose and James P. Beckwith, even became Crow

chiefs. The Crows were noted for their magnificent social discipline, which enabled them to spare themselves the ravages of liquor, use of which they long prohibited, while other tribes were weakened by it. They were, however, sexually dissolute.

[33] Dixon and R. Ewing followed much the same route as Parkman through the West, while R. G. Jacob went all the way to the Pacific Coast. All three went as far as Fort Laramie with W. H. Russell's or Lillburn W. Boggs' emigrant party, which Parkman saw assembling at Independence and later met at Richard's Post near Laramie. Here Jacob joined Edwin Bryant's horseback party to California, which was the first group of the 1846 emigration to reach the coast. Jacob then joined the California Battalion with Bryant, and went campaigning under Frémont. Dixon and Ewing went southward from Fort Laramie to Bent's Fort, and returned to Westport along the Santa Fe Trail. Parkman expected to keep them company, but they left without him while he was with the Sioux in the mountains.

[34] Pierre Chouteau (1758-1849), whose older half-brother Auguste accompanied Pierre Laclède to the site of St. Louis in November 1763, and in the following spring founded there the first center of a fur-trading enterprise which later covered the whole West. Chouteau and his son Pierre, Jr. (1789-1865), who acted as his father's clerk before he was sixteen and went into business for himself in 1813, lent their names to places as far north as Dakota and as far south as New Mexico; Kansas City was first known as Chouteau's Landing. Pratte, Chouteau & Company, of which the younger Chouteau was a leading partner, bought the Western Department and Upper Missouri Outfit of the American Fur Company in 1834, when John Jacob Astor sold out and a syndicate headed by Ramsay Crooks bought the Northern Department. Both outfits retained the old name in their field operations. By 1846 the St. Louis firm had become Pierre Chouteau, Jr. & Company, and it then operated Fort Laramie. Parkman found "the magic of a dream and the enchantment of an Arabian tale" in old Chouteau's memories of St. Louis' growth from outpost to metropolis, and gives an eloquent account of them in *Pontiac*, II, 274n. It would seem that he confused Pierre Chouteau, who only came to St. Louis in 1764, with Auguste, the co-founder.

[35] This sentence is taken almost word for word from the 1846 Account Book.

[36] Liguest P. Chouteau, a son of the elder Pierre, is quoted as an authority on Pontiac's death in *Pontiac*, II, 325. Pontiac led the Ottawas

at Braddock's defeat and was given a French officer's uniform by Montcalm shortly before the battle of the Plains of Abraham (*Pontiac*, I, 192*n*). Liguest was Pierre Laclède's last name, usually dropped.

[37] "Mr. Liguest P. Chouteau tells me, as coming from his father, that Pontiac had a high command over the Inds. in Montcalm army—that the English hired an Indian to kill him at Cahokia—that the Spanish requested his body, and buried it at St. Louis." (1846 Account Book.)

[38] The Kansa(s) or Kaw Indians were a tribe of Siouan stock who lived in the valley of the Kansas. Their mud-hut village stood a few miles above the river's mouth. The Kaws lived at peace with both whites and their Indian neighbors, growing corn and hunting. As they became more dependent upon the government, they grew lazy and demoralized, like those Parkman saw begging on the steamer.

[39] Henry Chatillon (1816-?), Parkman's hunter and guide on the Oregon Trail trip, was one of the St. Louis French who played so great a role in opening up the West. He had earned his living as a hunter on the plains and in the mountains since he was fifteen, and was considered one of the best hunters in the West. He was engaged for Parkman by P. Chouteau, Jr. & Company, whose trading posts he had long supplied with buffalo meat, as he later did the Missouri steamboats. The steamboat captains employed hunters to precede them up the river, leaving their kill on the river banks to be picked up by the boat's yawl and thus providing a welcome variation to the staple diet of pork and beans. H. M. Chittenden, the historian of the fur trade and of early navigation on the Missouri, mentions Chatillon as hunter for Captain Joseph La Barge, and calls him "a fine man, an excellent hunter, and sensible and gentlemanly in his relations" (*Early Steamboat Navigation on the Missouri* [New York, 1903], 126). Chatillon's real home was the plains and the mountains —he had just returned from four years there when Parkman engaged him at St. Louis, and he was perfectly willing to leave on another expedition after only three days in St. Louis—and like many another mountain man, he had taken an Indian wife. This woman, Bear Robe, who died during his expedition with Parkman, was the daughter of old Bull Bear, the great chief of the Oglalas—probably the chief here referred to by Parkman—and the relationship doubtless did much to explain the immunity with which the small party passed through the Indian country. It was certainly responsible for Parkman having the opportunity to live with an Indian village as it pursued its normal life. Chatillon was known as "Yellow Whiteman" by the Sioux, and as late as 1931 he was remembered by the descendants of Bull Bear's band (cf. G. E. Hyde, *Red Cloud's*

Folk [Norman, Oklahoma, 1937], 59). Parkman judged that Chatillon
had:

A natural refinement and delicacy of mind, such as is rare even in women. His
manly face was a mirror of uprightness, simplicity, and kindness of heart; he had,
moreover, a keen perception of character, and a tact that would preserve him
from flagrant error in any society. Henry had not the restless energy of an Anglo-
American. He was content to take things as he found them; and his chief fault
arose from an excess of easy generosity, not conducive to thriving in the world.
Yet it was commonly remarked of him, that whatever he might choose to do with
what belonged to himself, the property of others was always safe in his hands.
His bravery was as much celebrated in the mountains as his skill in hunting; but
it is characteristic of him that in a country where the rifle is the chief arbiter
between man and man, he was very seldom involved in quarrels. Once or twice,
indeed, his quiet good-nature had been mistaken and presumed upon, but the
consequences of the error were such that no one was ever known to repeat it. No
better proof of the intrepidity of his temper could be asked, than the common
report that he had killed more than thirty grizzly bears. He was a proof of what
unaided nature will sometimes do. I have never, in the city or in the wilderness,
met a better man than my true-hearted friend, Henry Chatillon. (*Oregon Trail*,
17-18)

Parkman gave Chatillon his rifle at the end of the trip; and though the
latter could neither read nor write—in one of the notebooks Parkman
wrote out his own name and Chatillon's, evidently for the latter's benefit—
he kept up a correspondence with Parkman through the aid of others until
1867. The two men then met again in St. Louis, where Chatillon had
retired to spend his last years.

⁴⁰ Independence, six miles from the Missouri, founded in 1827, was the
second starting point of the Santa Fe and California-Oregon trails, after
Franklin was washed away by the Missouri in 1828. It was the main
outfitting center of the westward movement from about 1832 to 1840.
It gradually lost ground before the rise of Westport, founded six years
later and ten miles farther west, which was near the good landing at Kansas
and beyond the Blue River (of the Missouri), which was hard for wagons
to ford.

⁴¹ Albert Speyer, a Prussian Jew who was a Santa Fe trader of many
years standing, carried two wagonloads of arms and ammunition con-
signed to Mexico on this trip. He was accompanied by Dr. Adolphe
Wislizenus, a German geologist, naturalist, and political refugee, who
had already followed the Oregon Trail as far as Fort Hall in 1839 and
written a book about it, and was now planning to investigate the flora and

fossils of the Southwest. After Speyer's train had set off, Colonel Kearny learned that these munitions were destined for General Manuel Armijo, the governor of New Mexico, with whose brother Speyer was probably in partnership. Kearny sent two troops of dragoons under Captain Benjamin Moore to intercept the shipment, but Speyer had too great a start and reached Santa Fe safely. On his way thence to Chihuahua the arms were seized by the Mexicans, against whom Speyer later made claim for payment, though he was escorted on this journey by General Armijo, who was fleeing from Santa Fe. George Frederick Ruxton met them on the trail. Speyer later quit the Santa Fe trade and set up business in New York, where he killed himself after going bankrupt.

[42] Westport, now part of Kansas City, stood approximately at the present intersection of the Santa Fe road and Grand Avenue. The landing on the Missouri near Westport was first known as Chouteau's and later as Kansas. Westport was predestined to be a center of the westward movement, for if freight for Santa Fe were landed farther up the Missouri, the Kansas River had to be crossed; if farther downstream, a longer wagon haul was demanded. Westport had the good grass, water, and wood essential for wagon trains, and its outfitting establishments soon rivaled those of St. Louis and Independence.

[43] Colonel Chick, who kept a store as well as a tavern at Kansas Landing, probably also speculated in land and outfits. He befriended all the westward-moving world, and his hospitality is frequently mentioned by travelers.

[44] The Sauks, like the Kickapoos and Pottowatomies, were of Algonkin stock and had been forced out of their home in northern Illinois and Wisconsin when the whites moved in. The Sauks and their close kinsmen the Foxes waged the Black Hawk War. These Eastern tribes were established on reservations in present-day Kansas and Oklahoma which were created by the government after 1830.

[45] The center of the Shawnee Methodist Mission was the large brick building which still stands two miles west of the Missouri line in the midst of Kansas City. The Shawnees and the Delawares were Algonkins from the eastern seaboard. The Wyandots (Hurons) had been driven out of their original home in Ontario near Georgian Bay by the Six Nations and the Sioux about 1650, and in 1842 they migrated to Kansas from Ohio and Michigan. In 1856 Parkman saw the other surviving section of the Huron nation at Lorette, near Quebec, where they had taken refuge with their Jesuit missionaries after the fall of Huronia in the seventeenth century. The Delawares, once the most important tribe of Algonkin stock

and hence given the title of "grandfather" by other Indians, were "made women" after their conquest by the Iroquois about 1720, and forbidden to make war or to hold land. They slowly migrated westward and south-westward, and became the only forest tribe that really mastered the Plains culture. In small bands they roved everywhere in the West, and were magnificent scouts, trailers, hunters, and trappers. They were the Ishmaels of the Plains Indians, since every man's hand had been against them and theirs was against every Indian's. They accompanied the fur-trapping brigades of the mountain men as trusted and valued master craftsmen of life on the plains and in the mountains. They were with Jim Bridger, Kit Carson, and Frémont, and later served as scouts for the U. S. Army. The Plains Indians had a healthy respect for the Delawares' prowess as warriors. Their Kansas reservation was established in 1835.

⁴⁶ This party, with which Parkman and Shaw joined forces, consisted of Captain Bill Chandler, a retired Irish officer of the British Army who had served in Canada and Jamaica; his brother Jack, an amiable non-entity; and Romaine, an English traveler who had "once been upon the Western prairies." The Britishers parted company with Parkman at the forks of the Platte, on June 10. Cf. *Knickerbocker Magazine* (June 1847) XXIX, No. 6, 506. Shaw later met the Captain in New York.

⁴⁷ The Noland House was run by Smallwood Noland, "Uncle Wood," who prided himself on the fact that his was the largest hotel in Missouri outside St. Louis. It was also the westernmost American hotel of the period, and the most famous of all frontier taverns.

⁴⁸ In *The Oregon Trail* (p. 9) Parkman identifies this party as being from Illinois. Many of the emigrants were men of substance and reputation, despite Parkman's low opinion of them, such as Jessy Quinn Thornton, James Frazier Reed, and the Donners, all well-to-do Illinois folk then in Independence awaiting the formation of a wagon train for Oregon. Cf. B. DeVoto, *Year of Decision* (Boston, 1943).

⁴⁹ McGee's establishment is not mentioned in other traveler's accounts of Westport.

⁵⁰ General Lewis Cass (1782-1866), after serving under Hull and Harrison in the War of 1812, became governor of the territory of Michigan in 1813, and during his eighteen years in that office collected documents on Pontiac's siege of Detroit, which he later put at Parkman's disposal. In 1839, while Minister to France, he commissioned Pierre Margry to collect papers in the Paris archives dealing with the old Northwest. A close friend and frequent companion of Schoolcraft, he was much interested in the Indians, about whom he wrote many articles for the *North*

American Review and his *Inquiries Concerning the Indians Living Within the United States* (n. p., 1823). He was an unsuccessful candidate for the Democratic nomination for the presidency in 1844, and in 1846 a leader in the Senate of the "54°40' or Fight" school of thought. He ran for president in 1848.

[51] Probably Albert G. Boone, a nephew of the great Daniel, who conducted an outfitting and trading business at Westport under the firm name of Boone and Hamilton. Daniel Boone, Jr. first explored this region, and three of his sons traveled westward with Boggs' or Russell's party, which Parkman frequently encountered. Boggs' wife, Panthea Grant Boone, was a granddaughter of the original Daniel.

[52] Vogel was probably one of the St. Louis Germans who worked their way westward as small traders, having emigrated from Germany after the disturbances of the 1830's. The Giessner Emigrant Society was established in Hesse in 1834 to aid those bound for America, and the first parties came to St. Louis in 1834 under the leadership of Frederick Muench and Paul Follenius.

[53] The first of five ferries, on the Kansas River between its mouth and Topeka. Fording was not practical at this point when the river was swollen in the spring, though calked wagons could be floated across without serious difficulty.

[54] This fort on the Missouri above Kansas City was then the westernmost outpost of the United States. It was built in 1827 by General Henry Leavenworth (1783-1834), who had led the punitive expedition against the Arikaras of the Upper Missouri four years before and who died while negotiating a peace with the Indians on the Southwest frontier. Fort Leavenworth was long the headquarters of the First Dragoons, a crack regiment and the only body of troops accustomed to Western conditions. In 1846 the fort became the base of the Army of the West for the Mexican Campaign.

[55] Colonel Stephen Watts Kearny (1794-1848), uncle of General Phil Kearny of Civil War fame, was the commanding officer on the Western frontier, with headquarters at Fort Leavenworth. In the preceding year he had led a party of the First Dragoons west to Laramie in a show of force designed to quiet the increasingly unruly Sioux—and perhaps to pave the way for American intervention in Oregon. Later in the summer of 1846, as general, he led the Army of the West against Santa Fe, and in the following year to California. Lieutenant Jefferson Davis, later president of the Confederate States, was adjutant of the First Dragoons.

[56] The Kickapoos were of Algonkin stock. They were first encountered

by the French in Wisconsin, and later moved to the Ohio Valley, where they fought for the British during the Revolution and the War of 1812. They had only recently been moved by the U. S. Government to this Kansas reservation.

[57] The Pottowatomies belonged to the central or Great Lakes division of the Algonkin linguistic group, like the Sauks, Foxes, and Kickapoos. Parkman had seen Ojibwa bark lodges at Sault Ste. Marie in 1845.

[58] A young Englishman with this uncommon name accompanied Father De Smet, S.J., into the buffalo country with Bidwell's Oregon party of 1841. References to him may be found in both De Smet's *Life, Letters and Travels* (New York, 1905), 276, 280, 295, 1,348-9; and in "De Smet's Letters & Sketch," *Early Western Travels*, XXVII (Cleveland, 1906), 198, 235-6. Father De Smet described Romaine as "jealous of the honor of his nation," and "of a good English family, and like most of his countrymen, fond of travel." He may have been one of the numerous British agents who were pursuing secret missions in the West at this period, before the Oregon question was settled, or simply one of the many well-heeled sportsmen who were drawn to the region by the magnificent hunting. Parkman gives a fuller account of him in the *Knickerbocker Magazine* (June 1847), 508.

[59] Captain Chandler, as a retired British officer who had served in Canada, may have had other purposes than sport in mind. He and his brothers reached the Oregon settlements, and visited the Sandwich (Hawaiian) Islands before returning home by way of Panama, New Orleans, and New York. Cf. *Knickerbocker Magazine* (November 1847).

[60] The "new fort up the Missouri," which two companies of the First Dragoons under Captain Philip St. George Cooke built just below Table Creek in the early summer of 1846, was Fort Kearney, which was soon abandoned. The name was then given to the fort on the Platte, not far from the junction of the Independence and St. Joseph trails with the Nebraska City road, which had been called Fort Child at its establishment in 1848. Through some error of the War Department or the Post Office, this placename has long been misspelled "Kearney," though it was intended to perpetuate the memory of Stephen Watts Kearny.

[61] The dragoon trail from Clough Creek to which Parkman refers was that followed by Kearny's First Dragoons in their sweep through the West in 1845.

[62] The St. Joseph's Trail commenced at Ellwood on the west bank of the Missouri, opposite St. Joseph, Missouri, and proceeded westward by Mosquito Creek, the Kickapoo Agency, Wolf Creek, and the Nemaha to

Marysville on the east bank of the Big Blue, where one route from Independence joined it. The junction with the Independence Crossing route was six miles to the west. St. Joseph, two days by steamer up the Missouri from Independence, was considered to be seventy miles farther west. The settlement was named in the French-Canadian fashion after Joseph Robidoux, who did much to promote its growth.

[63] There were no organized parties of Mormons ahead of Parkman on the trail—Parkman never encountered any until he reached the Pueblo—but the camp at Independence had been full of rumors of the proposed westward movement of the Latter-day Saints from their temporary resting place at Nauvoo. The emigrants from Illinois and Missouri, notably Lillburn W. Boggs (who as governor of Missouri had ordered his militia to exterminate the Mormons and had been filled with buckshot in his own home by a Destroying Angel) had reason to fear the Saints, who were supposed to be on the march in thousands, with "ten brass field pieces" and every man "armed with a rifle, a bowie knife, and a brace of large revolving pistols" (DeVoto, *Year of Decision*, 149). Boggs' or Russell's party had requested a military escort as protection against the Mormons, but Colonel Kearny had refused to supply it. Parkman evidently shared the emigrants' alarm, for he observed: "No one could predict what would be the result when large armed bodies of these fanatics should encounter the most impetuous and reckless of their old enemies on the prairie" (*Oregon Trail*, 47). He himself was later mistaken for one of the "fanatics" when he met emigrant trains on the trail, to his vast annoyance.

[64] Sorel, one of the Britishers' two hunters, was doubtless a French Canadian. The name is that of one of the oldest settlements on the St. Lawrence, at the mouth of the Richelieu.

[65] The Little Nemaha is about halfway between St. Joseph and Marysville. It was a steep-banked but not difficult crossing.

[66] Romaine, who had inspired the Chandlers to make the trip, proved to be "the most uncomfortable man" the Captain ever met, for he was "determined to have everything his own way." (*Knickerbocker Magazine*, June 1847, 505.) Jack Chandler, the brother of Captain Bill, was a nonentity among the members of the party. His easy-going good-nature, however, made him more popular with Parkman and Shaw than either the apprehensive Captain or the overbearing Romaine.

[67] The fur companies bought cheap and sold dear, in order to keep the trappers and hunters dependent upon them, after the classic company-store pattern. The account book (cf. Appendix, p. 491) shows that Park-

man paid $3 for a shirt at Laramie. This reduction and the compara-
tively low price for whiskey quoted by Chatillon show the effect of competition from the traders Richard and Bissonnette upon what had been a
monopoly of the American Fur Company. The independent traders sold
flour for 40% less, and bacon for 30% less, than the prevailing prices at
Fort Laramie. Osborne Russell estimated the usual mark-up in the
mountains as 2,000% on St. Louis prices (*Journal of a Trapper* [Boise,
1921], 63).

[68] This was the early practice in the fur trade, but the Indians now
brought most of their furs to the trading posts, as under the Hudson's
Bay Company system. Parkman met some of the old "winterers" at
Laramie, for every big company post still sent out a few traders to travel
with the various bands and to induce them to come to the post with their
furs.

[69] The Little Vermillion was sometimes known as the Black Vermillion.

[70] Chatillon seems to be alluding to the Owns-Alone feast, for women
who had reached the age of forty or more and had been strictly true to
the marriage relation. Cf. Clark Wissler, "Oglala Societies," *Anthropological Papers of the American Museum of Natural History*, XI, 1 (New York,
1916), 76-7. Chatillon, doubtless because of his Sioux wife, as Parkman
suggests, makes a little too much of Sioux chastity. Their women were
more promiscuous within the tribe, for instance, than the Cheyenne or
Arapaho women. The right of a brother-in-law to take liberties was
undisputed and universally practiced, and this right was often assumed
by nonrelatives. The Sioux girl here mentioned probably did not like
the young man in question, and felt insulted rather than degraded.

[71] Boisverd or Boisvert, the Britishers' second hunter, was also a French
Canadian.

[72] Wright, a St. Louis man, was the Britishers' muleteer. Missouri mule
skinners were already noted for the adequacy of their vocabulary.

[73] The main Oregon Trail left the Santa Fe Trail near Gardner, Kansas,
crossed the Waukarusa and the Kansas near Topeka, and struck overland
to the Little Vermillion and the Vermillion. One route then followed the
east bank of the Big Blue to the junction with the St. Joseph's road near
Marysville, Kansas, while another crossed the Big Blue at Independence
Crossing just short of it. It then followed the east bank of the Little Blue
and reached the Platte near Grand Island (Hastings, Nebraska), after
crossing the Pawnee Trail. It then continued along the south bank to the
forks of the Platte, from which various routes crossed to the North Platte,
whose south bank it followed well beyond Fort Laramie.

[74] Romaine might well be expected to know something about rafting across streams after his journey with Father De Smet in 1841, which he does not seem to have discussed with Parkman. The *Knickerbocker* version gives a fuller account of his annoying omniscience (June, 1847).

[75] Delorier, or Deslauriers, Parkman and Shaw's muleteer from Kansas Landing, was considered a true French Canadian—St. Jean Baptiste is the patron saint of French Canadians—by Parkman. He was loyal and indefatigable, cheerful and polite to his *bourgeois*, or boss, even when the going was rough, but somewhat stupid.

[76] Here Parkman probably garbled some of the wealth of information about the Indians which he was receiving. No such ceremony is known to have existed among the Plains tribes. A "white" buffalo—that is, an albino or unusually blond one—was about the most valuable object in the world to the Plains Indians, who regarded it as having great magical power. Its owner would only give it away under the compulsion of some dream or other magical instruction, or to obtain some even more greatly desirable object, or to propitiate the spirits after a disaster. Such an act called for a feast, and the guests would be duly impressed by the gift of the cherished possession. The *quid pro quo* inevitably expected by an Indian in return for a gift has given us the expression "Indian giving."

[77] Anything could be a "medicine," but usually personal medicines were parts of or objects associated with animals, birds, or insects. An Indian's personal medicine was usually revealed to him during the initiatory fast later mentioned by Parkman (p. 444). In the course of the trance produced by the various ordeals, a dream or vision occurred in which somebody or something analyzed the individual's character and forecast his future. The personal medicine was usually associated with the apparition, which if human was usually considered to be an animal or a bird which had temporarily taken on the form of a man, but the medicine might be merely some inanimate object involved in the vision—a tree, plant, or stone. Anything connected with these things was a medicine object. In his medicine bundle the Indian carried part of the bird or beast or thing in question, and perhaps some of the objects associated with his vision. This bundle was his most sacred possession, to be opened only by himself and usually only when alone, with the proper incantations and ritual.

Woodpeckers and rattlesnakes were no more powerful medicine with the Sioux and Kaws than with other Indians. All living objects were venerated for their medicine power, but special veneration was paid to the personal medicine.

[78] This passage indicates Parkman's anthropological naivete, in that he was still unfamiliar with personal medicines and the most nearly universal of primitive tabus, that affecting mothers-in-law. Not calling someone by his true name is a common practice among all primitives. Prince Maximilian of Wied displayed a much more profound understanding of Indian customs more than ten years earlier.

Parkman later witnessed Sioux mourning, for Chatillon's wife Bear Robe at his Chugwater camp, and for the warriors killed by the Snakes while in the Laramie Mountains. See pp. 448, 450, 459.

[79] Keatley, or Kearsley, the captain of the emigrant train that Parkman met near the Big Blue (the "Mormons" of earlier entries), resigned his charge because of the insubordination of his party. Such changes of leadership were typical of the emigrants, who carried the principle of the town meeting into the wilderness, and were restless under discipline. Kearsley joined Parkman's party with four ox-drawn wagons, an unwelcome addition since the emigrants moved at a much slower pace than the sportsmen.

[80] Bull Bear (Mahto-Tatonka in *The Oregon Trail*) was the head chief of the Oglala Sioux after 1835, and Henry Chatillon's father-in-law. His portrait was painted by Alfred Jacob Miller for Captain William Drummond Stewart in 1837. He was a good friend of the whites, but quarreled with the Pawnees over buffalo-hunting near the forks of the Platte in 1834, when his band were lured southward from the old Oglala Post on the south fork of the Cheyenne to trade at Fort William. From about 1840 Bull Bear's bands hunted west of the Laramie River, while Smoke's, the other division of the Oglalas, took over the Platte Forks range. The two divisions of the tribe met to trade horses, and in November 1841 Bull Bear was killed at Smoke's camp on the Chugwater in a drunken brawl. The tribe then split into two factions for forty years. After Bull Bear's death his band became "a body without a head," as old Red Water put it; for the chief's son of the same name, despite his courage, ambition, and activity, lacked his father's qualities of leadership. Among the Sioux the chiefs had little authority except in wartime, and the young warriors frequently disobeyed them.

[81] Henry Fraeb—the name frequently appears as Frapp—was a mountain man and small trader. He was a partner of Fitzpatrick in the Rocky Mountain Fur Company from 1830 to 1834, and later a partner of Peter A. Sarpy, with whom he built an American Fur Company fort on St. Vrain's Fork of the South Platte. While leading a group of free trappers in the Green River country, Frapp was killed in 1841 at Battle Creek, a

tributary of the Little Smoke near Dixon, Wyoming, by a mixed band of Sioux and Cheyennes in the first of a series of outbreaks which were increasing just as Parkman traveled through the West, because of the growing impatience of the Indians with the invasion of their hunting lands by the whites. This situation did much to hasten the decline of the roving trapper and hunter.

[82] Cf. Osborne Russell's dreams of "cool springs, rich feasts, and cool shade" (*Journal*, 39) while traveling on the prairie. Parkman was entering upon the subhumid region of the Plains, which appalled many an eastern forest-dweller. The increasing altitude produced mountain sickness in many travelers, with the usual symptoms of headaches, nervousness, and depression, or vomiting; while the alkali water gave almost every traveler dysentery.

[83] Similar self-mutilation, more common among the Cheyennes and the Mandans than the Tetons, is still practiced by the Canadian Sioux, as part of the sun dance. The idea of penance entered into such practices, but they were primarily coming-of-age ordeals, intended to demonstrate fitness and to induce a mystical consciousness. They were part of the highly symbolic sun-gaze dance, which most of the Plains Indians celebrated in some form as their great religious ceremony during the summer solstice. Cf. R. Walker, "Oglala Sun Dance," *Anthropological Papers of the American Museum of Natural History*, XVI (New York, 1921), 116-19. The participants were chosen by the priests, who were controlled by the war chief. Such selection was an honor. The ceremony lasted eight days, three or four of fasting and one to four of dancing to a ritual of chanted songs, and included both secret and public rites. The warrior societies paraded when the sun dance lodge was dedicated, and the chiefs then signaled out the bravest for public commendation. This lodge contained an altar on which a buffalo skull and pipe were placed; but the center pole, which represented the sun, was the focus of the dance, towards which the painted participants danced, blowing eagle-wing whistles to the accompaniment of chants and drums. At the conclusion of the ceremonies the dancers broke their fast and were purified in the sweat lodge. The sun dance lodge was usually abandoned to the elements as sacred after the ceremony.

[84] A grave marked "Mary Ellis—Died May 7, 1845. Aged two months." is mentioned in *The Oregon Trail*, 65. J. Q. Thornton notes several such graves of children who died on the trail during the long trek westward, in his *Oregon and California in 1848* (New York, 1849).

[85] The Indians' favorite method of hunting buffalo was to surround a herd with mounted men and break it up, so that the fat cows, which were

normally protected in the center of the herd by bulls on the flanks, could be killed easily. For excellent descriptions of "running" buffalo on horseback and "approaching" on foot, see *Oregon Trail*, 401-4. Henry Chatillon was considered the master of the latter technique; Kit Carson of the former. Later in the journal Parkman describes a surround in the Laramie Basin (p. 460).

[86] *Pommes blanches*, commonly called "prairie turnips" or "prairie potatoes," were breadroot (*Psoralea esculenta*), a near relative of skunkweed.

[87] Turner, a member of Robinson's Oregon train of some forty wagons, was known to Parkman from a meeting at Westport. Unarmed travel on the plains in the Pawnee country was distinctly dangerous (Cf. *Oregon Trail*, 73). This part of the trail was crossed by the north-south artery of Pawnee movement, the "Pawnee Trail" from the Platte villages to the Big Bend of the Arkansas which is shown on Frémont's map.

[88] "54° 40′ or fight" was the slogan of the warhawks who were ready to fight England for Oregon. Few New Englanders were of that persuasion.

[89] Pierre D. Papin, the *bourgeois* or boss of Fort Laramie, was a famous fur trader. His grave is six miles due south of the Mitchell Pass Museum, near Scott's Bluff, Nebraska. Of the eleven boats of the convoy which he took down the Platte, nine contained property of the American Fur Company—still so-called in the Indian country, though now really Pierre Chouteau, Jr. & Company—while the two others were laden with the furs of free trappers and hunters. Only eight boats arrived at St. Louis on July 7, after a two month's voyage which had taken a toll of one quarter of the shipment, according to the *Missouri Republican* of that date, which reported that the cargo was assigned to Chouteau & Company. The abandonment of beaver hats in favor of silk ones about 1840 and the virtual extinction of the beaver in the mountains had shifted the staple of the fur trade from beaver plews to buffalo robes and deerskins. By 1846 Fort Laramie's main trade was in robes, since the post was the center of the best buffalo country for five hundred miles. Each boatload probably consisted of 1,100 buffalo robes, since ten hides made a pack. This was a big load for any boat which could move on the Platte, whose navigation was always dangerous, and overloading may have been responsible for the heavy loss in transit.

[90] For Parkman's tour of Sicily in 1844, see the European Journal, p. 128.

[91] The Honorable Charles Augustus Murray's account of the Pawnees in his *Travels in North America* (London, 1839) was highly regarded by such Indian authorities of the day as George Catlin, who had also visited this tribe.

[92] For Parkman's experience in the Roman convent, see European Journal, p. 190.

[93] The Side or South Fork is now known as the South Platte. Parkman traversed it at the Lower California Crossing, near Brulé, Nebraska—the hardest ford of the trip.

[94] Ash Hollow is a canyon extending southward from the North Platte into the badlands between the two branches of the river. It was close to the scene of General William S. Harney's massacre of the Brulés in 1855, which won him the nickname of "Squaw Killer."

[95] Lawrence Fork is a southern tributary of the North Platte, near Bridgeport, Nebraska.

[96] Frédéric was one of Papin's assistants at Fort Laramie. Parkman had met him with the boats on the lower Platte (cf. *Oregon Trail*, 86-7).

[97] Chimney Rock, on the Platte opposite Bayard, Nebraska, was the first great landmark of the Oregon Trail encountered by the westbound traveler. It was a column of weather-worn marl and limestone. In 1842 Charles Preuss, who accompanied Frémont's expedition of that year, estimated that it towered some two hundred feet above the river.

[98] This refers to the fur company's practice of treating trappers or wintering traders when they returned to the fixed posts in the spring with their winter's catch. These Yellowstone blowouts were similar to the annual summer rendezvous held in the mountains for some sixteen years after 1825, when W. H. Ashley introduced the system of bringing a supply train out from the frontier to a prearranged meeting-place in the Rockies, where company trappers, free trappers, and Indians were all on hand to cash in on their winter's work. The first received their wages and a new outfit, while the free traders and the Indians bartered their furs for whatever equipment and supplies they needed. A blowout started while the trading was still going on, for an essential part of the train's equipment was the flat alcohol kegs, which were soon broached. There was much guzzling of food and drink and a great deal of gambling, usually at the trapper's expense and to the trader's profit. There were horse races, wrestling matches, shooting contests, and some real fights. In one way or another most of the trapper's year's earnings found its way back to the company before the train set out for the frontier with the furs.

[99] This party of five men returning to the East from the Oregon settlements was probably that of Joel Palmer, whose *Journal of Travels over the Rocky Mountains* is a classic description of the emigration of 1845.

[100] It is not clear which of the famous Robidoux brothers was guiding this party. Joseph, the founder of St. Joseph, Missouri, is the most likely

one, as Antoine joined the Army of the West as interpreter at Fort Leaven-worth on June 4, and accompanied it to Santa Fe and California.

[101] In 1846 the area known as Oregon included the present states of Oregon, Washington, and Idaho, with those parts of Montana and Wyoming that lie west of the Continental Divide. The goal of most of the emigrants in 1846 was the Willamette Valley. There, at Oregon City, the capital of the provisional government, modeled on that of Iowa, had been established in 1843, with a governor, a judicial system, and five counties. Oregon remained virtually an independent republic until it was given territorial status in 1848.

[102] Scott's Bluff, twenty miles west of Chimney Rock, was another landmark of the trail. It was named after a sick trapper who was brought down the Platte by bull boat one spring. The boat was wrecked and he was abandoned by his companions, who were unable to carry him. He struggled on sixty miles by himself to the spring rendezvous of the winterers at Scott's Bluff, but found them already gone. His bones were later discovered beside the spring at the Bluff.

[103] This probably refers to a warrior's voluntary announcement that he was tired of living or in love with death, which gave him complete freedom to do anything he liked with anyone's women or property until the next fight, when he had to "count a coup"—kill an enemy or perform a deed of great valor at the risk of his life—and was not allowed to flee. There was various rituals and private medicines practiced before a battle which were intended to make warriors invulnerable. Indians usually considered that they were so when they started to fight.

[104] The Apaches were of Athapascan stock, like the Kiowas and the Sarsi, and they ranged over southeastern Arizona and southwestern New Mexico. They were bitter enemies of the whites and systematically raided the flocks and herds of the New Mexicans, whom they con-temptuously called their sheepherders, for more than a century.

[105] James Kirker was an Irish-American who was hired by the Mexican governor of Chihuahua to destroy the Apaches. With a band of mountain men and Delawares, he gathered scalps, receiving a bounty of $50 per brave and $25 per woman or child. He appears by name in Mayne Reid's *Scalp Hunters*, and was probably the model for its hero.

[106] Old Smoke, chief of the other main division of the Oglalas besides Bull Bear's band, was a good friend of Henry Chatillon and proved a valuable informant to Parkman.

[107] Horse Creek, not far west of Scott's Bluff, flows into the North Platte from the southwest, near the Wyoming-Nebraska boundary. About 1815

the Kiowas held a fair there, trading the horses and Spanish goods which they brought up from the south to the northern tribes.

[108] Identified in *Oregon Trail*, 113, as the Hog. Later referred to as Lalamie. In the journal Parkman used the Indian names or their English or French equivalents at random; in the book he generally used English versions.

[109] Parkman evidently confused Fort Bernard, half-built in the summer of 1845 or in the following winter by the brothers John and Peter Richard, with the new Fort Laramie, built in 1841 about a mile up the Laramie from the old fort and named Fort John after John B. Sarpy, an officer of the American Fur Company. The Richard brothers traded under the license of Pratte, Cabanné & Company, and their fort was named after Bernard Pratte. Bissonnette represented the company there in 1845, and probably was trading under their license in 1846, since Parkman refers to his partnership with Richard. John Richard, probably the one Parkman encountered, was an explosive French Canadian in bad odor with his rivals. Such posts as this sought to break the monopoly of the American Fur Company by supplying the Indians with illicit liquor and by selling trade goods more cheaply than the company posts did.

[110] This was Fort Platte, a quarter of a mile up Laramie Creek from the old Fort Laramie (the name commemorates Joseph Laramée, a trapper drowned there in 1821). It was built in 1840 or 1841 by Lancaster P. Lupton, a lieutenant of dragoons who went west with Colonel Dodge in 1835 and resigned from the army in the following year to enter the fur trade. The fort was sold to Sabille, Adams & Company in 1842. This small firm had some sort of working arrangement with Pratte, Cabanné & Company, and both the Richards and Bissonnette worked for it. In the following year Pratte, Cabanné & Company took over direct control of Fort Platte, which offered lively opposition to Fort Laramie. The Indian agents, bribed by the American Fur Company, made the trade too hot for the opposition, however, and in 1845 Pratte, Cabanné & Company abandoned Fort Platte and established Fort Bernard, six or eight miles to the east.

[111] This was the second Fort Laramie, three-quarters of a mile up Laramie Creek from Fort Platte and a mile above the site where the original fort was built by Sublette & Campbell, who named it Fort William after Sublette. In the following year the Rocky Mountain Fur Company, which was supplied with outfits by Sublette & Campbell, ceased to exist; and three former partners of it, Milton Sublette, Jim Bridger, and Thomas Fitzpatrick, formed a new company which bought

Fort William. This firm, which operated as a trapping and trading company, first contracted with Lucien Fontenelle to sell its furs and buy its supplies, and then with Pratte, Chouteau & Company, who bought it out in 1836 and acquired the fort. In 1846 the successor of this company, Pierre Chouteau, Jr. & Company, operated Fort Laramie, while the former partner Pratte ran the opposition establishment at Fort Bernard. In 1841 Fort Laramie was rebuilt on the new site upstream where Parkman found it. It was at first called Fort John on the Laramie, after John B. Sarpy, but usage gradually condensed its name to Fort Laramie, as in the case of Fort William on the Laramie.

Charles Preuss, who visited the new fort with Frémont in 1842, thus describes it:

. . . a quadrangular structure, built of clay, after the fashion of the Mexicans, who are generally employed in building them. The walls are about fifteen feet high, surrounded with a wooden palisade, and form a portion of a range of houses, which entirely surround a yard of about one hundred and thirty feet square. Every apartment has its door and window—all, of course, opening on the inside. There are two large entrances, opposite each other, and midway the wall, one of which is a large and public entrance; the other smaller and more private—a sort of postern gate. Over the great entrance is a square tower with loopholes, and, like the rest of the work, built of earth. At two of the angles, and diagonally opposite each other, are large square bastions, so arranged as to sweep the four faces of the walls.

When the whites first established themselves at Fort Laramie, no one Indian tribe claimed the surrounding territory, though many hunted there, so the importance of the site for trade purposes was obvious. It was the crossroads of the old Indian route through South Pass which became the Oregon Trail, and of the north-south trade route along the Front Range of the Rockies which is as old as Indian legend in the West. It was the center of a country rich in beaver and buffalo. All these favorable conditions were responsible for the bitter competition among the fur companies for the control of the Laramie trade.

[112] James Bordeaux, acting bourgeois of Fort Laramie in Papin's absence when Parkman visited it, is mentioned by many Western travelers. He was the "author" of a description of the Gratton Massacre which may be found in the 1854 Report of the Commissioner for Indian Affairs.

[113] "Colonel" Pierre Louis Vasquez (1798-?), the St. Louis-born son of Don Benito Vasquez, a Spanish grandee and militia captain of Louisiana, was one of the leading mountain men. He was a partner of Jim Bridger, and married an American wife.

Simoneau was a noted French-Canadian mountain man, who was considered Henry Chatillon's chief rival for the title of best hunter in the West.

Monthalon, the clerk of the fort, was notable in the illiterate West for his ability to read and write and keep books.

[114] These Iroquois had been brought West as trappers by the North-West Company, but they failed to adapt themselves to a country so radically different from any they had known. They introduced the idea of Christianity among the Western Indians, and the desire of the Flatheads and the Nez Percés to have the Bible and "blackrobes" probably stems from them. It is a curious coincidence that Parkman should be greeted at Fort Laramie with news of the Iroquois, after he had traveled two-thirds of the way across the continent in order to be able to recreate their history in the East.

VOLUME II

[115] The high prices charged for provisions and supplies at Fort Laramie by the American Fur Company were notorious. The company paid good prices for buffalo robes and such few furs as were still taken, but got most of its money back by exorbitant charges for supplies, of which it had a virtual monopoly. Few mountain men could get their provisions from the nearest settlements, eight hundred miles to the east, and the company had ways of dealing with the feeble opposition offered by such rivals as Pratte, Cabanné & Company. Parkman had good reason to be bitter at the prices, for he had to make extensive purchases at Fort Laramie, amounting to $105.50. Chatillon, wise in mountain ways, bought some supplies from the opposition at Fort Bernard, who charged ten cents less a pound for flour and three and a half cents less a pound for bacon. Cf. Appendix, p. 494.

[116] Many mountain men took squaws, both for domestic comfort and occupational security. They fed them and supplied them with work curing robes and skins, in exchange for the wilderness version of the comforts of home. Sometimes they had more than one "wife," since a solitary white man's safety among the Indians was partly dependent upon the number of his savage relatives who might be expected to avenge his death. When a trapper made a trading visit to a normally hostile or semihostile tribe, he was usually given a squaw for the duration of his visit by the chief, who wanted to trade and to protect the trapper. In such cases the squaw was

a business asset, but also a liability because her relatives had to be shown with presents that he loved her. From the squaw's point of view, trappers were extremely desirable husbands, gentler than any Indian and furnishing their wives with store clothes and ornaments, knives and utensils, and other articles that they would never otherwise have seen.

117 Parkman gives an account of the role of the "soldiers," the misnamed Indian police, on p. 445. (See also *Oregon Trail*, 263, 301, 303.) The Indian term *akiata*, usually translated "soldier," means "those who see there is general order in camp, when traveling, and who oversee the buffalo hunt." Among the Sioux the "soldiers" were chosen from the most reputed warriors by the chiefs. Before their contact with the British, the Sioux had no chiefs and were controlled by the "soldiers." Cf. C. Wissler, "Oglala Societies," *Anthropological Papers of the American Museum of Natural History*, XI, 1 (New York, 1912), 7-74.

118 Finch, a trapper, had been held up by the Pawnees earlier in June.

119 Jack Hill was a trapper allied by marriage to Smoke's band.

120 Old Lalamie or Lomalomie, the Hog, is described at length in *Oregon Trail*, 113-14. He offered to become Parkman's uncle by swapping a niece for his horse, but this alliance was declined.

121 Paul Dorion was the grandson of the half-breed voyageur Pierre Dorion, who had briefly assisted Sacajawea on Lewis and Clark's expedition, and with his Iowa squaw Marie Aioe had accompanied Wilson Hunt's Astorians. Parkman had read about the elder Dorions in Washington Irving's books. He named the mare, for whom he traded his horse Pontiac, Pauline, so evidently he ranked Paul Dorion with his other Indian heroes: Pontiac, the great chief of the Ottawas, and Hendrick, the Mohawk leader who was killed at Bloody Pond.

122 Raymond, a willing but timorous and thick-skulled *engagé*, was hired by Parkman when he left Fort Laramie for the Chugwater camp at the end of June. He was the only member of the party to accompany Parkman during his stay with the Sioux in the mountains, and he stayed with him until Bent's Fort, where he was paid off with $38 at the end of August, having received a $3 shirt as advance wages when engaged at Laramie. Raymond died in 1848 on Frémont's criminally foolish attempt to cross the Rockies in the winter. Cf. Appendix, pp. 494-95, and *Oregon Trail*, xvi.

123 Parkman first met Reynal at Fort Bernard. The trader joined forces with him when he left Fort Laramie to meet the Whirlwind (Tunica)'s village. Reynal's squaw Margot and her two nephews, the Horse (His Horses), and the Hail Storm were also members of the party; and it was their village of the Oglalas that Parkman joined in Laramie Basin, after

the proposed war party broke up. Chatillon's relatives did not cross the mountains to hunt buffalo, and since he stayed behind with Shaw at Fort Laramie, Reynal replaced him as Parkman's interpreter.

124 This was the *travois* or *traineau* used by most of the Plains tribes. The lodge poles were bound together with rawhide to form an A-shaped frame, to which a basket for carrying baggage was tied. The heavier ends of the poles were fastened on either side of a rude packsaddle, while the other ends dragged on the ground.

125 The Laramie Mountains were called the Black Hills on Frémont's map, which Parkman had with him, and in common speech at this time, because of the thick growth of cedar which covered them as it does the Black Hills of Dakota, where the name has survived. Cedar made excellent lodge poles, which was one reason why this region was a favorite resort of the Indians.

126 Wild sage and absinthe are the same plant. There are numerous species of sage, and their relationship was not always recognized.

127 Practically all of the secret societies were "mystic associations," and tricks with fire were performed by the medicine men among their other jugglery. The subject has received little study from ethnologists, but it is clear that the Plains Indians, like all Indians and most primitives, made a cult of prestidigitation.

128 This might be merely a reference to the desperate deeds of valor performed by any Indian while on the warpath under the compulsion of some omen or dream. But more probably it refers to the cult of dedication to death described in note 103. Some members of the cult did everything by contraries and were known by that name. A contrary would say: "I do not want the best part of that deer," and the owner of the deer was obliged to give him the choicest part. Followers of the cult were much in demand as good warriors and war party leaders. If they failed, they were subject to intolerable derision; but if they succeeded, they gained great honor and were privileged characters.

129 Cf. note 83, p. 621.

130 Parkman here confuses the sun dance, the purification rituals required by some medicines before going to war, and the initiatory ordeals of puberty. Fasting was part of most Sioux religious ceremonies, for it helped to bring on the desired visions.

131 The war bonnet was a dress uniform and a lodge garment, and not war medicine as Parkman here suggests.

132 La Bonté's camp was at the mouth of Big Timber or La Bonté's Creek, on the Platte about sixty miles above Fort Laramie. It marked the

beginning of the worst stretch of the Oregon Trail east of the Continental Divide. La Bonté was a historical person who became the fictional hero of George Frederick Ruxton's *Life in the Far West* (London, 1848).

[133] The scalp of the Whirlwind's son hung in Papin's room at Fort Laramie, which Parkman and Shaw occupied in the *bourgeois'* absence. It had been taken, along with those of nine other Oglala warriors, during the previous summer by the Shoshonies (Snakes), who had left it at the fort in an attempt to propitiate the Whirlwind, with whom they had asked Vasquez to intercede. Revenge for the Snake victory of the previous year was the motive of the great muster of the Sioux, which to Parkman's disappointment failed to come off.

[134] Mentioned earlier as the Man Afraid of his Horses. Called the Horse in *Oregon Trail*. He later became a head chief of the Oglala. Cf. G. E. Hyde, *Red Cloud's Folk*.

[135] Tunica is earlier referred to as the Whirlwind; in *The Oregon Trail* he is also called by the latter name.

[136] This was the emigrant train which Parkman had seen assembling at Independence in May. It was first headed by Colonel W. H. "Owl" Russell, veteran of the Black Hawk War, former secretary of Henry Clay, and an orator with a low flashpoint. Much given to drink, he had earned his nickname by bellowing in reply to the whooing of owls one exalted night: "Colonel William H. Russell of Kentucky, sir, a bosom friend of Henry Clay." The company, which included the annalists Jessy Quinn Thornton and Edwin Bryant as well as the famous Donner Party, had rejected Russell's leadership in favor of that of Lillburn W. Boggs, former governor of Missouri, mortal enemy of the Mormons, and the husband of Daniel Boone's granddaughter. It was the most notable emigrant party to travel the Oregon Trail this year, and contained a far higher proportion of educated and cultivated people than most trains.

[137] The Miniconques, or Minneconjous, were a band of Sioux who belonged to the same Teton division of the nation as the Oglalas. The Sioux had long ranged from the Missouri westward, but under pressure from Eastern tribes pushed out by the whites, they had for some years been moving southwestward again, thus impinging upon the Cheyennes to the south and the Crows to the northwest.

[138] William P. May, a trader, was killed by the northern Arapahos this same year. He was the May who was robbed of his furs on the Yellowstone by Kelsey in 1843.

[139] The Minneconjous, who arrived after Parkman left Fort Bernard, did break up and return home, having lost their warlike purpose in floods

of liquor supplied by the emigrants, according to Parkman, and perhaps by Richard, who had a bad name for selling drink to the Indians. Paul Dorion and the Canadian free trappers were displeased, since liquor made normally friendly Indians untrustworthy.

[140] This party included Jim Clyman, returning from California after crossing the Salt Desert and Wasatch Mountains with Lansford Hastings, whose new cutoff trail to California was to lead the Donner Party to its doom. The veteran Clyman urged the emigrants at Richard's post to take the old Fort Hall route, but in vain. Clyman was an epitome of the new West, as DeVoto has pointed out in *Year of Decision*. He was born in Virginia in 1792 on a farm belonging to George Washington. By way of Pennsylvania, Ohio, and the Sangamon he worked his way westward, reaching St. Louis in the spring of 1823. He joined the second expedition of W. H. Ashley in that year and spent the next four years in the Rockies, helping to blaze the South Pass route. He then returned to Illinois, keeping a store and serving as a private in the same company as Abraham Lincoln during the Black Hawk War. Then he took up a timber claim in Wisconsin, where he spent six years. In 1844 he went to Oregon with Ford's company, and 1845 to Sutter's Fort in California. Such a man had much to tell Parkman, but the latter was too much concerned with his letters to Boston to waste time on uncouth non-Indians.

[141] Tucker was one of the mountain men who had greeted Henry Chatillon on his arrival at Fort Laramie on June 15.

[142] Identified as Rouleau in *Oregon Trail*, 161. The two traders killed by the Arapahos were Boot and May, the latter of whom Parkman had met at Fort Laramie.

[143] There is a full account of Bear Robe's death and funeral in *Oregon Trail*, 165-68.

[144] Bissonnette was trading in the summer of 1846 on the license of Pratte, Cabanné & Company, and probably was in partnership with the Richard brothers of Fort Bernard. He was a friend of Paul Dorion and Nat Sabille, and may have been a son of Antoine Bissonnette, the *engagé* of Manuel Lisa on his expedition to the Upper Missouri, who was killed as a deserter by Lisa's aide Drouillard at the mouth of the Osage in 1807.

[145] The party included Morin, Séraphin, Rouleau, and Gingras. Cf. *Oregon Trail*, 169.

[146] This quarrel between Bordeaux and the trapper Perrault is described in *Oregon Trail*, 156-57.

[147] Wife-stealing was sometimes ritualistic—at least one secret society among the Crows made it a prerogative—sometimes a kind of joke, and

sometimes a quite legitimate way of getting a wife, under the proper circumstances. Sometimes it was purely a business transaction, when a man wanted a particular woman. It was not, as Parkman thought, "a way of becoming great," though refusing to make payment for a stolen wife indicated a certain toughness; the injured husband would demand or take compensation unless afraid of the offender.

[148] Le Borgne ("One Eye") in *Oregon Trail*, where he is called "the Nestor of the tribe" (179).

[149] Mad Wolfe was a nephew of Le Borgne. Parkman judged that he "seemed, but for his face, the Pythian Apollo himself." (*Oregon Trail*, 190).

[150] Shaw had a homeopathic medical kit and applied simple remedies to the Indians, as a means of winning their goodwill. This incident takes place in Smoke's lodge in the book.

[151] Liberties might be taken with a young girl by a brother-in-law. Cf. note 70.

[152] The Strong Hearts, like the Arrow Breakers whose activities Parkman later records, were one of the secret societies, partly religious and partly military in character, which extended through the tribes. Each had a tutelary deity or totem, to whom respect was paid in the ritual, described in *Oregon Trail*, 198, 302, 358. Among the Plains Indians these societies were largely military.

[153] Bitter Cottonwood Creek, near Wendover, Wyoming, was named after the narrow-leaved cottonwoods of bitter taste which line its banks. This was the third camp site for the emigrants after Fort Laramie, though the faster outfits usually pushed on to Horseshoe Creek, where there was better grass.

[154] Parkman had visited Dixville Notch in the White Mountains in 1841 and 1842. Cf. pp. 24, 33-34, 82, 83.

[155] Mt. Auburn, a pleasant stretch of countryside along the Charles River on the outskirts of Cambridge, Massachusetts, has long been the Valhalla of the Bostonian as an exclusive cemetery.

[156] It was not likely that they would meet Snakes here, although it was possible; but in any case the Snakes were well disposed toward the whites at this time. It was only barely possible that they might encounter Gros Ventres, while Arapahos were much more likely to be found in this region. Raymond was clearly reluctant to wander further into the mountains with only one companion, and seems to have tried to frighten Parkman into returning to Fort Laramie.

[157] This was one of the periodic breakups which had given the Oglalas their name of Scattered or Divided People. Le Borgne and all Bull Bear's

relations had remained behind with the Whirlwind, who had lost his zeal for warring on the Snakes. Cf. *Oregon Trail*, 235.

[158] Practically all the tribes had many thunderbird myths. The Thunderbird was usually considered a great spirit, whose conflict with another deity—usually a monster—produced thunder and lightning. The swastika was a thunderbird symbol.

[159] Heap of Hail is called Hail Storm in the book. His great crony was the Rabbit.

[160] Red Water, the elder statesman of the reduced band, is also called Mene-Seela in *Oregon Trail*, 271, where Parkman gives a fuller account of him.

[161] These were the "Mormon crickets," the black crickets who were the victims of Brigham Young's miracle of the sea gulls at Great Salt Lake.

[162] Red Water's story is given in finished form in *Oregon Trail*, 271-72.

[163] The Plains Indians made pemmican by drying strips of buffalo meat in the sun, pulverizing it, mixing it with tallow and some such flavoring matter as crushed wild cherries, and packing it in intestines or rawhide bags with more tallow. It was the best of all concentrated foods, the mainstay of the early explorers and the fur traders when fresh or ordinary meat failed.

[164] This was the White Shield, whose brother had been killed the previous year by the Snakes and who became Parkman's friend. Cf. pp. 461-65 and *Oregon Trail*, 287-91.

[165] Reynal's wife was following Indian etiquette when she gave the feast for her helpers. Ceremonies were prescribed for the occasion, and one of the women was there because she had the ritualistic right to cut and shape the skins.

[166] The ordinary trapper's rifle—the best was made by the Hawken brothers of St. Louis and sold for $40—was only accurate at ranges of two hundred yards or less. It was shorter and heavier than the long Kentucky rifle. It was not a much better weapon than the Indian's bow, which could kill at seventy-five to hundred and fifty yards, though the rifle was more accurate within this range and could be discharged much more rapidly. The maximum range of the Hawken was five or six hundred yards, and it fired a 32-to-the-pound bullet. Parkman had a superior rifle, which Chatillon liked to use and which he received as a gift at the end of the trip.

[167] Rouville was a trapper who had once been an acrobatic rider in the circus. This may have given him a bond with Parkman, who had taken lessons from a circus rider while a Harvard student. Parkman's party now

consisted of Shaw, Chatillon, and Deslauriers, whom he had rejoined at Fort Laramie, and Raymond.

168 Nathaniel Sabille was one of the famous brothers whose name was well known though continually misspelled in the West. Frémont's map assigns it in the form "Sibille" to one of the southern tributaries of Laramie Creek, which has retained this version, though the modern town on the North Fork of this stream is called "Sibylee." "Sybil" is another common variant.

169 Antoine Le Rouge was a half-breed. Cf. *Oregon Trail*, 356-57.

170 Probably Andrew Sublette, since Milton had died in 1835 and William in 1845, and Solomon was presumably guiding emigrants this year. Parkman credits this hold-up to Smoke's young men (cf. *Oregon Trail*, 347).

171 This was Wales B. Bonney, returning alone from Oregon to get his family. Near Fort Bridger he was met by Lansford Hastings, who got him to carry an open letter to the emigrants about the Hastings Cutoff on the California Trail. Parkman later referred to Bonney as a "bare-faced rascal," which he was.

172 During his sweep to South Pass in 1845, Colonel Kearny had announced his intention of returning the following summer, but the outbreak of the Mexican War in the spring of 1846 called him to the command of the Army of the West, while it took the First Dragoons to Santa Fe, Taos, and San Diego.

173 The movement of the Army of the West along the Santa Fe Trail, and Zachary Taylor's victories of Palo Alto (May 8) and Resaca de la Palma (May 9), which resulted in the American occupation of Matamoras. The news had taken three months to reach Parkman. Cf. *Oregon Trail*, 354-55.

174 Another reference to the sun dance, of which Parkman had evidently gained no clear understanding.

175 Another reference to the Owns-Alone ceremony. Cf. note 70.

176 This cluster of abandoned forts was a memorial to the vanished trade in beaver plews (from the French *plus*, for top-grade skins), which had once centered in the South Park region. It was also evidence of the keen competition in the trade. After coming West with Colonel Dodge's dragoons in 1835, Lieutenant Lancaster P. Lupton resigned his commission—supposedly after cursing Andrew Jackson—and entered the fur trade on the South Platte in the following year. In 1837 the American Fur Company, disturbed at this invasion of its Fort Laramie territory, subsidized Peter Sarpy and Henry Fraeb in the building of a competing

post, Fort Jackson, six miles from Fort Lupton. In 1839 it also subsidized the building of the third post by Andrew Sublette and Louis Vasquez, which was named after the latter. The Bent brothers, who also drew furs from this region, established Fort George in this region in 1841, under Marcellin St. Vrain. The forts had been abandoned when Parkman saw them because the trade had shifted to buffalo robes, while beaver had become scarce. Fort Lupton was on the right bank of the South Platte, ten miles above the mouth of St. Vrain's Fork, opposite which on the right bank stood Fort George or St. Vrain.

177 Parkman thus camped near the site of Denver, Colorado. He was following southward the established trail linking Fort Laramie, the Pueblo, Bent's Fort, and Taos.

178 Richard, the *bourgeois* of Fort Bernard, was taking some buffalo robes to Taos, and guided William Crosby and John Brown's party of Mississippi Mormons from the Platte to the trapper's winter stockade at the Pueblo. Here they were later joined by the sick detachment of the Mormon Battalion and another group of unfit sent back from Santa Fe by Captain Philip St. George Cooke after he took over command of the battalion. Crosby and Brown's party left Fort Bernard soon after their meeting with Jim Clyman at Ash Hollow on July 2, when they learned that there were no other Mormons ahead of them on the trail. The party consisted of nineteen wagons, twenty-four men, women, and children, and five Negro slaves. They had left Mississippi in April, under instructions to meet the main Mormon body—which did not move until the following year—along the Oregon Trail.

179 Possibly the camp of Dr. Edwin James, who accompanied Major Long's expedition to the Rockies in 1820. On July 12 he camped on the Fontaine qui Bouille, twenty-five miles from Pikes Peak, which he and two other men then climbed, returning to their camp on July 15.

180 The Lower Pueblo (Pueblo, Colorado), was chiefly a trapper's winter quarters, although it was also a natural stopping place on the north-south trade route which linked Mexico and the Platte. There had been some sort of post at this place since 1806, when Zeb Pike built a breastwork there. During 1846 it accidentally became a Mormon outpost. The fort Parkman visited was probably that built in 1842 by Jim Beckwith.

181 Any Indian was apt to make a brother of a white whom he liked, by exchanging knives or other gifts (any Indian expected a gift in return for the one he gave). The Sioux made brothers among the whites as well as the Crows, but the latter did it more frequently and meant more by it. The Crows really liked the whites and saw that it was to their

advantage to get along well with them. Their refusal to wage war on the whites made them unpopular among other Indians, but it helped them to keep more of their original country than any other Plains tribe. Their reservation in their original homeland—Absaroka, in the Big Horn and Little Big Horn country—is on extremely good agricultural and grazing land, among the best set aside for reservations.

[182] Bent's Old Fort, or Fort William, five hundred and thirty miles from Independence by the mountain route of the Santa Fe Trail, stood on the north bank of the Arkansas near the mouth of the Purgatoire or "Picket-wire." It was a crossroads of the West like Fort Laramie and, until the Oregon and California emigration really got under way, far more important and better known. A little to the southwest the trail forked, one branch leading to Taos. To the west a trail led up the Fontaine qui Bouille to South Park. Northward was the route to the Platte.

Bent's was one of the largest of the trading posts and the first permanent settlement in Colorado. It boasted warehouses, a smithy, a wagon shop, storerooms, dormitories, and such unlikely luxuries as a billiard table and an icehouse. A staff of 150 men was permanently employed at the fort. It was a magnet for mountain men, Santa Fe traders, and the Cheyennes, Arapahos, Utes, Kiowas, and Comanches. Parkman bought $49 worth of supplies and paid off Raymond while at Bent's.

[183] Holt, the trader in charge of the fort in the absence of the Bents, invited Parkman and Shaw to dinner, which was served on a table covered with a white cloth—their first civilized meal since dining with Colonel Kearny at Fort Leavenworth in May.

[184] Seventy-five invalid officers and soldiers had been left behind at Bent's by the Army of the West, whose raw militia suffered heavy losses from dysentery on the march to Santa Fe.

[185] Evidently a rumor about James Magoffin's mission to conquer Santa Fe by fifth-column tactics was abroad, although this may have been simply the judgment of experts on Governor Armijo's fortitude. The courage of the Mexicans was not highly regarded by Americans in the Southwest. The garrison of Santa Fe was known to be small and worthless, and there was a question whether militia could be raised to reinforce it. Part of Kearny's command and many natives of Santa Fe thought that the Mexicans would not fight.

[186] Hodgman, christened "*Tête Rouge*" by Chatillon because of his red hair, was a slightly unbalanced young Missourian who found marching to the Halls of Montezuma too much for his constitution. He was one of the casualties left at Bent's by Kearny.

[187] Munroe, an Iowan, had found the West less promising than reputed, and was heading homeward. Parkman characterized him as "open, warm-hearted, and intelligent" (*Oregon Trail*, 379).

[188] Ben, called Jim Gurney in the book and Jim hereafter in the journal, was a Boston sailor who had reached California by sea, and probably was a deserter from his ship, preferring to beat his way home overland rather than around Cape Horn. Parkman liked him best of the four new members of the party.

[189] The homesick emigrant, who was really lovesick according to Jim Gurney, was a Missourian named Ellis.

Bridger's Fort was in the valley of Black's Fork of the Green River. It was established in the summer of 1843 to cater to the emigrants, to whom it offered a blacksmith's shop for wagon repairs, horses, and supplies.

[190] Probably Marcellin St. Vrain, since Parkman later met Céran on the Santa Fe Trail. Céran, who had useful connections from his marriage into the New Mexican gentry, helped Colonel Sterling Price to put down the Taos Rising in January 1847, as a captain of volunteers.

[191] Originally there were four Bent brothers in the trade. One was dead by August 1846, and two more were killed within a year. Charles Bent, American governor of New Mexico, was murdered on January 19, 1847 in his own home at Taos by a Pueblo mob. William Bent and a number of his trappers had been engaged as scouts by Kearny when he set out for Santa Fe on August 1.

[192] William Magoffin, a younger brother of James and Samuel, who were magnates of the Santa Fe carrying trade. William later studied medicine, served in the Confederate Army, and eventually settled in Minnesota.

[193] Ewing was the Kentuckian whom Parkman had met at St. Louis and again at Fort Bernard, and with whom he had planned to travel from Laramie to Bent's and Westport. But Ewing had become impatient while Parkman was in the mountains with the Indians and had gone ahead, probably with Richard's Mormon party. Between the Caches and Pawnee Fork, on the homeward stretch of the Santa Fe Trail, he killed a Pawnee who tried to steal his horses, and by thus arousing the Indians once more caused Parkman to run risks.

[194] Parkman's "poison" was dysentery, very prevalent on the Plains and a cause of much illness in the Army of the West. It was often caused by the alkali water and the change to an exclusive diet of fresh meat. This is the first specific reference to Parkman's illness in the journal. In the book he depicts himself as struggling against collapse from it soon after his arrival at Fort Laramie.

[195] Here Parkman encountered the main part (later known as the Great Southern Herd) of the Plains buffalo herd, which was gradually being divided into two parts by the emigrant traffic. Before this he had only encountered small bands.

VOLUME III

[196] Colonel Sterling Price's Second Missouri Volunteers were mounted infantry, hastily recruited for the Mexican War from Monroe, Platte City, and St. Louis counties. Price was made commandant of New Mexico when Doniphan moved on Chihuahua with the First Missouri late in 1846. He suppressed the Santa Fe Conspiracy of December 1846 and the Taos Rising of the following January, which his "undisciplined raga-muffins" had done much to cause. The Second Missouri was consider-ably inferior to the First, which under the inspired leadership of Doniphan performed military miracles, although its discipline never appealed to West Pointers.

[197] The Ridge Road was a short cut on the Santa Fe Trial across a long bend in the Arkansas River, to the west of Pawnee Fork and the Big Bend.

[198] The Mormon Battalion, on its march from Fort Leavenworth to Santa Fe, was under the command of Lieutenant Andrew Jackson Smith of the First Dragoons. Smith was replaced on October 2 by Captain Philip St. George Cooke, who marched the battalion from Santa Fe to California. The detachment had been born in May 1846, when President Polk welcomed Elder Little's suggestion that a Mormon battalion be enlisted for the defense of California. This amounted, from the Mormon point of view, to the free transportation westward of five hundred men and a sum in pay and allowances which would enable the main body to move. Brigham Young recruited over five hundred men, who were accompanied by a good many wives, relatives, and children. Since many of the young Mormons were unwilling to serve a government they had cursed for years, the ranks were filled with unfit elders; and when Cooke took over from Smith, he weeded out nearly a third of the command and sent them to the Pueblo, where some women and children had already been sent by Smith. Beset by mumps, dysentery, and the irreconcilability of the ways of Saints with West Pointers, they nevertheless made better time from Fort Leavenworth to Santa Fe than Price's command. They constituted without doubt one of the oddest units which ever saw service in the United States Army. During their entire service they saw no action,

except when they were attacked on the Arizona desert by a large herd of wild cattle, who gored some of the brethren, and when at Los Angeles they were ordered to massacre the bloodthirsty dogs of the town. Cf. DeVoto, *Year of Decision*.

[199] The Santa Fe Trail, a well-established trade route of eight hundred miles from Independence to Santa Fe by way of either Bent's Fort (the Mountain Route) or the Cimarron Crossing (the Desert Route), saw its busiest season in the summer of 1846. In addition to the regular traders' trains of enormous wagons, twice the size of the prairie schooners of the Oregon emigrants, Kearny's army, his wagon trains and those of his supports, Price's Second Missouri, the Mormon Battalion, commissary trains, scouts, couriers, ambulances, and detachments of discharged and invalided soldiers passed over it. The Army chose the less vulnerable Mountain Route and used Bent's Fort as a base. From this point onward, Parkman encountered wagon train after wagon train, and grew weary of answering the same inevitable questions. He might have paid the price of civility more cheerfully if he had realized that the volume of traffic over the trail probably saved his small party from mishap at the hands of the Indians, who were far more dangerous on the Santa Fe route than on the Oregon Trail. The southern part was within reach of the Apaches, while the eastern was the land of the thieving Pawnees, who still took scalps as readily as horses at this period. The middle section was a no man's land raided by the southern Arapahos, the southern Cheyennes, and most notably the Kiowas and Comanches, the most dangerous Indians of the West at this period, who fortunately for Parkman were more concerned with the vulnerable Texans and Mexicans this year. In the following summer the Comanches killed forty-seven men and burned three hundred wagons on the trail, including Army supply trains. As Parkman saw, traffic along the trail followed established routines, except for such parties of greenhorns as the Second Missouri. Beyond Council Grove the trains traveled in formation of two or four parallel lines. A corral was formed at night. The route, which had even been surveyed, was mostly through country bountifully supplied with buffalo, and offering abundant grass in normal years, and water in reasonable plenty, except on the Cimarron Crossing Route. Forty-five or fifty days was the usual running time from Independence to Santa Fe.

[200] This train was making very poor time. It was half a day out from Council Grove, and thus had covered only a sixth of the total distance. At the same rate of progress, it would take almost twice as long as usual to make the trip to Santa Fe.

[201] Bent & St. Vrain freighted their own goods from Independence to their trading post of Bent's Fort, whose trade extended far to the north, west, southwest, and southeast. They had smaller posts in the Indian country, and agents living with the tribes. The original partnership was formed in 1831 by Charles Bent and Céran de Hault de Lassus de St. Vrain (1802-70), the son of a French naval officer who had settled at Ste. Geneviève near St. Louis. Céran St. Vrain early entered the fur trade, working for Bernard and Sylvestre Pratte. Like most Santa Fe traders, he became a Mexican citizen, and he married an aristocratic New Mexican girl. With Cornelio Vigil, he owned some four million acres in the Purgatoire and other valleys. Charles Bent had likewise married a Mexican wife, while his brother William, the resident manager of Bent's Fort, was the husband of the Cheyenne Owl Woman. Thus through marriage the firm had excellent connections with Santa Fe, Taos, and one of the main tribes on the trail which was its lifeline. Their wagon train was late this year, because Kearny had held up the traders until his army reached Santa Fe.

[202] George Catlin (1796-1872), author of *Manners, Customs, and Institutions of the North American Indians* (1841) and *The North American Indian Portfolio* (1844), was a painter and ethnologist, who abandoned his early career as a lawyer in 1832 to study the Indians, who he realized were beginning to die out. His paintings were widely exhibited in the United States before he took them to Europe in 1840, where Parkman had seen them in London in 1844. They are now in the National Museum at Washington, D. C.

Joe Chadwick was Catlin's companion on some of his Western travels. He was killed in Texas in 1838, one of four hundred prisoners shot on Santa Anna's orders. Bernard DeVoto points out that this same train included Lewis Garrard, whose *Wah-To-Yah*, a forgotten classic, is a better book about the West in 1846 than Parkman's famous work.

[203] Perhaps Major John Dougherty, long Indian agent for the Pawnees, who supplied Catlin with his views on the Indian question (Cf. *Manners*, II, 26). These are summed up in a sentence in one of his reports to the Secretary of War, which Catlin quotes approvingly: "It is my decided opinion, that, so long as the Fur Traders and trappers are permitted to reside among the Indians, all the efforts of the Government to better their condition will be fruitless; or, in a great measure, checked by the strong influence of these men over the tribes."

[204] The Wyandots had been granted lands in Ohio and Michigan under a treaty of 1817, only to have much of this land sold to white settlers two

years later, regardless of the agreement. This payment in 1846 was a reparation. The Wyandots moved to Kansas in 1845 and later established themselves in Oklahoma.

205 John B. Clapp signed Parkman's and Shaw's "passport" to the trading posts on behalf of Pierre Chouteau, Jr. & Company.

206 Robert Campbell (1804-79) had been Thomas Fitzpatrick's partner in the only firm which gave serious opposition to the American Fur Company. Like his partner, he was an Irishman who drifted to St. Louis. He was with Ashley on the second Missouri expedition in 1825, and became one of his principal lieutenants. He later was associated with Fitzpatrick, Jed Smith, Jim Bridger, and the Sublettes. He saved William Sublette's life in the fight against the Blackfeet at Pierre's Hole in 1832, which was chronicled by Washington Irving. In 1835 he returned to St. Louis, and until 1842 devoted himself to the affairs of the firm which he formed with Fitzpatrick in that year. He then went into real estate and banking, and became active in politics. He did much to train and equip the Mounted Volunteers in 1846. He was an Indian commissioner in 1851 and 1869.

207 Brantz L. Mayer wrote on Mexican history and archaeology and was the founder of the Maryland Historical Society.

208 John Ledyard (1751-89) of Connecticut was the famous explorer who left Dartmouth to become a sailor. He was with Captain Cook on the latter's last voyage in the Pacific, and formed the dream of opening up the trade of the Pacific Northwest. Jefferson knew him, and shared his interest in the Northwest. Ledyard's most ambitious effort in a colorful career was his attempt to walk across Russia and Siberia, which was frustrated by Catherine the Great's police. His story was familiar to Parkman from Jared Spark's *Life* in the Library of American Biography.

209 John Romeyn Brodhead collected papers bearing on the colonial history of New York from the French archives. These papers were of vital importance to Parkman's work.

210 Parkman contributed five sketches of frontier life to the *Knickerbocker Magazine* in 1845. The editor, Gaylord Clark, was rewarded for his encouragement of the young writer by the opportunity to serialize *The Oregon Trail*, which first appeared in the *Knickerbocker* from 1847 to 1849.

211 Ramsay Crooks knew better than anyone else the whole empire of the American Fur Company, of which he was the administrative head for many years.

212 These notes refer to sources for *The Conspiracy of Pontiac*, and reveal

the wide range of Parkman's research for the work which did not appear until 1851.

²¹³ Dr. Edwin James was Major Long's annalist and one of the first men to climb Pikes Peak. Cf. note 179.

²¹⁴ This note suggests that Parkman had been offered the use of W. L. Stone, Sr.'s collection of materials for a life of Sir William Johnson. The work was eventually undertaken by Stone's son.

VIII. 1856 & 1866 NOTEBOOK

¹ Parkman was seeking a title for the great history to which he had decided to devote his life. These tentative titles are not far removed from his final choice, "France and England in North America," but evidently his concept of the history as a struggle between two colonial systems for domination in the New World had not yet clearly emerged.

² This work of Faillon saw the light as Part II of the first volume of his *Histoire de la Colonie française en Canada* (Montreal, 1865-66). Abbé Etienne-Michel Faillon (1799-1870), a Sulpician, first came to Canada in 1849 as official visitor of his order. He went back to Paris in the following year, but returned to Montreal in 1854 and again 1858, when he spent three years in historical work. His history, which he did not live to complete, stops short at 1600, although he had prepared the materials up to 1710. "His other Canadian works to which Parkman refers include biographies of Madame d'Youville (1852), Soeur Bourgeoys (1853), and Madamoiselle Jeanne Mance (1854). Parkman opened a correspondence with him early in 1856, and on March 13 Faillon, then in Paris, wrote that he put himself at Parkman's disposal and offered to persuade the Bishop of Boston to open the ecclesiastical libraries to the young Protestant historian.

³ The publication of Schmitt's *Catalogue de l'Histoire du France* was begun in 1855 by the Bibliothèque Impériale in 1855. Parkman probably got this information from Faillon.

⁴ While a political exile in Paris from 1840 to 1845, L. J. Papineau did research on the old regime of New France at the Archives de l'Etat. He had many important documents copied, and brought them back to Canada when he returned. The greater part were destroyed with the Parliamentary Library in the fire of 1849, when an English mob sacked the government buildings in Montreal.

This entry was crossed out, probably indicating that Parkman had examined the collection.

[5] General Lewis Cass, while Governor of the Michigan Territory (1813-31) collected materials on the early history of the region. In 1839 Cass, while Minister to France, employed Pierre Margry to compile relevant documents from the French archives. Cass had placed his Detroit MSS. in Parkman's hands for the writing of *Pontiac*, while Parkman had visited Detroit in the summer of 1845 for firsthand information.

This entry was crossed out, probably indicating that Parkman had examined the collection.

[6] Charles Etienne Arthur Gayarré (1805-95) collected historical material from public and private archives while spending eight years in France under doctor's orders. This was used as the foundation of his *Histoire de la Louisiane* (1846-7) and of his later and more complete *History of Louisiana* (New Orleans, 1851-66).

[7] Benjamin F. French collected documents for his *Historical Memoirs of Louisiana* (New York, 1853).

[8] Pierre-Joseph-Marie Chaumonot, S.J. (1611-93), *La vie du R. P. Pierre Joseph Marie Chaumonot, De la Compagnie de Jésus, Missionaire dans la Nouvelle France, Ecrite par lui-même par ordre de son Supérieur, l'an 1688* (*Nouvelle York, Isle de Manate, A la presse Crémoisy de Jean-Marie Shea, MDCCCLVIII*). *Bib. Can.* 101.

Nicolas Perrot (1644?-1717?), *Mémoire sur les moeurs, coustumes et religion des sauvages de l'Amérique Septentrionale par Nicolas Perrot publiée pour la première fois par le R. P. J. Tailhan de la Compagnie de Jésus* (Leipzig & Paris, 1864). *Bib. Can.* 130. Evidently Shea did not print Perrot, if Parkman was correct in supposing that he intended to do so.

Claude Dablon, S.J. (1619?-97), *Relation de ce qui s'est passé de plus remarquables aux missions des pères de la Compagnie de Jésus en la Nouvelle France les années 1672 et 1673. Par le R. P. Claude Dablon, Recteur du Collège de Québec & Supérieur des Missions de la Compagnie de Jésus en la Nouvelle France* (*A la Nouvelle York, De la Presse Crémoisy de Jean-Marie Shea, MDCCCLVI. Bib. Can.* 70. Also his *Relation de ce qui s'est passé de plus remarquables aux missions des pères de la Compagnie de Jésus en la Nouvelle France les années 1673 à 1679. Par le R. P. Claude Dablon, Recteur du Collège de Québec & Supérieur des Missions de la Compagnie de Jésus en la Nouvelle France* (*A la Nouvelle York, De la Presse Crémoisy de Jean-Marie Shea, MDCCCLX*).

Mère St. Augustin [Marie de Tranchepain], *Relation du voyage des premières Ursulines à la Nouvelle Orléans et de leur établissement en cette ville. Par la Rev. Mère St. Augustin de Tranchepain, Supérieure. Avec les lettres circulaires de quel-*

ques-unes de ses Soeurs, et de la dite Mère. (Nouvelle York, Isle de Manate, De la Presse Crémoisy de Jean-Marie Shea, MDCCCLIX). This last volume carries a note that it was printed after *"la Chronique du monastère."* Marie Hachard's *Relation du voyage des religieuses Ursulines de Rouen à la Nouvelle Orléans en 1727* was reprinted at Rouen in a small edition in 1865.

[9] George Bancroft wrote to Parkman on August 9, 1856: "As to what papers there are at Rome, there can be no difficulty. Were my old friend B. U. Campbell alive, he would undertake it for us. I think Mrs. George Ripley, wife of George Ripley of the *Tribune*, will easily interest Archbishop Hughes in your behalf. . . . I don't believe much remains in Rome, But the search is worth making." (Massachusetts Historical Society Parkman Papers, cxxvii, 89).

[10] The Biddle Papers in Bancroft's possession were thus described in his letter of July 31, 1856 to Parkman: "I have also three MS. volumes relating to the French settlements on the St. John, in Florida, given to me by Mr. Biddle, the historian of Cabot." In his letter of August 9, 1856 to Parkman, Bancroft speaks of the pleasure he takes in lending him "the family papers obtained by Mr. Biddle." (Massachusetts Historical Society Parkman Papers, cxxvii, 88.)

[11] F. X. Garneau's picture of the colonization of New France, in his classic *Histoire du Canada*, has not been greatly changed by subsequent investigation, though the topic is one which has received a great deal of attention among French-Canadian historical workers.

[12] Parkman seems to have heard in Quebec of the plan to publish Perrot, perhaps from Père Félix Martin, S.J., who was the most historically-minded of the small group of Jesuits who resumed the work of the order in Canada in 1842.

[13] Montcalm was buried in an unmarked grave in the chapel of the Ursuline Convent at Quebec. Lord Aylmer, in visiting the convent in 1830, was surprised to find that no memorial marked the last resting place of the great general. At his own expense he caused the present marble plaque to be installed during the following year, at the spot traditionally supposed to be the grave. In 1833 only one 82-year old nun, Soeur St. Ignace, still remained who remembered Montcalm's funeral and the place where he was buried. Under her guidance, the grave was found and opened. Only some fragments of the bier and some bones were discovered and these fell into dust except for the skull, which was perfectly preserved and since has been carefully guarded, almost as a sacred relic, by the convent. (Martin, *Montcalm*, 267 n.)

[14] Dablon, in Chapter IV of his *Relation* of 1670-71, describes Père

Chaumonot's Huron colony at Lorette and the image to which Parkman refers:

Their village is situated near a Chapel which they built in union with the settlers of the place, and in which honor is paid to a picture in relief of the Blessed Virgin, made from the wood of an oak in whose heart there was found, sixty years ago, one of like size,—in the village of Foye in the province of Liége, one league from the Town of Dinant. It is a precious pledge of the affection of the Queen of Heaven toward this Tribe and all the settlers of the district. That Mother of mercy has already made herself known there by so many favors, which pass for miracles in the opinion of all their recipients, that all Canada has recourse to her. (Thwaites, *Jesuit Relations*, LIV, 287).

In Père Félix Martin's edition of Chaumonot's *Autobiographie* (Paris, 1885), there are two mentions of this image: "l'image de la sainte Vierge, faite sur celle de la vraie Lorette, d'où on nous l'a envoyée" (p. 198) and "le P. Poncet, ayant repassé en France, a eu soin de m'envoyer non seulement une Vierge faite sur celle de Lorette (ainsi que je l'ai déjà dit), mais aussi une coiffe ou bonnet de taffetas blanc qui a été sur la tète de l'image, laquelle est dans la Sainte Maison d'Italie" (203).

[15] C.-P. Drolet (1795-1873), whose mother was English-speaking, was deputy clerk of the Court of Appeals and registrar of the Vice-Admiralty Court in Quebec. He was admitted to the bar in 1827 and sat in the Legislative Assembly as member for Saguenay from February 1836 until the dissolution of 1838. He was one of the most active *Patriotes* in the Quebec district during the Papineau Rebellion, and helped the Americans Dodge and Theller to escape from the Citadel on the night of October 15, 1838.

[16] Charles Panet, Jr. (1838-86) was admitted to the bar in 1859 and became clerk of the House of Commons in 1875. He was a brother-in-law of F. R. Angers. At the time of Parkman's visit to Quebec he lived at 67 St. Louis St., not far from Parkman's customary stopping place, Russell's Hotel (now the St. Louis) on the same street.

[17] Narcisse Fages had his notary's office at 6 St. George (now St. John's) St.

[18] Thomas Sterry Hunt (1826-92) was a native of Norwich, Connecticut. He was a student of Benjamin Silliman at Yale, and soon after his graduation became chemist and mineralogist for the Geological Survey of Canada under Sir William Logan. He was the first professor of chemistry at Laval University in Quebec, and a fellow of the Royal Society of London, the Geological Society of France, the Imperial Geological Institute of Vienna, and the Imperial Leopold Academy of Germany.

He became a naturalized British subject, but died in New York City, after spending most of his life in Canada.

[19] Mgr. Charles-Félix Cazeau (1807-81) was a native of Quebec. He was ordained in 1830 and immediately was attached to the archbishop's staff as a secretary. He became vicar-general in 1850 and a domestic prelate in 1875. He was an honorary canon of the chapter of Quebec. Mgr. Cazeau and Mgr. Hamel, rector of Laval, were brought into Parkman's circle of friends by Abbé Casgrain and Dr. LaRue.

[20] Henry Black (1799-1873) was judge of the Vice-Admiralty Court of Quebec for more than fifty years. He was admitted to the bar in 1820, and nominated for the bench by the Imperial Government shortly afterwards. He was a member of the Special Council under Poulett Thomson, from April 1840 to February 1841, and was one of Quebec's two members in the Assembly under the Union.

[21] Georges-Barthélemi Faribault (1789-1866) was the founder and "perpetual" archival secretary of the Quebec Literary and Historical Society, in whose work of publishing historical documents he took a leading part. Faribault knew much of Quebec history at first hand: as a boy he was a pupil of John Fraser, a Scots veteran of Wolfe's army, and he studied law with J. A. Panet, first Speaker of Quebec's Assembly. Faribault became associated with the assembly as a clerk and translator in 1822, and was its assistant clerk 1840-55. He was an impassioned collector of books and documents relating to the history of Canada. His first collection of 1,600 volumes was lost in the Montreal Parliamentary fire of 1849. Faribault was sent to Europe by the assembly in 1851 to acquire a new library. He assembled 2,000 volumes, of which 700 were lost in the Quebec Parliamentary fire of 1854. Discouraged and broken in health by this double tragedy to his lifework, he resigned his official post. Nevertheless, before his death he had amassed another notable collection, for he left 400 MSS., 1,000 volumes, and an album of maps, plans, portraits, and views relating to Canada to Laval University.

[22] Félix Martin, S.J. (1804-86), was born in Brittany, ordained in Switzerland, and came to Canada in 1842, when the Jesuits returned to their best-known mission field. After serving at Sandwich as superior for Ontario (1844-47), he became superior of the Montreal house in 1847, a post he held for ten years. He was the founder and first rector of the Collège Ste. Marie on Bleury Street. In 1857 he was sent abroad by the government to search the French and Roman archives for materials bearing on the early history of Canada. On his return he was named rector of the Jesuit residence in Quebec, and there he remained until he

was finally recalled to France in 1862. Père Martin was an earnest historical worker and the author of *Le Marquis Montcalm au Canada* and of biographies of the Jesuit martyrs Jogues, Brébeuf, Chaumonot, etc.

[23] Jacques Viger (1787-1858) was a journalist, militia officer, antiquarian, and the first mayor of Montreal. A son of a member of the Legislative Assembly, he first took to political journalism as an editor of *Le Canadian* of Quebec (1808-9). In the War of 1812 he served as a captain of the *Voltigeurs*; and after long service as inspector of streets and bridges in Montreal, he became mayor in 1833. For fifty years Viger copied notes, MSS., letters, maps, plans, and everything which might possibly serve history into a collection of notebooks, which he refered to as *Ma Saberdache*. This collection of forty-four notebooks, five opuscules, and an album of views is now in the Archives de la Séminaire de Québec. Many of Viger's materials were published by Michel Bibaud in his *Bibliothèque Canadienne*, to which Viger was an anonymous contributor.

[24] Louis-Joseph Papineau (1786-1871), the first great political genius of the French Canadians, was a lawyer, long Speaker of the Legislative Assembly, and the leader of the *Patriote* uprising of 1837, which is commonly known by his name. He was first elected to the Assembly in 1808, served as a captain in the militia in 1812, and became Speaker in 1815, a post that he held almost continuously until the Assembly was dissolved on the outbreak of the rebellion twenty-three years later. Papineau went to London with John Neilson in 1822-23 to combat the project of joining Upper and Lower Canada in one Union. As the spearhead and spokesman of the French-Canadian resistance to the autocratic rule of the English governors and their placemen, Papineau at first favored constitional resistance and an anti-British embargo rather than revolutionary means. But in his speeches he was frequently carried away into more violent utterances than he intended; and upon the outbreak of the troubles in the autumn of 1837, Lord Gosford ordered his arrest and put a price upon his head. Papineau fled from Montreal to St. Denis and then to St. Hyacinthe, finally taking refuge in the United States about November 25 when he was indicted for treason. He then spent two years at Albany, Philadelphia, and Saratoga Springs; but after all hope of resistance in Canada had collapsed, he went to Paris, where he became intimate with Béranger, Louis Blanc, and Lamennais. He did research work in the Archives d'Etat and had copies made of many documents concerning the French regime in Canada. Thanks to Lafontaine's efforts, Papineau was permitted to return to Canada in 1845, and to retire to his seigneury

of Petite Nation at Montebello, where Parkman visited him in 1856. Here he had one of the best historical libraries then existing in Canada.

[25] John Tanner (1780-1847), *A Narrative of the Captivity and Adventures of John Tanner* (*U. S. Interpreter at the Saut de Ste. Marie*) *during thirty years residence among the Indians in the interior of North America* (New York, 1830). *Bib. Can.* 1612.

[26] Philip Alegambe, S.J., *Bibliotheca scriptorum societas Jesu, post excusum anno MDCVIII catalogum P. Ribadeneirae, nunc novo apparatu librorum ad annum reparatae salutis MDCXLII editorum concinnata et illustrium virorum elogiis adornata, a P. Alegambe* (Antwerp, 1643). See also his *Mortes illustrae, et gesta eorum de Societate Iesu* (Rome, 1657). Cf. Thwaites, *Jesuit Relations*, LXXXI.

[27] Samuel de Champlain (1570-1635), the navigator, geographer, founder of Port Royal (Annapolis Royal) and of Quebec, the "Father of New France."

[28] Viger's *Album* was a collection of pictures and prints which formed part of its owner's collection of Canadiana. The *Album* is now in the Bibliothèque Municipale of Montreal, while the rest of the collection is in the Archives de la Séminaire de Québec.

[29] Père Pierre-François-Xavier de Charlevoix, S.J. (1682-1761), the first historian of New France. Born in France, he was sent out in 1720 to investigate the true boundaries of Acadia and the possibilities of explorations in the West. Leaving Quebec in early March 1721, he traveled by way of Montreal, the upper St. Lawrence, and the Great Lakes to Michilimackinac; thence by Fort St. Joseph, the Kanakakee, and the Illinois to the Mississippi at Cahokia; and thence to New Orleans, which he reached on January 5, 1722. Returning to Paris by way of Santo Domingo early in the following year, he published his *Journal d'un Voyage fait par ordre de la Cour dans l'Amérique Septentrionale par le Père de Charlevoix, S.J.*, together with his *Histoire et Description générale de la Nouvelle-France*, at Paris in 1744.

[30] Père Joseph-François Lafiteau, S.J. (1681-1746), the missionary, teacher, and writer. He came to Quebec in 1711 and spent five years studying the Iroquois at the mission of Saut-St.-Louis near Montreal. He was the discoverer of ginseng in Canada. He returned to France in 1717, where he remained as procurer of the Canadian missions in Paris and as a historical writer.

[31] Abbé François Picquet (1708-81) was a Sulpician missionary, the founder of La Présentation. He came to Canada in 1734 and began the study of Indian dialects while ministering to the Indians at Montreal. In

1739 he was attached to the mission at the Lake of Two Mountains (Oka), and devoted himself to developing the colony, which included Algonquins, Nipissings, Hurons, Ottawas, and even Iroquois. In 1744 he replaced the primitive fort by a small modern one constructed on European lines, using his own money and royal funds. His Indians were active in war from 1743-48. In 1749, under La Galissonière and Bigot, Picquet decided to build a fort at the mission of La Présentation (Ogdensburg, New York), with the aim of drawing the Iroquois away from the English. In 1753 he took three Iroquois to France and introduced them to Louis XV, who gave him books and a silver statue of the Virgin for the church at Oka. Early in the following year Picquet returned to his post, strongly favored by Vaudreuil and by Montcalm, who called him the "Patriarch of the Five Nations." After Picquet had accompanied his warriors to Oswego and Fort George in 1757 and to Ticonderoga in the following year, the English put a price on his head. Nothing daunted, Picquet built and launched two 10-gun corvettes on the lakes in the spring of 1759; and in May and June accompanied La Corne's force in the attack on Oswego. After its failure, Picquet moved his mission to Ile Picquet (Big Isle), and until the summer of 1760 tried to check the desertion of the Indians to the English. On September 8 of that year he left Montreal with twenty-five French and two groups of Indians for New Orleans, by way of the Ottawa Valley, lakes Huron and Michigan, and the Wisconsin and Mississippi rivers. He reached New Orleans in July of the following year and remained there until the peace of April 1763 sealed the fate of New France. He then returned to France.

[32] Père Emmanuel Crespel (1703?-75), a Recollet, was at Quebec from 1724 to 1726; accompanied an expedition against the Foxes west of Lake Michigan in 1728; visited Niagara, Fort Frontenac, and Fort Frédéric (Crown Point); and was shipwrecked on Anticosti Island while returning to France in 1736. He published a journal of his experiences, *Voyages du R. P. Emanuel Crespel dans le Canada, et son naufrage en revenant en France. Mis au jour par le S*r*. Louis Crespel son Frère (A Francfort sur le Meyn, MDCCXLII. Bib. Can.* 183. This was republished at Amsterdam in 1757, and an English translation appeared in London in 1797. The French version was republished at Quebec in 1884 by Abbé L.-E. Bois.

[33] Luc de La Corne, Sieur de Chaptes et de St. Luc (1711-84), early adopted the military life. He served against the Sauks and Foxes of Wisconsin in 1734, at Fort Clinton in 1741, at Crown Point and Saratoga in 1746-47, at La Présentation in 1752, and at Ticonderoga in 1758. He organized the ambush of Abercromby's wagon train at Fort Lydius and

the less successful attempt to intercept Haldimand's march on Niagara in 1759. He was a brilliant leader of mixed parties of French and Indians, and was a favorite of the tribes, whose languages he spoke. He was wounded at Ste. Foye in 1761 and in the following year was one of the seven survivors of the wreck of the *Augusta*, which was returning to France with most of the officials of the colony. From 1775 until his death he sat in the Legislative Council, and he served in command of the savages at Wood Creek under Burgoyne in 1777. His third wife was Marguerite Boucher de Boucherville, whose daughter Marie-Marguerite Lennox married Jacques Viger in 1808, after the death of her first husband.

³⁴ The Caughnawaga fort was begun in 1747 and completed in 1754. There is a plan of it in the Public Archives at Ottawa. For a description, see E. J. Devine, *History of Caughnawaga* (Montreal, 1922), 243-44.

³⁵ The Mission of Two Mountains near Montreal was settled by some nine hundred Iroquois about 1720, after the abandonment of Saut-au-Recollet. They were later joined by Nipissings and Algonquins from Ile-aux-Tourtes.

³⁶ The Hôpital-Général, or Monastery of the Religieuses Hospitalières de la Miséricorde de Jésus, was founded at Quebec in 1692 by Bishop Saint-Vallier as a home for the old and infirm, under the direction of a sister of the Congrégation de Notre Dame. In 1693 he put four nuns from the Hôtel-Dieu in charge of the new establishment, and in 1710 added two wings to the original quarters in the old Recollet Convent of Notre-Dame-des-Anges. During his thirteen years of exile in France he raised funds for the hospitalization of thirty persons. Provision was made for the care of the insane there until the Beauport asylum was opened in 1846; and the nuns also conducted a boarding school for girls until 1868. Part of the buildings were reserved for those who chose to spend the remainder of their lives there, as Bishop Saint-Vallier did.

³⁷ Bishop Jean-Baptiste de Saint-Vallier (1653-1727) was one of the most remarkable prelates of New France. After serving as a court chaplain under Louis XIV and as a military chaplain in Flanders in 1678, he refused the bishoprics of Tours and Marseilles. He first visited Canada in 1685 as bishop-elect and grand-vicar. He was consecrated at St. Sulpice in Paris in 1688 and reached Quebec that autumn. After conflicts with Frontenac, the governor, he was captured by the English while on his way to France in 1704, and spent five years in England and four in France before he could return to his diocese. He spent 600,000 livres, a third of the sum being his own, on the works of the Church in Quebec. He was buried in the chapel of the Hôpital-Général.

[38] The Soeurs de la Congrégation were founded at Montreal in 1658 by Venerable Marguerite Bourgeoys (1620-1700). The congregation is devoted to the education and instruction of youth.

[39] The Soeurs de la Charité de l'Hôpital-Général de Montréal (Soeurs Grises), or Grey Nuns, were founded at Montreal in 1737 by Madame d'Youville (Venerable Marie-Marguerite Dufrust, dame d'Youville) (1701-71). Madame d'Youville, born at Varennes and educated by the Ursulines of Quebec, was the daughter of an officer killed in service. She married a spendthrift, who left her penniless and with two children to support. Founding a successful small business, she gave much of her time to devotions and to charity. In 1737 she formed, with three other Montreal women, a community devoted to the service of the poor, and in 1747 took on the Hôpital-Général when the Frères Charon gave it up because of financial difficulties. The court had ordered the combination of the Hôpitals-Généraux of Montreal and Quebec, but Madame d'Youville managed to have this order rescinded through petition to the Bishop and to the Intendant Bigot. Before her death in 1771 she paid off all except 7,000 livres of the total debt of 48,000 which she had inherited from the Frères Charon; and had established two new wards for poor patients, an asylum for the insane or perverted, and a home for foundling children. All this was accomplished despite the effort of founding and developing her new community, the wartime trials of 1759-60, and the destruction of the hospital by fire in 1765.

[40] The Soeurs Servantes du Coeur Immaculé de Marie founded the Asile du Bon-Pasteur de Québec in 1850 as a refuge for repentant young girls and for the education and instruction of children.

[41] The Hôtel-Dieu of Quebec was founded in 1639 at Sillery by Mères St. Ignace, St. Bernard, and St. Bonaventure (the oldest of whom was then 29), of the Congrégation des Hospitalières de la Miséricorde de Jésus. The institution was moved to Quebec in 1646.

[42] The Quebec house of the Religieuses Ursulines was founded in 1639 by Madame de la Peltrie, with Venerable Mère Marie de l'Incarnation as the first superior. The Ursulines are famous for their education of girls.

[43] At present this division of the land at Charlesbourg can best be observed from the church steeple or from a plane.

[44] *Lettres de la Vénérable Mère Marie de l'Incarnation, Première Supérieure des Ursulines de la Nouvelle-France, divisées en deux parties* (Paris, 1681). This edition by Dom Claude Martin, which was exceedingly scarce, has been superseded by Dom Jamet's, in Vol. III-IV (1935-1937) of his *Escrits Spirituels et Temporels de Marie de l'Incarnation.*

On November 1(?), 1857 Parkman referred to his difficulties in finding this volume in a letter to George Bancroft (M.H.S., Bancroft Papers, 1857, June to December):

Dear Sir,

I observe, cited by you, the name of a book which I have chased in vain in the United States, Canada, and France—the *Lettres de Marie de l'Incarnation*. It is rare, and though I know of one or two copies, they are fast locked up in convent libraries. I should be very much your debtor, if you can aid me in gaining an opportunity to consult either this or another kindred book—Juchereau's *Histoire de l'Hôtel-Dieu de Québec*. The latter is comparatively numerous: but, being chiefly in unaccomodating hands, I fear I must go to Canada to consult it.

I remain, Dear Sir,

Respectfully yours,

Francis Parkman.

The Know-Nothing disturbances and the rise of that party to complete power in Massachusetts had not left Boston Catholics in a mood to be helpful to Protestant students.

[45] Abbé Edouard-Gabriel Plante (1813-69) became chaplain of the Hôpital-Général de Québec in 1851, after serving for eleven years as vicar of the Basilica. He was passionately devoted to Canadian history and amassed a remarkable library, which included the original editions of Champlain, Sagard, Lescarbot, a collection of the *Jesuit Relations*, Denys, Boucher, Lafiteau, and Leclerq. He left his books to Laval University.

[46] R. P. P.-F.-X. de Charlevoix (1682-1761), *Vie de la Mère Marie de l'Incarnation* (Paris, Chez Claude Briasson, 1724). According to Dom Jamet, the modern editor of Marie de l'Incarnation, this is merely an "easy and intelligent popularization" of Dom Claude Martin's biography.

[47] Louis Bertrand Latour (1700-80), *Histoire de l'Hôtel-Dieu de Québec* (Montaubon, Chez Jerome Legier, 1751).

[48] Jeanne-Françoise Juchereau [Mère de St. Ignace] (1650-1723), *Les Annales de l'Hôtel-Dieu de Québec, 1636-1716, Composées par les Reverends Mères Jeanne-Françoise Juchereau de St. Ignace et Marie Andrée Duplessis de Ste. Hélène, Anciennes Religieuses*. This was the basis, after much cutting and alteration, of Latour's *Historie*. It has recently been edited from the original text by Dom Jamet (Quebec, 1939).

[49] Père Paul Ragueneau, S.J. (1608-80), *La Vie de la Mère Catherine de Saint-Augustin, Religieuse Hospitalière de la Miséricorde de Québec en la Nouvelle-France (A Paris, Chez Florentin Lambert, M.DC.LXXI)*. A facsimile was printed at Quebec in 1923.

[50] Margry's list of documents on Louisiana cannot be traced.

[51] *Les Voyages Aventureux du Capitaine Jan Alfonce Santongeois*, an abridgement of his *Cosmographie*, was published at Poictiers in 1559 and translated in Hakluyt's *Voyages*, (Glasgow, 1904) VIII, 275. It also appears in French in M. Musset's *Récueil de Voyages et documents pour servir à l'histoire de la Géographie*. Alphonse, who served as pilot to Roberval in 1542-43 gives some account of the Saguenay, which he took for an inland sea and a possible northwest passage.

[52] M. Adolphe de Puibusque (?-1863) was a French writer who married an English Canadian, and spent three years in Canada.

[53] This passage is crossed out.

[54] Pierre Margry (1818-94) was drawn into his lifework in 1839 by his employment by General Lewis Cass, then U. S. Minister to France, to collect documents in the French archives relating to the history of the Old Northwest. When John Romeyn Brodhead came to Paris to gather documents bearing on the early history of New York, Margry was recommended to him by Cass. At some uncertain date Margry became attached to the Archives de la Marine et des Colonies, of which he eventually became the conservator. Exhausting his own archives, he sought further materials on the colonial history of France wherever they were to be found, in public or private hands. After his death his immense collection of transcripts went to the Bibliothèque Nationale. There is an account of it in the library's *Inventaire Sommaire* for 1898-99. The existence of this treasure house of materials became known to historians by the publication of *Relations et mémoires inédites pour servir à l'histoire de la France dans les pays d'outremer* (Paris, 1867), and Margry was besieged by requests to use it, which he refused. Parkman had many dealings with Margry in the late 1860's and early 1870's, and obtained the appropriation by the American Congress of $10,000 to underwrite the publication in six volumes of Margry's *Découvertes et établissements des Français dans l'ouest et dans le sud de l'Amérique Septentrionale, 1614-1754* (Paris, 1876-86).

[55] Penicaut, *Relation ou annales véritables de ce qui s'est passé dans le pays de la Louisiane . . . 1669, continué jusqu'en 1722* (in Margry's *Découvertes*, V, 375-586).

[56] Pierre-Joseph-Oliver Chauveau (1820-90), lawyer, statesman, and man of letters, studied law in Quebec under Parkman's friend Judge George O'Kill Stuart. He was Superintendent of Public Instruction from 1855-67, and was the first Prime Minister of Quebec under Confederation. His most famous book is *Charles Guérin* (1853), one of the first French-Canadian novels. He was also the author of a study of Garneau (1883).

[57] This collection is no longer preserved at the Parliamentary Library

in Quebec. It may have been among the papers taken to Ottawa when the government moved to the new capital in 1867.

[58] *La Bibliothèque Canadienne, ou Miscellanées Historiques, Scientifiques, et Littéraires* (Vol. I, 1822; Vol. II, 1825-26), edited by Michel Bibaud.

[59] *La Revue Canadienne*, the longest-lived French-Canadian magazine, was first published in January 1864 by E. Senécal.

[60] David Dale Owen (1807-60), the geologist son of Robert Owen and Ann Dale of New Lanark, made a survey of the Dubuque and Mineral Point districts of Wisconsin and Iowa for the Federal Land Commissioner. His report was published in *House Document No. 239 (26 Cong. I Sess.)*, April 2, 1840. He made a more complete survey of Wisconsin, Iowa, and Minnesota which may be found in his *Report of Geological Survey of Wisconsin, Iowa, and Minnesota . . . 1852.*

[61] Munsell's Historical Series, No. VIII: John Dawson Gilmary Shea (1824-92), *Early Voyages Up and Down the Mississippi by Cavelier, St. Cosme, Le Sueur, Gravier, and Guigues* (Albany, 1851). *Bib. Can.* 167.

[62] Abbé Henri-Raymond Casgrain (1831-1904), completing his studies at the Quebec Seminary, traveled in France and Italy before serving as a vicar at Beauport and at the Basilica of Quebec. In 1861 he became chaplain to the Convent of the Bon Pasteur, where he made his home until his death. In that same year he published his *Légendes Canadiennes*, and in 1864 his *Histoire de la Mère Marie de l'Incarnation*, as well as several of the biographical sketches which were later collected in *Biographies canadiennes* (1879), which includes a life of Parkman. He was the leading spirit of the literary revival of the 1860's, which was largely the work of Quebec writers. He was to become Parkman's closest friend in Quebec, and his rival in the same historical field.

[63] Jacques Duperron Baby of Windsor, Ontario, a prominent trader who supplied the garrison of Detroit with provisions during the siege of 1763. He was a friend of Pontiac, the great Indian leader. Parkman visited his grandson at Windsor in 1845.

[64] *Le Foyer Canadien*, the organ of Abbé Casgrain's literary group, began publication in January 1863 and ceased to appear in December 1866.

[65] Chevalier James Johnstone (1720-1800), *A Dialogue in Hades, a parallel of military errors, of which the French and English armies were guilty during the campaign of 1759 in Canada* (Quebec, 1866). In Quebec Literary & Historical Society *Documents*, II Series.

[66] Philippe Joseph Aubert de Gaspé (1786-1871), *Mémoires. Bib. Can.* 4464.

[67] Eugene Vétromile (1819-81), *The Abenakis and Their History, Or*

Historical Notes on the Aborigines of Acadia (New York, 1866). *Bib. Can.* 4546.

[68] Abbé Joseph-Pierre-Anselme Maurault (1819-71), *Histoire des Abenakis depuis 1605 jusqu'à nos jours* ([Sorel?] 1866). *Bib. Can.* 4520.

IX. FIRST PARIS NOTEBOOK

[1] Pierre Margry had lived on the same street, formerly known as Rue de la Harpe, in 1845, at the outset of the studies which brought him into contact with Parkman. (Note by Margry in his presentation copy of the *Jesuits*, dated "25 Jan. 1869" by Parkman.)

[2] This portrait of Anne de La Grange-Trianon, Comtesse de Frontenac (1632?-1707?), painted as Minerva, is reproduced as the frontispiece of *Frontenac and New France* (Part V of *France and England in North America*). An account of the portrait and of the Countess herself is given in the opening pages of that work.

[3] Parkman evidently changed his opinion of this bust of Montcalm, for it does not figure among the illustrations to *Montcalm and Wolfe*.

[4] Henri Joutel (1640?-1735), *Journal historique du dernier voyage que feu M. de La Salle fit dans le Golfe de Mexique* (Paris, 1713). Joutel, who accompanied La Salle as intendant on his expedition of 1684-87, repudiated this altered and abridged version of his journal, which Margry printed in full in *Découvertes*, III, 91-534. An English translation of the first printed text was published at London in 1714, and reprinted at Albany in 1906 in a new edition by Henry Reed Stiles. The Caxton Club of Chicago also issued an English version, c. 1895. (*Bib. Can.* 96, 230).

[5] This baptismal certificate furnished the basis of a footnote on the first page of *La Salle*.

[6] These letters of La Salle and Beaujeu, who was in charge of the ships, are printed in *Découvertes*, II, 519-52.

[7] The passage in the *Histoire de M^r. de La Salle* upon which Margry based his accusation against Nicolas Perrot (1644-1717), the interpreter, is cited in *La Salle*, 116 n.

[8] Parkman did not accept Margry's view of Beaujeu. Cf. *La Salle*, 389-90 n.

[9] The copies sent to New York were those selected by John Romeyn Brodhead in 1841-45, in his capacity of historical agent for the State.

They were printed in E. B. O'Callaghan, *Documents Relating to the Colonial History of New York* (Albany, 1853-83), IX-X ("Paris Documents"). In 1845 the Canadian government authorized Louis Joseph Papineau, then in Paris, to obtain copies of documents in the French archives relating to the history of Canada. Of the ten MS. volumes he gathered from the Archives des Colonies, six were destroyed in the Montreal Parliament fire of 1849, while four volumes, calendared in the *Catalogue de la Bibliothèque du Parlement* (Quebec, 1858), 1448, were preserved in the library of the Quebec Literary and Historical Society. In 1851 Georges-Barthélemi Faribault gathered what were known as the second and third series of Paris documents, to replace those lost in the fire of 1849. These are calendared in the 1858 *Catalogue*, 1499-1611.

The letters of Antoine Laumet de la Mothe Cadillac (1658-1730), who commanded at Michilimackinac, Detroit, and in Louisiana, were used by Parkman in *The Old Regime* (Part IV of *France and England in North America*). In the preface he mentions his reliance upon the Archives de la Marine et Colonies and upon Margry's aid. These papers were later printed in Margry, *Découvertes*, V, 75-346. It evidently did not take Parkman long to discover that Margry was holding back the La Salle papers, which were not made available until the publication of the first three volumes of the *Découvertes* in 1879.

[10] While American Minister to Paris from 1836 to 1842, General Lewis Cass collected materials on the history of the old Northwest—the Great Lakes region. Papineau made a selection from the Paris archives in 1845.

[11] L. Dussieux, *Le Canada sous la Domination Française* (Paris, 1862), 283-376.

[12] Sir Thomas Phillips, as Margry told Parkman on February 25.

[13] As later entries in this notebook indicate, Parkman established relations with the Marquis de Montcalm and was given permission "to copy all the letters written by his ancestor, General Montcalm, when in America, to members of his family in France." (*Montcalm and Wolfe*, Preface, viii).

[14] Frontenac's dispatch to Colbert of November 2, 1672 is cited in *Frontenac*, 25.

[15] R. Thomassy, "De la Salle et ses Relations inédites," in *Géologie pratique de la Louisiane* (Paris, 1860).

[16] Cited *La Salle*, 374.

[17] This map, rudely sketched by Parkman in his notebook, is Harrisse No. 228. Harrisse, in his *Notes sur la Nouvelle France* (Paris, 1872), 205, like Parkman (*La Salle*, 383 n.), assigns it to the engineer Minet, Beaujeu's

chartmaker, and considers it a copy of No. 226. Harrisse found it among the working drawings of the great cartographer Guillaume Delisle (1675-1726); and hazards the guess that "Minet" became "Minuty" either through the copyist's misreading, or through an attempt to latinize the engineer's name.

[18] Probably a preliminary sketch for Harrisse No. 241: "Carte de l'Amérique Septentrionale, dressée par Raudin, l'ingénieur et l'obligé du Cte. de Frontenac," 1689. Harrisse was only able to find an outline tracing of this lost map (reproduced in J. Winsor, *Narrative and Critical History of America*, IV, 235). The tracing is now in the Barlow Collection. J. Winsor, *The Kohl Collection* (Washington, 1904), 110.

[19] Parkman may have seen the lost map of Raudin, which, like the sketch, shows the Mississippi as the Buade. Harrisse dates this map 1689.

[20] Harrisse No. 263: "Carte de la Rivière de Mississippi sur les mémoires de M. le Sueur qui en a pris avec la boussole tous les tours et détours depuis la mer jusqu'à la Rivière St. Pierre et a pris la hauteur du pôle en plusieurs endroits. Par Guillaume De L'Isle Géographe, de l'Académie Royale des Sciences, 1702." This map was based on information supplied by Pierre Charles Le Sueur (1657-1702?), long a fur trader among the Sioux of the upper Mississippi, who ascended the river from Louisiana in 1700 in search of a copper mine in the same region, after his fur trading activities had been banned by Louis XIV's edict of 1698.

[21] In 1730 Pierre Gaultier de Varennes, sieur de la Vérendrye, came down to Quebec from his post of command at the trading posts on Lake Nipigon. While urging his plans of discovery in the West, he showed the governor, the Marquis de Beauharnois, a map drawn by the Indian Aughagah or Ochagach. This map was evidently sent to France, for a tracing of it was reproduced in Philippe Buache's "Carte Physique des terrains les plus élevés de la partie occidentale du Canada, 1754." The original "Carte tracée par les Cris" is reproduced in L. J. Burpee, *Journals and Letters of La Vérendrye and His Sons* (Toronto, 1937), 192; while Buache's map, with its inset "Carte tracée par le Sauvage Ockagach," is found in the same work, p. 53. A further "Carte contenant les nouvelles découvertes de l'Ouest, 1737," which went to France with De Beauharnois' letter of October 14, 1737, is reproduced opposite p. 116. There are four variants of this map, two of them copies by La Galissonnière, head of the department of nautical charts at Paris. Christopher Dufrost, sieur de La Jemeraye —La Vérendrye's nephew, who died in 1735 while trying to establish a new post west of the Lake of the Woods—is supposed to have drawn the "Carte d'une partie du lac Supérieur, avec la découverte de la rivière

depuis le grand portage A jusqu'à la barrière B," (*ibid*, 488), but it contains information which must have been obtained after his death.

[22] This map, to which Parkman refers in *La Salle* (469 n.), seems to be distinct from Harrisse No. 260: "Carte du Mississipy à la Coste de la Floride avec ses environs, 1700." The latter shows La Salle's fort and a route marked "Chemin Par où les Espagnols ont Esté à la Baye St. Louis." Since Parkman refers to the map he saw as a manuscript in Margry's collection, it may have been a tracing from that listed by Harrisse, with an altered legend.

[23] Harrisse No. 360: "Carte de la Rivière Longue et de quelques autres qui se déchargent dans le grand fleuve de Mississippi, 1689." This map, which is found in the first volume of Lahontan's *Nouveaux Voyages* and reproduced in *Narrative and Critical History*, IV, 261, shows an east-west route marked down the "Rivière des Ilinois" from the village of the "Oumamis de Chegakoi." On the "Carte générale de Canada" in the second volume, the river is still given as the "Ilinois," but the "Portage Ilinois" of the first map becomes "Portage de Chegakou V[ers] des Ilinois" and the "Chegakou Oumanis" village is shown. Parkman's "Chacagou" might well be a misreading or a phonetic equivalent, but where he got "Rivière à la Roche" from Lahontan remains a mystery.

[24] This "Tabula Novae Franciae Anno 1660" (Harrisse No. 329; Kohl No. 210) appeared in *Historia canadensis, seu Novae Franciae Libri Decem, ad annum usque Christi M.DC.LVI. Auctore P. Francisco Creuxio, e Societate Iesu* (Paris, 1664). Père du Creux's work was based upon the *Jesuit Relations*, which he followed in too detailed a fashion for Charlevoix's taste. The map was reproduced in Père Bressani's *Relation abrégée* (*Bib. Can.* 45), translated and edited by Père Félix Martin, S.J., at Montreal in 1852. It is also given in facsimile in J. G. Shea, *Mississippi Valley* (New York, 1853), 50, and partially in *Narrative and Critical History*, IV, 148 & 389. It almost corresponds in extent to Champlain's great map of 1632 (Harrisse No. 322).

[25] Harrisse No. 348; Kohl No. 178: "Le Canada faict par le Sr. Champlain où sont la Nouvelle France, la Nouvelle Angleterre, etc., avec les nations voisines et autres terres nouvellement découvertes suivant les mémoires du P. du Val Géographe du Roy," 1677. Duval's map was based on Champlain's of 1632. An earlier version appeared in 1664 (Harrisse No. 331), while Winsor (*Narrative and Critical History*, IV, 388 n.) mentions one of 1660 in the Kohl Collection.

[26] Harrisse No. 359; Kohl No. 213: "Partie occidentale du Canada ou de la Nouvelle France où sont les nations des Illinois, de Trace, les

Iroquois, et plusieurs autres Peuples; avec la Louisiane Nouvellement découverte etc.," 1688. This map was republished in the following year on a reduced scale, annexed to the "Partie orientale, 1689" (Harrisse No. 361), as "L'Amérique Septentrionale, ou la Partie Septentrionale des Indes Occidentales" (Harrisse No. 362). The western portion is sketched in *Narrative and Critical History*, IV, 232. Coronelli was the Venetian cartographer; and his work was "corrected and augmented" by the Sieur Tillemon.

[27] Kohl No. 240: "Partie de l'Amérique Septentrionale qui comprend le cours de l'Ohio, etc.," 1755, by Robert de Vaugondy. De Vaugondy (1688-1766), the cartographical heir of the Sansons, was royal geographer in 1760.

[28] Atlas F & G: "Carte du Canada et de La Louisiane qui forment La Nouvelle France et des Colonies Angloises où sont représentés les Pays contestés Dressée sur les observations et sur plusieurs Cartes particulières et même Angloises Par J. B. Nolin Géographe . . . 1756."

[29] Kohl No. 240: "Canada et Louisiane par le Sieur le Rouge, ingénieur géographe du Roi," 1755.

[30] N. Bellin's "Carte de la partie orientale de la Nouvelle France ou du Canada, 1744" appeared in the first volume of Père Charlevoix's *Histoire et description de la Nouvelle France* (Paris, 1744).

[31] Harrisse No. 354; Kohl No. 127: "Partie de la Nouvelle France . . . par . . . Hubert Jaillot, 1685." This map, based almost entirely on Canadian sources according to Kohl, shows the French and English posts on Hudson's Bay. Jaillot was royal geographer in 1736.

[32] Harrisse No. 238; Kohl No. 233: "Parties les Plus Occidentales du Canada. *Pierre Raffeix Jesuite*," 1688. The map is sketched and the marginal inscriptions are given in *Narrative and Critical History*, IV, 233. Raffeix's suggested route runs from Lake Ontario, not Lake Erie, up the Cheneseco, with a portage to the headwaters of the Alleghany, and thus by the Ohio to the Mississippi.

[33] "Canada, Louisiane et terres Angloises. Par le sr. d'Anville. 1755." This is a three-sheet map (pl. 28-28a-28b) from Jean Baptiste Bourguignon d'Anville's *Atlas général* (Paris, 1743-80). Cf. P. L. Phillips, *Geographical Atlases* (Washington, 1909), 573.

[34] "Amérique Septentrionale. Par le sr. d'Anville, 1746." A one-sheet map (No. 10-11) in D'Anville's 1727-80 *Atlas général* and two sheets (pl. 27) in the 1743-80 edition (Phillips, 571).

[35] "Carte de l'Amérique Septentrionale Depuis le 28 degré de latitude jusqu'au 72. Par N. Bellin Ingénieur de la Marine et du Depost des

Plans . . .," 1755. In Library of Congress; photo-lithograph copy in Public Archives, Ottawa, Tray 54.

[36] "Nouvelle Carte particulière de l'Amérique où sont exactement marquées la Nouvelle Bretagne, le Canada ou Nouvelle France, la Nouvelle Ecosse, la Nouvelle Angleterre, la Nouvelle York, la Pensilvanie, Mary Land, La Caroline Septentrionale, l'Ile de Terre Neuve, le Grand Banc, etc.," from Henry Popple, *Atlas* (Amsterdam, 1733).

[37] Parkman's account of Montcalm in *Montcalm and Wolfe*, I, 351-60, is based chiefly on an unpublished autobiography, *Mémoires pour servir à l'Histoire de ma Vie*, "preserved by his descendents." Parkman uses the current Marquis' characterization of his ancestor's mother—"a woman of remarkable force of character and who held great influence over her son" (*Montcalm and Wolfe*, I, 359)—without adopting the suggestion that Madame de St. Véran induced him to take the American command offered by D'Argenson. The family name was De Montcalm-Gozon de St. Véran; the Marquis' wife was known as Madame de Montcalm, his mother as Madame de St. Véran. The portrait is reproduced as frontispiece to *Montcalm and Wolfe*, I.

[38] Sir Thomas Phillips (1792-1872) was one of the great book and manuscript collectors of his day, and maintained a private press at his residence, Middle Hill, at Broadway. He later removed to Thirlestane House, Cheltenham, where Parkman saw him.

[39] The original draft of this letter, pasted in Margry's presentation copy of *The Jesuits*, came to light in Rutland, Vermont, in the spring of 1942. Through the courtesy of the present owner of the volume, Richard B. McCormack of Chicago, the text of this important letter is here given in full:

–Cette lettre a été adressée par moi à Ste. Beuve qui m'avait prié de lui donner les moyens de répondre à Parkman sur un sujet qu'il ne connaissait pas–

Monsieur

Vous trouverez avec ce billet le Volume de M. Parkman sur lequel vous m'avez fait l'honneur de me demander un mot. Ce volume, intitulé, comme vous le savez, *Les Jésuites dans l'Amérique du Nord*, fait partie d'une série de livres de cet auteur sur l'action de la France dans ce continent, action dont il me semble avoir été amené à reconnaitre l'importance par son [livre] de La Conspiration de Pontiac–La révolte des Hurons et des autres nations voisines des Lacs contre les Anglais, qui eut lieu sous les ordres de ce chef après la [?] perte du Canada, ayant dû montrer à M. Parkman l'attachement de ces nations pour les Français. Il a voulu sans doute étudier les circonstances dans lesquelles s'étaient formées nos relations avec les tribus indiennes, et comment notre puissance s'était établie dans le continent qu'elles parcouraient plus qu'elles ne le possédaient, suivant l'expression du Général Cass.

Le premier volume que M. Parkman a donné en conséquence sur ce sujet contient la tentative d'établissement des Français à la Caroline du Nord sous Charles IX et la vie de Samuel de Champlain fondateur de la puissance française sur le Saint Laurent.

Le second volume est celui que vous m'avez confié.

Et il précède, à qu'il paraît, un troisième ouvrage qui aura pour sujet la Découverte de l'Ouest.

Il est difficile de juger une de ces parties sans les autres. Néanmoins pour vous être agréable, je vous dirai ce que j'ai aperçu du second volume.

Dans cette partie l'auteur Américain a cru pouvoir détacher comme présentant un tableau capable de frapper l'attention le rôle des Jésuites dans l'Amérique du Nord pendant 20 ans de 1634 à 1654.

Il lui a paru que durant ce temps ils ont prétendu former en Canada un Empire analogue à celui qu'ils avaient fondé au Paraguay. Et il attribue aux victoires des Iroquois, ennemis des Hurons et des nations Algonquines dont les Jésuites étaient les missionaires, d'avoir eu pour résultat la chute du projet de La Compagnie.

Suivant moi, l'auteur a raison quand il expose ce dessein des Jésuites. Ils l'avouent eux-mêmes, mais il se trompe quand il ne voit qu'une cause aussi indirecte à la fin de la domination des Jésuites là où il y en a plusieurs bien plus nettement apparentes pour ceux qui ont suivi les faits de plus près que M. Parkman.

La première de ces causes a été la Cession d'Indépendance des colons qui ne pouvaient se faire à un tel régime de compression que celui qu'avaient établi les Jésuites. Et lorsque le nombre des colons augumente, les R.R.P.P. eurent la main forcée, parce que les habitants s'aidèrent contre eux d'autres forces contraires aux vues de la Société de Jésus.

La création du gouvernement Royal, en se substituant à celui des compagnies commerciales absorbé par les Jésuites, favorisa naturellement les habitants pour établir sa propre indépendance, et à cet effet il opposa également les Sulpiciens et les Récollets aux Jésuites.

Ce qui prouve à la fois la justice de la vue de M. Parkman sur le but des Jésuites, et son erreur sur ce qu'il croit avoir amené le fin de leur domination, c'était le rôle de cette Société dans l'ouest même, et dans la vallée du Mississippi après l'établissement du Gouvernement Royal sur les bords du Saint Laurent—Les français étant restés peu nombreux dans l'ouest et au sud. Les Jésuites prétendirent bien y demeurer les maîtres. Et ils firent une guerre acharnée, rarement ouverte, presque toujours souterraine, à ceux qui vinrent dans ces régions en rivaux, soit pour établir l'autorité Royale, soit pour élever des missions, soit pour trafiquer en dehors d'eux, tandis que la Société continuait de lutter sur les bords du Saint Laurent pour garder du pouvoir tout ce qu'elle pourrait. Pendant 30 ans je la vois dans toutes les cabales, dans tous les remuements des partis qui divisent le pays, et peu s'y faut que ses menées n'aient pas pour conséquence la ruine entière de la colonie.

Le livre de M. Parkman est donc un livre insuffisant et faux dans ses déductions par l'insuffisance de ses lumières—Néanmoins il a ceci de bon qu'il laisse apercevoir une partie de la vérité, ce qui rendra aux autres plus facile de la faire entendre toute entière—D'un autre côté il concourt à faire reconnaître sous certains aspects la grandeur de notre colonisation et par là, Monsieur, il mérite que vous lui encouragiez à continuer son oeuvre, quoiqu'à mon sens également il ne fasse que résumer avec un peu plus de lest d'esprit les travaux historiques publiés tant en France qu'en Canada par des ecclésiastiques—Seulement il est nécessaire que vous sachiez au moins pour vous que tout est loin d'être dit sur ces matières.

Je pense, Monsieur, que ces quelques mots vous suffiront pour répondre à M. Parkman. Et pour justifier auprès de vous le plaisir que me conféra toujours l'occasion de vous témoigner les sentiments avec lesquels

J'ai l'honneur d'être

Votre très humble et très obéissant serviteur

J'espère, parce que je le souhaite, que votre santé est meilleure que le jour où j'ai eu l'honneur de vous voir après un contretemps.

Pierre Margry,
11 Rue du Mont Thabor

After receiving this letter, Ste. Beuve wrote a brief and guarded note to Parkman, congratulating him upon his work but not criticizing it. Cf. Massachusetts Historical Society, Parkman Papers, 128, 60.

[40] Cf. *La Salle*, 317 n., for Parkman's account of the small fieldpiece found at Ottawa, Illinois, and for a comparison of it with the Paris specimens.

[41] In the spring of 1759 Bougainville brought the news, which he had heard before sailing from France, that one of Montcalm's daughters had died (*Montcalm and Wolfe*, II, 179).

[42] J. E. Roy, in his *Rapport sur les Archives de France relatives à l'histoire du Canada* (Ottawa, 1911), 324, says that the Archives de Guerre go back continuously to the reign of Louis XIV, with a few scattered dossiers, documents, and registers of earlier date.

[43] No mention of this map is found in the standard works on French cartography.

[44] This might be any of a dozen or more plans of Louisbourg. N. Bellin did a "Port de Louisbourg dans l'Isle Royale, 1764" which is mentioned in J. S. McLennan, *Louisbourg* (London, 1918), 433, as being in the Bibliothèque Nationale (FF. 4693 pl. 23). The manuscript Parkman saw may have the basis of this engraved map.

[45] In *Montcalm and Wolfe* (I, 76) Parkman refers to his use of the Detroit

map made c. 1750 by the French engineer Gaspard Chaussegros de Léry (1682-1756). N. Bellin's "La Rivière du Detroit" and its inset "Plan du Fort du Detroit," in *Le Petit Atlas Maritime* (Paris, 1764), are based upon two manuscript sketches of De Léry, made in 1749 and 1752.

[46] Probably maps by Robert de Vaugondy from his *Atlas Universel* (Paris, 1757).

[47] The papers upon which Margry based his views were published in his *Découvertes*, II, 357-471, and were used by Parkman in the eleventh edition of *The Discovery of the Great West*, which was reentitled *La Salle and the Discovery of the Great West*.

[48] Harrisse No. 225: "Carte de la Louisiane, May 1685," by Minet. Harrisse says that Minet cut partially away the original outline of the river's mouth, and pasted the second version beneath it. He also thinks that the map was made after Minet's return to France, and that it was based upon Franquelin's manuscript map of 1684. Cf. Thomassy, 208; J. G. Shea, *Peñalosa* (New York, 1882), 21; G. Gravier, *La Salle* (Paris, 1870), 283; Delisle, *Journal des Savans*, xix, 211. The map is sketched in *Narrative and Critical History*, IV, 237.

[49] Cf. *La Salle*, 114.

[50] Cf. T. Chapais, *Montcalm* (Quebec, 1911), 226.

[51] *Lettres de monsieur le marquis de Montcalm . . . 1757, 1758, 1759* (London, 1777). *Bib. Can.* 289. These are the Roubaud letters, given to George III about 1764 by the renegade Jesuit, circulated in manuscript in 1775, and then printed. Roubaud claimed the author was an Englishman known to Chatham (cf. *Canadian Archives Report*, 1885, xiii-xxi, cxxxviii-cxliii). Parkman and Justin Winsor uncovered Roubaud's forgery in Massachusetts Historical Society *Proceedings*, XI(1869), 112-28; *ibid*, II Series, 3 (1887), 202-5.

X. MT. DESERT NOTEBOOK

[1] Mt. Desert Island, off the Maine coast near the mouth of the Penobscot, was discovered and named by Champlain in 1604. It was first settled by the Jesuits in 1609, but their colony was destroyed four years later by Samuel Argall. In 1688 the island was granted to the Sieur de la Mothe Cadillac, but no general settlement was established until 1762, when Massachusetts granted half the island to Governor Francis Bernard.

Despite its growing popularity as a summer resort, in 1870 the island was still reached only by stage from Bangor or by steamer twice a week from Portland.

2 Grand Manan Island, off the New Brunswick coast near the entrances of Passamaquoddy Bay and the Bay of Fundy, was discovered by Champlain in 1604 and is mentioned by Lescarbot (1609) and Biard (1611).

3 Pemaquid was an early settlement on the Maine coast, near the modern town of Boothbay Harbor, which fell victim to the French and Indians. See *Frontenac*, 235-37, 397-401.

4 Mt. Katahdin, the unattained goal of Parkman's youthful excursion along the Canadian boundary in the summer of 1842, evidently still held some lure for him. It can hardly be said to be "very accessible" even today. The region about Katahdin was first explored in 1837 by Dr. Charles T. Jackson, the state geologist, whom Parkman met in the White Mountains in 1841; and Thoreau visited it in September 1846. At the entrance of Somes Sound on Mt. Desert Island was the site of the settlement of St. Sauveur, founded by the Jesuits Biard and Massé in 1609 and destroyed by Samuel Argall in 1613.

5 Parkman first visited Center Harbor on Lake Winnepesaukee in New Hampshire in 1838 with his father. He describes the place in the 1841 Journal.

XI. ACADIAN NOTEBOOK

[Parkman probably used "A New Map of Nova Scotia Compiled from the Latest Surveys expressly for the *Historical and Statistical Account of Nova Scotia*, 1829," which serves as frontispiece to T. C. Haliburton's book of that title (Halifax, 1829). This map gives the old French and Indian names in italics, along with the current English names.]

1 Digby or Annapolis Gut is the narrow entrance to the Annapolis Basin, the Port Royal of the French first settlers.

2 A fort was built on this site about 1643 by Charles de Menou de Charnisay, Sieur d'Aulnay (Parkman prefers the spelling "d'Aunay"). The place was always fortified until Port Royal was surrendered to the English under Colonel Nicholson in 1710. The Annapolis River was variously known under the French regime as Rivière du Port Royal and Rivière du Dauphin (Lescarbot). Allen's River was called Rivière de

Notes—Acadian Notebook 665

l'Equille, "because that was the first fish caught there" (Lescarbot, II, 234). *Equille* is a local Norman word for sand eel.

³ Perhaps Judge Chipman of Halifax, Haliburton's informant.

⁴ These French remains on the Lequille may have been the ruins of the mill which appears on Lescarbot's "Figure du Port Royal en La Nouvelle France, 1609."

⁵ There is still a small Micmac settlement on the Bear River reservation, partly in Digby and partly in Annapolis County. The river's name is a corruption of Hébert, the name given to it by Champlain after the apothecary Louis Hébert, later the first habitant of Quebec.

⁶ The French Acadian settlement at Clare, the region between the Sissiboo River and St. Mary's Bay, dates from 1768, when, on the recommendation of Lieutenant Governor Michael Francklyn, grants there were given to returning Acadians who took the English oath of allegiance. Joseph Dugas was the first settler, but he was soon joined by many compatriots, including numbers returning from exile in Massachusetts. More lands were granted in 1771, 1772, and 1775; and today the bulk of the French population of Nova Scotia is concentrated in this region.

⁷ Minas Basin was named by Champlain after the mines he sought in the region.

⁸ Lyon's Cove does not appear on most maps. Cape Blomidon stands at the entrance of the Minas Basin and is the landfall for vessels approaching from the Bay of Fundy.

⁹ In 1621, Sir William Alexander obtained from James I a grant of the whole peninsula (in which the name of Nova Scotia was first used instead of Acadia) as a fief of the Scottish Crown. James' grant was based on the claim that the territory belonged to England by right of Cabot's discovery. This claim had also served as the legal excuse for Samuel Argall's descent upon Port Royal in 1613, when he and his Virginian freebooters laid waste the Sieur de Monts' settlement of Port Royal. This settlement, like that of Sir William Alexander which replaced it, was at Lower Granville, opposite, not on, Goat Island. The Scots arrived in 1628, and made their headquarters on the site of the old French fort which Argall had destroyed. The little colony, never very successful, surrendered to De Razilly in August 1632 under the terms of the treaty of St. Germain-en-Laye, and thus closed the short-lived attempt to make a New Scotland.

¹⁰ Perreau is undoubtedly a phonetic equivalent for Perrot, in which form the name is given on Haliburton's map. François-Marie Perrot was governor of Acadia, 1684-86, and remained as a trader after his dismissal from office.

[11] The Gaspereau was named after the small herring which frequent this tidal stream.

[12] The Triassic red sandstone formation of the Minas Basin culminates in the basaltic promontory of Cape Blomidon.

[13] The Jemseg River flows into the St. John about thirty-five miles upstream above the city of St. John. In 1659 Colonel Thomas Temple, acting under a grant given him by Oliver Cromwell and as governor of Acadia, established a fort at the mouth of the Jemseg as a trading post with the Indians. When Acadia was restored to France in 1667 by the Treaty of Breda, Fort Jemseg was taken over by the French. In the summer of 1674 it was captured by a Dutch force under Captain Jurriaen Aernouts. The fort was rebuilt by Villebon in 1690, after having returned to French hands, but was abandoned in favor of the fort at Nashwaak in 1692.

[14] Fort Nashwaak or St. Joseph, built by Villebon in 1692, at the Junction of the Nashwaak River with the St. John, was the headquarters for many French and Indian raids on the New England settlements. After Villebon's attack in 1696 on the English stronghold of Fort William Henry at Pemaquid, a retaliatory expedition under Colonel John Ha(w)thorne who supplanted Captain Ben Church in command after the latter's attack on Chignecto, was sent from New England to attack Fort Nashwaak, but retired without having done more than ineffectually bombard the French stronghold. In 1698 Villebon abandoned Nashwaak in favor of the fort at the mouth of the St. John.

[15] Parkman here confuses the sites of Latour's and D'Aulnay's forts, a common error until the matter was settled by Dr. W. F. Ganong's exhaustive research, to the early results of which a footnote in *The Old Regime* (39) refers. The place called "Old Fort," at Carleton on the west side of the harbor, overlooking Navy Island, was the site of D'Aulnay's fort and later of a succession of French and English establishments. Latour's fort was on the east side of the harbor at Portland Point. Its site is now marked by a brass tablet at the head of Portland Street. D'Aulnay destroyed Latour's fort in 1645 and built a new one on the opposite side of the harbor. After D'Aulnay's death by drowning in 1650, Latour returned to St. John as governor of Acadia, and lived there until his death in 1666. Since he made his headquarters at the fort built by his rival, it became known by his name; and thus arose the confusion into which Parkman, like many others, fell. (For Ganong's evidence, see *Transactions* of the Royal Society of Canada, IX, 1891, Pt. II, 61, and V, 1899, 276; and *New Brunswick Magazine*, I, 20, 165. Hannay's case against the Old

Fort site is in *New Brunswick Magazine*, I, 89. See also Ganong's note in Denys, *Acadia*, 114-15.)

[16] This French fort at the mouth of the Nerepis River was variously known as Fort Boishébert, Beauhébert, or Nerepis. It was built in 1749, upon the site of an ancient Indian fort and village, by Charles des Champs de Boishébert et Raffetot, who had served under his uncle M. de Ramezay at the unsuccessful siege of Annapolis Royal in 1746 and at the defeat of the British under Colonel Noble at Grand Pré in January 1747. Boishébert's original orders in 1749 were to rebuild and garrison the fort at the mouth of the St. John; but meeting opposition from the Nova Scotian government, which claimed the territory as British, he moved upriver to Nerepis. Here he built the small fort which goes by his name and contented himself with keeping watch on the English and preventing their settlement in the region by encouraging raids by the Indians, whom he secretly supplied with arms and supplies. As delivery of these by sea was difficult, De la Jonquière, the governor of Canada, tried to improve the land route from Quebec to Lake Témiscouata. In 1754, under a more aggressive French policy, Boishébert was ordered to rebuild Villebon's old fort at St. John, and the fort at Nerepis was abandoned.

[17] Pierre-Louis Morin was a Quebec surveyor and cartographer, who made maps for Parkman.

[18] Thomas Sterry Hunt (1826-1892), geologist and pioneer organic chemist, early became absorbed in the natural sciences, and was a private student and assistant of Professor Benjamin Silliman, Jr. at Yale. In 1846 he was appointed to the Geological Survey of Vermont, and in the following year became chemist to the Geological Survey of Canada under Sir William Logan, which post he held until 1872. He was professor of chemistry at Laval University in Quebec when Parkman met him.

[19] Digby is a township in the county of Annapolis, which includes the township of Clare where the bulk of the French population of the province is concentrated, though descendents of the Acadians are also found in Cape Breton and Halifax County. It is probable that Parkman meant to write "The French in Annapolis Cty."

[20] Horace Gray (1828-1902), Massachusetts jurist and United States Supreme Court justice, was, like Parkman, a lover of sport and country life. Since he was a member of the Harvard class of 1845, he had probably known Parkman since the latter's law school days. Gray was, with C. C. Langdell, an early advocate of the case system.

XII. SECOND PARIS NOTEBOOK

[1] These working drawings of the cartographer Guillaume Delisle (1675-1726) are mentioned by Harrisse in his account of the French archives (*Notes*, xxvii). Photostats in Public Archives, Ottawa.

[2] No record of this study has been found. Sebastien Crémoisy (1585/6-1669) was the printer of the *Jesuit Relations*, which appeared in annual volumes from 1632 to 1673. The books which bear his imprint are often called by his name.

[3] Le Rocher was the site of Fort St. Louis of the Illinois, and was later known as Starved Rock (cf. *La Salle*, 314). In Margry, *Découvertes*, III, 607-22, there are documents relating to the fate of La Salle's other colony, Fort St. Louis of Texas, which was often confused with Le Rocher. Parkman may have made, in this instance, the very error which he later warned his readers against, since no papers of the sort he describes seem to exist.

[4] Harrisse (*Notes*, xxiii-xxiv) mentions twenty-three portfolios, No. 122-43, devoted to North America, which contained materials relating to La Salle, Joliet, Bourgmont, Le Gardeur, and the La Vérendryes. Parkman's reference is correct.

[5] Probably Harrisse No. 208: "Carte de 80 x 50 c., représente le 'Messipi' du 49 au 42 d. où la revière 'Misconsing' vient aboutir. Le Lac Supérieur est nommé: Almepigou," 1679. Cf. *La Salle*, 481-482, where Parkman maintains that this map was "made by or for Du Lhut."

[6] Harrisse No. 209: "Carte de 68 x 43 cent. représentant tous les grands lacs. Le cartouche est vide, et on remarque à l'Ouest un grand nombre d'animaux tels que chameaux et rennes. La rivière des Illinois ne porte que la légende suivante: 'Rivière descendante dans le fleuve Mississippi,'" 1679. Harrisse considers this map to be the work of Franquelin.

[7] Jean Baptiste Louis Franquelin (1652-1718), who came to Canada in 1672, was the first *"hydrographe du roi"* in Canada. He made his first map in 1678; was named *"hydrographe royal"* in 1687; and left Quebec in 1695, probably to work for Vauban. He was succeeded by Louis Joliet. A great number of his maps and sketches are preserved in the Dépôt des Cartes de la Marine. For a list of his published maps, see C. de La Roncière, *Catalogue général des Manuscrits des bibliothèques publiques de France, Bibliothèques de la Marine* (Paris, 1907).

[8] Harrisse No. 258: "Carte en quatre sections de 90 x 53 cent. chacune,

dressée par M. de Fonville, Enseigne d'une compagnie de volontaires de la marine et dédiée au comte de Maurepas. Elle est datée de Québec 1699." De la Roncière (227) notes that this map includes views of Quebec from the east and northwest.

9 Harrisse No. 240: "Carte de l'Amérique Septentrionale entre les 25 et 65 degrés de latitude et depuis environ 240. jusqu'aux 340 de longit. . . . Par Jean Baptiste Louis Franquelin," 1689. Harrisse notes that this map includes a very fine view of Quebec from the east.

10 Harrisse No. 214: "Carte gnlle. de la France Septentrionale contenant la découverte du pays des Ilinois Faite par le Sieur Jolliet," 1681. Parkman notes: "This map, which is inscribed with a dedication by the Intendant Duchesneau to the minister Colbert, was made some time after the voyage of Joliet and Marquette. It is an elaborate piece of work, but very inaccurate. . . . This map, which is an early effort of the engineer Franquelin, does more credit to his skill as a designer than to his geographical knowledge, which appears in some respects behind his time." (*La Salle*, 480-81).

11 Harrisse No. 219: "Carte de l'Amérique Septentrionale et partie de la Méridionale Depuis l'embouchure de la Rivière St. Laurent jusqu'à l'Isle de Cayenne, avec les nouvelles découvertes de la Rivière Mississippi, ou Colbert," 1682. Parkman dates this map 1682 or 1683, and believes that Du Luth supplied data for it (*La Salle*, 455).

12 In the *"grandes archives,"* Harrisse found many boxes of "instructions, reports, travel notes, and memorials, for the most part unpublished." (*Notes*, xxiii-xxiv). Carton 5, No. 18, contained material relating to Le Gardeur and La Vérendrye.

13 Carton 5, No. 15, contained manuscript material dealing with Joliet's voyage to Labrador in 1694 (*Notes*, xxiv).

14 Harrisse Nos. 253 & 254: "Plan de la ville et du Château de Québec en la présente année 1695." and "Plan de Québec en 1699. Fait ce 30 Mars par Levasseur de Neré, Ingénieur."

15 Harrisse No. 240: "Carte de l'Amérique Septentrionale . . . par Jean Baptiste Louis Franquelin," 1689.

16 Harrisse No. 259: "Partie de l'Amérique Septentrionale . . . par Jean Baptiste Louis Franquelin, Géographe du Roy, 1699."

17 Harrisse No. 219: "Carte de l'Amérique Septentrionale et partie de la Méridionale," 1682.

18 Harrisse No. 421: "*Trés-humble remontrance et mémoires des choses nécessaires pour l'entretien et exécution de l'entreprise faicte en la Nouvelle France, présentées au Roy, et du temps qu'elle a été découverte,*" 1621.

[19] Harrisse No. 443: "Dépêche du Cardinal de Richelieu à M. de Châteauneuf, Ambassadeur à Londres, lui recommandant la poursuite de la restitution du Canada," 1629.

[20] Harrisse No. 501: "Lettre du P. Nickel, Général des Jésuites, au P. Cellot, Provincial de la Compagnie en France. Rome 16 Octobre 1656."

[21] Cf. Harrisse, *Notes*, 151.

[22] Margry had the "Relation de Joutel" well "mislaid," since it was not "found" until the publication of *Découvertes* was under way. It was printed for the first time in full in *Découvertes*, III, 91-534.

[23] There is a Brienne Collection of 362 volumes in the Bibliothèque Nationale, Nos. 6972-7328, which may be what Parkman meant, since there is no collection of this name in the British Museum.

[24] The Jesuits had no special collections of documents in their Paris house. In 1864 Père J. Tailhan had published Nicolas Perrot's *Mémoire sur les Moeurs, Coustumes, et Religion des Sauvages de l'Amérique septentrionale*, one of Charlevoix's manuscript sources.

[25] Probably "A *correct plan* of the environs of Quebec, and of the battle fought on the 13th sept., 1759 together with a particular detail of the French lines and batteries and also of the encampments, batteries and attacks of the British army [etc.]. Engraved by Thomas Jefferys. 16 x 35. [London], T. Jefferys." A. Doughty & G. W. Parmelee, *Siege of Quebec* (Quebec, 1901), VI, 292, No. 39.

[26] "Carte Des Environs de Québec En La Nouvelle France Mesurée très exactement en 1688 Par le Sr. De Villeneuve Ingr." Cf. Harrisse No. 230. This map gives a table of the names and surnames of the inhabitants of Quebec by parishes.

[27] Harrisse No. 230: "Carte Des Enuirons De Québec En La Nouvelle France Mesuré Sur Le Lieu Très-Exactement En 1685, Et 1686. Par Le Sr. Devilleneuve Ingénieur Du Roy."

[28] Cf. Harrisse No. 195: "Véritable plan Québec Comme il est l'an 1664 et la fortification que l'on y puisse faire."

[29] Harrisse No. 251: "Carte de la Coste de la Nouvelle Angleterre depuis le Cap Anne jusqu'à la Pointe Nevresing, où est compris le Chemin par Terre et par Mer de Boston à Manathes. Par J. B. L. Franquelin. Hydrographe du Roy, 1693." Harrisse notes that this map contains a "Plan de Manathes ou Nouvelle Yorc. Vérifié par le Sr. de la Motte."

[30] Harrisse No. 259: "Partie de l'Amérique Septentrionale où est compris la Nouvelle France . . . Par Jean Baptiste Louis Franquelin, Géographe

du Roy 1699." Harrisse believes this to be a copy made by F. de la Croix, for Franquelin was succeeded as royal hydrographer by Joliet in 1695.

[31] Harrisse No. 240: "Carte de l'Amérique Septentrionale . . . Franquelin," 1689.

[32] Harrisse No. 258: "Carte en quatre sections de 90 x 53 cent. chacune, dressée par M. de Fonville . . . 1689."

[33] Cf. *Frontenac*, 12-13.

[34] Abbé Faillon's papers were later transferred to the Montreal Sulpicians, and number much more than the "4 Ms. vols." shown Parkman.

[35] The Archives of the Dépôt des Cartes de la Marine, No. 359, contained two plans of Quebec in 1694 and 1695 (Harrisse Nos. 252 & 253). No. 369 probably held later plans of the city and of the fortifications.

[36] D'Avezac had recently published an essay on the Cabots in J. G. Kohl's *History of the Discovery of Maine* (Portland, 1869).

[37] Probably Nicolas de la Salle's *Récit* of 1685, published by Margry in *Découvertes*, I, 547-70, and in an English translation by the Caxton Club of Chicago in 1898 (*Bib. Can. 88*). Nicolas de la Salle was also the author of the letter dated Toulon, 3 Sept. 1698, which gives an account of Louisiana. He was "the son of a naval officer at Toulon, and was not related to the Caveliers." (*La Salle*, 463 n.)

[38] These notes indicate that Parkman had discovered that the missing La Salle papers were concentrated in Margry's hands.

[39] See note 37.

[40] Samuel L. M. Barlow was a noted collector of Americana.

[41] The Fonds Clerembault was one of the manuscript collections, named after the individuals who formed them under Louis XIV and Louis XV, which contained some of the most valuable Canadian material in the Bibliothèque Nationale. Cf. Harrisse, *Notes*, xxix.

XIII. 1878 NOTEBOOK

[1] These lines, on the ridge which crosses the plateau half a mile from the fort, were first formed by the abatis built by Montcalm's army in a single day against Abercromby's attack in 1758 (cf. *Montcalm and Wolfe*, II, 104-6). They are clearly shown on Lieutenant E. Meyer's "Sketch of the Country Round Tyconderoga" (*Montcalm and Wolfe*, II, 99) and in Skinner's "A Perspective View of Lake George" (Samuel, *Seven Years'*

War in Canada, 44), but are best seen in Engineer Lieutenant Thérbu's "Plan du Fort Carillon."

² The Indian path over Mt. Defiance to Lake Champlain was probably used by Sir William Johnson and the Indians, who were stationed on the mountain during Abercromby's attack on Ticonderoga. The path to Trout Brook is shown on Meyer's "Sketch" (*Montcalm and Wolfe*, II, 99).

³ Lord George Augustus Howe (1724-58) was killed on July 8 near the junction of Trout Brook with the outlet of Lake George, not far from the portage to the sawmill and the lower falls. Cf. *Johnson Papers*, II, 872.

⁴ The best map of the head of Lake George is "A Plan of Fort William Henry and the English Camps and Retrenchments with the French different Camps and Attack there upon" (*Johnson Papers*, II, 728). This is from the famous "Set of Plans and forts in America, reduced from actual surveys" (London, 1763). Unfortunately the plan is poorly reproduced and most of the legend is unreadable. A more useful map of the battlefield is Engineer Lieutenant Thérbu's "Attaques du Fort William-Henri". Samuel Blodget's "A Perspective View of the Battle Near Lake George" has been frequently reproduced, *e.g.*, Bancroft, *History of the United States*, IV, 210. On this map, see Massachusetts Historical Society *Collections*, II Series, IV, 153.

⁵ Fort George was laid out by Amherst and Montresor in June 1759, on the hill at the head of Lake George which had formed part of Johnson's camp in 1755, of Munro's in 1757, and of Abercromby's in 1758. It was finished about a month later, but the capture of Ticonderoga and Crown Point rendered it useless.

⁶ According to Blodget's "Perspective View" the old road did run into Johnson's camp.

⁷ Artillery Cove and Lévis' camp are shown on Thérbu's "*Attaques*."

⁸ Brown's was a crossroads tavern near the toll gate on the plank road to Lake George.

⁹ The site of Fort William Henry was first fortified by Sir William Johnson on the advice of Captain Eyre in 1755. Robert Rogers used the camp as his base in 1755-56. The fort was surveyed by Montresor in March 1757 and captured by Montcalm in the following July.

¹⁰ The Whitehall–Fort Anne–Fort William Henry area is best shown in the map supposedly used by Montcalm, "Carte, depuis le fort St-Frédéric jusqu'à Orange ou Albanie, du Lac de St-Sacrement & de la situation des Forts construits dans cette partie de l'Amérique Septentrionale, 1757," which is reproduced in *Knox's Historical Journal*, III, 28.

¹¹ The stream that enters the head of South Bay is Mt. Hope Brook.

[12] Fort Anne (Fort de la Reine), a military post on Wood Creek on the portage from the head of South Bay to Fort Edward, was built by Colonel Nicholson in 1709. It was later captured and destroyed by the French, but rebuilt.

[13] Wood Creek, called Rivière-au-Chicot on Montcalm's plan, is now a canal between Whitehall and the Hudson. Half-Way Brook is a tributary which joins the main stream at Fort Anne.

[14] These are the Drowned Lands, near the northern end of which are the Two Rocks (Deux Rochers).

[15] Pierre de Sales de Laterrière (1747-1815), *Mémoires de Pierre de Sales Laterrière et de ses traverses* (Edition intime. Quebec, 1873). *Bib. Can.* 832. This book was published in 1871 in an edition of one hundred copies by Alfred Garneau, the historian's son, who doubtless brought it to Parkman's attention. It is a valuable source for the social history of the post-conquest period, and a most entertaining book.

[16] In Abbé Casgrain's *Histoire de l'Hôtel-Dieu de Québec* (Quebec, 1878), he lists Mere Juchereau de St. Ignace's work of the same name (Montauban, 1751) in his bibliography and remarks: "*Cette histoire a été écrite d'après les renseignements de la mère de St-Ignace et rédigée par la mère Duplessis de Ste-Hélène.*" The original manuscript, in the writing of Mère de Ste-Hélène and signed by Mère de St. Ignace, is in the Hôtel-Dieu of Quebec.

[17] Possibly a descendent of John Neilson (1776-1848), editor of the Quebec *Gazette*, friend of Louis-Joseph Papineau, delegate to London of the Quebec Asembly, and Speaker of the Legislative Council in 1844.

[18] The Archives de la Séminaire de Québec contain a rich store of historical material on the French and English periods. Parkman's friend Abbé Casgrain knew them well, and used their resources both to help and to refute his friend's work.

[19] James Macpherson Le Moine (1825-1912), *Maple Leaves: Canadian History—Literature—Sport. New Series* (Quebec, 1873).

[20] The Buttes à Neveu is the highest point on the Plains of Abraham.

[21] Wolfe's Ravine is where the British troops climbed the Heights of Abraham on the night of September 12, 1759.

[22] Major Robert Stobo (1727-?), a Scots officer of the Virginia Regiment, held hostage by the French in the Fort Necessity affair of 1754, was condemned to death for breaking his parole by corresponding with the British forces. He was reprieved; twice escaped to Louisbourg in 1756 and 1759; and came back to Quebec as a spy. He was not involved in the Battle of the Plains, for he left Wolfe to join Amherst on September 7.

De Vitré's son, Lieutenant John Denis De Vitré, memorialized William

Pitt for losses suffered as a result of his father's action (cf. Viger, *Siège de Québec en 1759* [Quebec, 1836] 38-41), so it seems clear that his share in Wolfe's victory was established.

[23] Abbé Louis-Edouard Bois (1813-89) developed an interest in historical pursuits while vicar at St. Jean-Port Joli, where he saw much of the historically minded Aubert de Gaspé family. He worked as an antiquarian and compiler while curé of St. François de Beauce and of Maskinongé. He had a major part in the production of the Laverdière edition of the *Jesuit Relations* (Quebec, 1858) and of the *Collection des anciens documents*. He was a member of the Literary and Historical Society of Quebec and was awarded the degree of *docteur-ès-lettres* by Laval. His admirable library is now in the Séminaire de Nicolet.

[24] *Siège de Québec en 1759. Copié d'après un manuscrit apporté de Londres par l'honorable D. B. Viger, lors de son retour en Canada en Septembre 1834—Mai 1835. Copié d'un manuscrit déposé à la bibliothèque de Hartwell en Angleterre* (Quebec, 1836). *Bib. Can.* 299. Viger made a copy of this MS. in the library of Dr. John Lee at Hartwell House, who got it from Captain Alex Schomberg, an English naval officer present at the siege, who edited the MS. The journal, written at four ten-day intervals by one of the besieged, covers the period from May 1 to September 10, 1759, just before the Battle of the Plains.

[25] Frédéric-Georges Baby (1832-1906), lawyer, cabinet minister, judge. He was Sir John MacDonald's Minister of Internal Revenue in 1878, and later became a Supreme Court justice. He was a founder of the Société Historique de Montréal and president of the Numismatic and Antiquarian Society of Montreal. His papers now belong to the University of Montreal and are being calendared.

[26] Théophile-Pierre Bédard (1837-1900), lawyer, journalist, and historian, began with *Journal de Québec*, but turned to the civil service and became archivist and registrar. In 1869 he published his *Historie de cinquante ans* (1791-1841), which shares more of the vices than the virtues of Robert Christie's history, to which it was a rejoinder. He published a "Table analytique des Jugements et Deliberations du Conseil Superieur, 1717-31" in the *Rapports du Secrétaire et Registraire de Québec pour 1892 et 1893*.

[27] James Macpherson Le Moine (1825-1912), born in Quebec of a French-Canadian father and a Scots mother, wrote with equal facility in English and French. He was a lawyer, but did not long practice, since he became inspector of internal revenue for Quebec in 1869 and held this office until his death. His five series of *Maple Leaves*, *L'Album du Touriste* (Quebec, 1872), *Quebec Past & Present* (Quebec, 1876), *Chronicles*

of the St. Lawrence (1888), and *The Explorations of Jonathan Oldbuck* (1889) are perhaps the best known of the almost innumerable books, pamphlets, and discourses he produced. In addition to his historical interests, he was an ornithologist, and he wrote widely for Canadian and American magazines. His home, Spencer Grange, in Sillery was a center of hospitality for the artistic and the literary. He was president of the Royal Society of Canada and several times president of the Literary and Historical Society of Quebec. He was knighted by Queen Victoria in 1897.

[28] Lieutenant Colonel R. S. Beatson, *Notes on the Plains of Abraham* (Gibraltar, 1858). According to Doughty (*Siege of Quebec*, VI, 155): "The book is exceedingly rare and the only copies we have knowledge of are in the possession of the Gibraltar Garrison Library and Sir J. M. Le Moine."

[29] Montcalm died in the home of M. André Arnoux, St. Louis Street (probably on the site of No. 59) at 5 A.M. September 14, 1759, the day following the battle, and was buried in the Ursulines' Chapel at nine that night (cf. Chapais, *Montcalm*, 666-75). Chapais supports De Folignée's story of the shell-hole grave (cf. Doughty, *Siege*, IV, 207).

[30] George Robert Gleig (1796-1888), *Lives of Eminent British Military Commanders* (London, 1831-32).

[31] This "Plan of the Town & Basin of Quebec" is No. 14 in Doughty's list of plans and engravings, *Siege*, VI, 285 & n.

[32] The relevant portion of Parkman's letter to Le Moine, dated Montreal November 17, 1878, is as follows:

> Your Historical Society has done a great deal for Canadian history, but there is, I think, no particular in which it has done better service than in collecting and printing memoirs and journals concerning the great crisis of 1759. I trust it will continue this good work. A great deal may thus be saved that would otherwise perish and be forgotten. There must be a great number of letters, papers and maps in private hands, subject to fire and all sorts of accidents, which might be saved at moderate expense and the preservation of which is essential to a full knowledge of that important period.

This letter is printed in Literary and Historical Society of Quebec *Transactions*, New Series, XIII (1877-79), 159.

[33] Joseph Marmette (1844-95), historian, novelist, and archivist, presented Parkman with copies of most of his books. His chief works were *François de Bienville* (Quebec, 1870), *Le Chévalier de Mornac* (Montreal, 1873), and *Bigot* (Quebec, 1874), as well as other popular romantic novels about the French Regime. In 1880 Chapleau made him joint commissioner with Hector Fabre at Paris, where he studied in the French archives.

Upon his return to Canada in 1884, he became assistant director of the Ottawa archives, for whom he later visited Paris in search of documents.

34 Mgr. Thomas Hamel (1830-1913) was associated with Laval University all of his life, except for four years of graduate study in Paris. He became superior of the Seminary and rector of the University in 1871 and held the post until 1880, and again from 1883 to 1886. He was librarian from 1886 to 1908. A scientist, he was president of the Royal Society of Canada.

35 Dr. Hubert La Rue (1833-81), one of Parkman's closest friends in Quebec, was a physician, professor, and man of letters. He did graduate work at Louvain and Paris after completing his classical course at Laval, and then returned to occupy a new chair which he held until his death. He wrote a vast number of pamphlets and magazine articles, gave innumerable lectures, and was a founder of the *Soirées Canadiennes* of 1860. His wife was a daughter of Judge Panet and Lucie Casgrain.

36 Louis Dupont du Chambon de Vergor (1710-?), an Acadian who was an accomplice of the Intendant Bigot and plundered both people and government, was in ill repute for his surrender of Fort Beauséjour in 1755 to Monckton after Pichon's betrayal. Bougainville gave him command of the post at Anse au Foulon (Wolfe's Cove), and he is suspected of having been bought by the English.

XIV. 1879 & 1885 NOTEBOOK

1 This is a list of the children of Dr. Hubert La Rue, Parkman's friend and frequent host in Quebec. Alphonsine died the following year; and only four of the ten La Rue children survived their father, who died at the age of forty-eight in 1889.

2 It is not clear on what text these notes are based, for the *Journal de Franquet* was first published in the *Annuaire du Institut Canadien de Québec* (1885), 29-240. A note in the foreword reads: "Une copie en fut transcrite et mise dans nos archives nationales en 1854." Parkman evidently made his notes from a text in Quebec. In 1889 a general edition was published: Louis Franquet (1697-1768), *Voyages et Mémoires sur le Canada par Franquet* (Quebec, 1889). *Bib. Can.* 229. Parkman's page references do not agree with either of these editions.

3 Jean C. Langelier (1845-1910) was a journalist and publicist who

became deputy registrar of Quebec in 1887. As a young man he wrote for *La Minerve* and *Le Courier de St. Hyacinthe*; and then produced a long series of pamphlets on agriculture, colonization, railroads, and public works. His most scholarly work was a *Liste des terres concedées par la couronne, 1763-1870.*

⁴ Luc Letellier de St. Just (1820-81) was lieutenant governor of Quebec from 1876-79. In the latter year a dispute over his powers with the premier, Charles de Boucherville, was settled against him by the governor general in council, and it was established that the lieutenant governor, like the king whom he represents, reigns but does not govern. Letellier, who had fought for Maximilian in Mexico and traveled widely, was a friend of Sir James Macpherson Le Moine; and Parkman saw much of him during his visits to Quebec.

⁵ Wolfe's line of battle was drawn up somewhat nearer the city than the site of the prison. His deathplace is about as far in the opposite direction.

⁶ Parkman had met Abbé Louis-Edouard Bois, for forty-one years the historically minded *curé* of Maskinongé, in the previous year. Bois was a friend of Le Moine, who gives a biographical sketch with bibliography in *Monographies et esquisses*, 467-68.

⁷ Joseph-Eudore Evanturel (1852-1919) was one of Parkman's copyists in Quebec. He published his *Premières Poésies* in 1878. He later became a civil servant in Quebec, and died a pillar of the Boston St. Jean-Baptiste Society.

⁸ Narcisse-Henri-Edouard Faucher de St. Maurice (1847-97) was one of the most colorful figures of Quebec at this period. A son of the seigneur of Beaumont, he had fought for Maximilian in Mexico in 1864 and was twice wounded. He was clerk of the Legislative Council of Quebec from Confederation until 1881, and a member of the Assembly. As a yachtsman he sailed the lower St. Lawrence and described his voyages in several books, as he also did his travels in Europe and North Africa. He was later editor of the *Journal de Québec* and of *Le Canadien*. As a historically minded sportsman, he was a welcome addition to Parkman's circle of Quebec friends.

⁹ "A view of the Fall of Montmorenci and the attack made by General Wolfe on the French Intrenchments near Beauport, with the Grenadiers of the Army, July 31st, 1759." Engraved by William Elliott (Coverdale Collection, No. 21). One of Smyth's St. Lawrence set, "Six Elegant Views of the Most Remarkable Places in the River and Gulph of St. Lawrence, from the Originals drawn on the spot by Captain Hervey Smyth, Aid de Camp to the late General Wolfe, 1760." The others, some of which

Parkman mentions, are: "A View of the City of Quebec," "A View of Cape Rouge," "A View of Gaspe Bay," "A View of Miramichi," and "A View of the Pierced Island" (Coverdale Collection, Nos. 19-25).

10 Alfred Garneau (1836-1904), the son of François-Xavier Garneau, the first great French-Canadian historian, was a poet and an antiquarian who served the provincial government as a translator and as librarian of the Parliamentary Library.

11 The Academy of Inscriptions was a section of the French Academy.

12 William M. McPherson was Quebec agent for the Dominion Line Steamships, with offices at 92 St. Peter Street.

13 This letter of December 29, 1757 from Wolfe to Pitt is not given in Doughty's *Siege of Quebec*. Grant's *Memoir of Wolfe* is not listed in *Bib. Can.*

14 The French-Canadian word for codfish, *morue*, is supposedly derived from the Gascon *mouru*. Spaniards, Basques, and Gascons were active in the St. Lawrence fisheries before the period of French settlement, as a few place names along the lower St. Lawrence indicate. Lescarbot gives the Basque word for cod as *bacaillos* (II, 24).

15 Fort Lawrence, named after Major (later Governor) Charles Lawrence, who built it in the autumn of 1750, stood on or near the site of the village of Beaubassin (burned in that same year) on a ridge parallel with the higher ridge of Beauséjour, about a mile and a quarter across the marshes of the Missequash River. It was square, consisting of four bastions connected by curtains, with a ditch and picket palisade. After Monckton captured Beauséjour in 1755, the latter replaced Lawrence as the British stronghold. Fort Lawrence was dismantled and evacuated in 1756, but part of the ditch on the south side can still be seen.

16 Fort Beauséjour (called Cumberland, after its conquest by Monckton in 1755) was named after an early settler of the place. It was begun in 1751 as a counterweight to Fort Lawrence and was still unfinished at the time it was besieged by Monckton, thanks to Abbé Le Loutre's insistence that all available men work on the *aboiteaux* or dikes on the marsh west of Beauséjour. The fort was a "pentagon of earthworks about 280 feet in width," consisting of five bastions and connecting curtains. It was surrounded by a deep ditch and a fifteen-foot picket palisade. Casements were built along the walls for protection from cannon fire, but during Monckton's siege these were found not to be bombproof. De Vergor, the commandant, and Le Loutre, who played a role reminiscent of the modern Russian Army political commissars, surrendered the fort on June 16, 1755 after a siege of twelve days. The fort was greatly strengthened by the English, as indicated by Lieutenant Colonel Moore's report in

1784. The "immense stone structure" which Parkman noticed was the magazine, built of stone and brick outside the main entrance, this being the best preserved portion of the fortifications in an 1870 watercolor sketch. See J. C. Webster, *Forts of Chegnecto* (Shediac, 1930), 78. Its base still remains, Barracks stood within both the pentagon and the extension of the glacis in a spur toward the south, which was added by the English. The walls still stand, but the buildings have disappeared, the glacis has been leveled, and the casements have fallen in.

[17] Cumberland Basin is now called Chegnecto Bay.

[18] The reversing falls of St. John, New Brunswick, are one of the great sights of the Maritime Provinces.

1885

[19] For Parkman's use of these notes on Beaufort, South Carolina (the Port Royal of Jean Ribaut in 1562), see *Pioneers*, 39-41.

[20] Not Ribaut's "Charlesfort." Cf. *Pioneers*, 41 n.

[21] For Ribaut's arrival at Fernandina, Florida, see *Pioneers*, 38-39.

[22] The St. John's River was Ribaut and Laudonnière's "River of May." Cf. *Pioneers*, 51-52.

[23] Pelican Bank was the sand bar which Ribaut (*Pioneers*, 36) and Laudonnière (*ibid*, 50) crossed in their boats, since it blocked the entrance of ships to the harbor which has since become the port of Jacksonville.

[24] For the Vale of Laudonnière see *Pioneers*, 55 & n.

[25] Cf. *Pioneers*, 59-60 for the use Parkman made of these notes.

[26] Parkman used these notes in his description of Menendez' march on Fort Caroline in 1565 (*Pioneers*, 121).

[27] Anastasia Island was the scene of Menendez' massacre of the shipwrecked French in 1565 (*Pioneers*, 133-47).

XV. 1889-1892 NOTEBOOK

[1] Sir John George Bourinot (1837-1902), a Nova Scotian educated at Toronto, became Clerk of the House of Commons in 1880 and for many years was honorary secretary of the Royal Society of Canada. He was a historian and an authority on constitutional government. His chief works are *Canada under British Rule*, a *Manual of the Constitutional History of Canada*, and *Parliamentary Procedure and Government in Canada*.

[2] Theodore Roosevelt (1858-1919) dedicated *The Winning of the West*,

which he had written in an interlude of his political career, to Parkman, saying that "your works stand alone and that they must be the models for all historical treatments of the founding of new communities and the growth of the frontier here in the wilderness." He found it difficult to thank Parkman for the gift of *A Half-Century of Conflict:* "It must have been rather hard for any one to whom Gibbon, for instance, sent his work to find perfectly fit words to use in acknowledging the gift."

³ Captain Samuel Vetch (1668-1732), a Scot who came to New York in 1699, was accused of illicit trade while acting as Governor Dudley's emissary to Vaudreuil in the matter of the Deerfield captives in 1705. He was the author of the plan for the reduction of Canada during the War of the Spanish Succession, and with Colonel Nicholson was joint leader of the expedition of 1709. The statement to which Parkman refers appears in *A Half-Century of Conflict*, I, 103-4.

⁴ Benoni Stebbins, a sergeant in the county militia, was killed in the Deerfield massacre of 1704. See *Half-Century*, I, 63-6.

⁵ Miss C. Alice Baker of Cambridge, Massachusetts, a descendent of one of the Deerfield captives, did considerable research on the massacre.

⁶ For Vetch's military qualifications, see *Half-Century*, I, 122.

⁷ William Smith (1728-93), *The History of the Late Province of New-York, from its first discovery* (London, 1756 and New York, 1829). *Bib. Can.* 266.

⁸ Jeanne-Françoise Juchereau, Mère de St. Ignace (1650-1723). *Histoire de l'Hôtel-Dieu de Québec.* Ed. by Dom Latom. (Montaubon, 1751.)

⁹ John R. Bartlett, "The Four Kings of Canada," *Magazine of American History*, March 1878. This is an account of the five Mohawk chiefs whom Peter Schuyler took to London in 1710. One died on the voyage; the others were presented to Queen Anne, one as emperor of the Mohawks and the others as kings. See *Half-Century*, I, 142.

¹⁰ Samuel Vetch and Colonel Francis Nicholson were the joint leaders and instigators of the campaign against Canada in 1709. Nicholson commanded the force moving north by the Champlain route while Vetch was to accompany the British fleet which was to sail to Quebec from Boston. After the collapse of this campaign, Nicholson was named to command the expedition against Port Royal in the following year, with Vetch as his adjutant general. This effort was successful. See *Half-Century*, I, 120-55.

¹¹ *Mémoires des Commissionaires du roi et ceux de Sa Majesté britannique Sur les possessions & les droits respectifs des deux Couronnes en Amérique.* 4 vols. (Paris, 1755-7). *Bib. Can.* 235.

¹² Benjamin Perley Poore had collected and copied documents in Paris

bearing on the colonial history of the Commonwealth. These copies, kept at the Statehouse in Boston, are commonly called the Paris Documents.

[13] Dr. Douglas Brymner (1823-1902) was the Dominion Archivist from 1872 until his death. His annual reports were eagerly awaited by Parkman, who provided the Public Archives at Ottawa with copies of his own collection of Paris documents.

[14] The letters of De Goutin, a magistrate who acted as intendant at Port Royal and reported to Paris, are valuable sources on Acadian history from 1700 to 1710. The originals are in the Archives de la Marine et des Colonies at Paris, with some copies in the *Correspondance Officielle* at Ottawa. See *Half-Century*, I, 119 n.

[15] E. Rameau de St. Père (1820-99) was the author of *La France aux Colonies* (Paris, 1859), of which a new edition appeared as *Une Colonie Féodale* in 1889. Parkman reviewed the earlier book in the *Nation* for December 27, 1877 (XXV, 400) and April 4, 1878 (XXVI, 230). Parkman and Rameau held violently opposing views on the Acadian question.

[16] The character of Colonel Francis Nicholson is sketched in *Half-Century*, I, 148.

[17] *Le Canada-Français*, a magazine published by Laval University at Quebec, printed in three separate volumes, *Collection de Documents inédits* (Quebec 1888-90), Abbé Casgrain's Acadian material, before it was collected in *Un Pèlerinage au Pays d'Evangéline*.

[18] Dr. Convers Francis' "Life of Rale" may be found in Jared Sparks's *Library of American Biography*, New Series, VII.

[19] Abbé Cyprien Tanguay (1819-1902), *Dictionnaire Généalogique des Familles Canadiennes* (Quebec, 1871).

[20] The original of the Reverend Henry Flynt's *Common Place Book* is in the library of the Massachusetts Historical Society. It is quoted in *Half-Century*, I, 222, 230-1. Père Sebastien Rale, Rasles, or Rasle, S.J. (1657-1724) was assigned to the Abenaki Mission in 1691, after spending two years in the Illinois country, and devoted the rest of his life to keeping the Abenaki loyal to the French. He took an active part in their war efforts and was killed in a New England raid on one of their villages.

[21] The letter of the Rev. Joseph Baxter to Rale (April 1719), belonging to the Massachusetts Historical Society, is summarized in *Half-Century*, I, 229-30. Baxter was Rale's rival as spiritual guide and political director of the Abenakis, and carried on a polemical correspondence in Latin with him on the relative merits of their faiths, their Latin, and their tempers.

[22] Rale's papers were seized by Colonel Westbrook's expedition against

Norridgewock in 1721, which had the capture of the missionary as its main object. Rale escaped, but his strongbox was captured; and the papers it contained supplied clear evidence that he was acting as an agent of the Canadian authorities in exciting his flock against the English. Some of these papers, including a letter from Vaudreuil to Rale (Quebec, Sept. 25, 1721), are preserved in the Archives of Massachusetts. See *Half-Century*, I, 238 & n.

[23] Rale was a good linguist, like many of the other Jesuit missionaries. His *Abenaki Dictionary* is preserved in the Harvard College Library. It was published in 1833.

[24] Niles based his *Indian and French Wars* largely on Penhallow's *History of Wars of New England with the Eastern Indians*, but frequently blundered in his copying. See *Half-Century*, I, 46 n.

[25] Benjamin Crafts (?-1746) was a private in Colonel Hale's Essex Regiment. His journal is quoted in *Half-Century*, II, 148.

[26] William Vaughan (1703-?) of Damariscotta, son of the lieutenant governor of New Hampshire, was second in command of Pepperrell's expedition against Louisbourg in 1745. He is the supposed author of the attack, and played a leading role in the siege. See *Half-Century*, II, 64-5, 98-118.

[27] Sir William Pepperrell (1696-1759), born in Maine and a member of the General Court of Massachusetts from 1727 until his death, commanded the expedition against Louisbourg and captured the fortress in 1745. He was subsequently made a baronet, and lieutenant general in 1759. His papers are in the Massachusetts Historical Society. A journal appended to Shirley's letter to Newcastle (Oct. 28, 1745) bears the names of Pepperrell, Waldo, Moore, Lothrop, and Gridley, who attest its accuracy. This may be the journal referred to by Parkman. See *Half-Century*, II, 144 n.

[28] William Douglass (1691?-1752), *A summary, Historical and Political, of the First Planting, Progressive Improvements, and Present State of the British Settlements in North America* (London, 1760). *Bib. Can.* 225. Originally issued serially in Boston, 1747-52.

[29] Robert Hale Bancroft was a descendent of Colonel Robert Hale of the Essex regiment in the Louisbourg expedition of 1745. See *Half-Century*, II, 107 n. The letter from John Payne of Boston to Colonel Hale is given in II, 88-9 n.

[30] The Rev. Stephen Williams (1693-?) of Longmeadow, Massachusetts, son of the Rev. John Williams of Deerfield, was captured as a boy of eleven at the time of the massacre. He was the author of an *Account of the*

Captivity of Stephen Williams and of manuscript diary of the winter after the capture of Louisbourg, where he served as chaplain. Parkman owned the later diary, and refers feelingly to its "detestable" handwriting. See *Half-Century*, II, 150 n.

[31] These "Latour books" were the materials upon which Parkman based the new section, "The Feudal Chiefs of Acadia," which he added to the 1893 edition of *The Old Regime*.

[32] "*Good Government* was the organ of the Civil Service Reform League. Parkman's support was probably recruited by his friend E. L. Godkin of the *Nation* or by Theodore Roosevelt, who had been named a Civil Service Commissioner in 1889 by President Cleveland. It was a period of revolt on the part of the established elements of the community against boss and machine rule in politics. The object of the League was close to Parkman's heart. See his "The Failure of Universal Suffrage," *North American Review*, July-August 1878 (CXXVII, 1-20).

Index

Abbot, Elisha, 343
Abbot, James, 68 ff., 343
Abbot, Lt., 474
Abbotsford, 225, 226
Abenaki Dictionary, 597, 682
Abenakis, 274, 276, 349, 350, 352, 391, 559, 681
Abenakis, Histoire des, 655
Abenakis and Their History . . . , 521, 654–55
Abercromby, James (Gen.), 48, 61, 261–62, 264, 270, 327, 337–38, 339, 340, 346, 380, 649, 671, 672
Abert, J. J. (Col.), 608
Abert, James William (Lt.), 412, 608
Absaroka, 636
Acadia, 324
Acadia, 232, 233, 667
Acadians, 366
Account of the Captivity of Stephen Williams, 682–83
Account of the Countries adjoining to Hudson's Bay, 368
Account of the European Settlements in America, 378
Account of the Gospel Labours . . . of John Churchman . . . , 324, 378–79
Account of the Remarkable . . . Colonel James Smith . . . , 378
Account of Two Voyages to New England, 351, 352
Adams, Daniel, 597
Adams, Henry, xii, 594, 596
Aeneas, 158
Aernouts, Jurriaen (Capt.), 666
Aetna, Mt., *see* Mt. Aetna
Agathocles, 160, 355
Agawam R., 43
Agniers, 275, 365
Agrigentum, 151, 245
Aimable, 528, 530
Akins, Thomas, 547–48

Albano, 188, 189, 190
Albano, Lake, 189
Albany, N.Y., 41, 44, 87, 90, 273, 355, 359, 362, 376
Albion tavern, 128, 354
Album (Viger), 519, 648
Album du Touriste, 674
Alegambe, Philip, 519, 648
Alexander, William (Sir), 665
Algeciras, 118, 119, 122
Algic Researches, 306, 374, 375, 604
Algonkins, 374, 375, 396, 482, 579, 608, 609, 613, 615, 616
Algonquins, 274, 559, 580, 649, 650
Alhambra, 10, 330
Alleghany Mts., 408
Alleghany R., 407
Allegro, Mt., 246
Allen, Ethan, 50, 338, 341
Allen, Ira, 338
Allen's R., 549, 664–65
Alloa, 597
Aloüez, Claude, 324, 377, 534
Alphonse, Jan (Capt.), 653
Alps, 205, 209, 213, 216
Alton, N.H., 7, 8, 330
Amariscoggin R., 25
"Ambitious Guest," 331
"America," 42, 65
American Archives, 362, 370
American Fur Co., 373, 374, 375, 388, 397–98, 401, 440, 604, 607, 608, 610, 618, 620, 622, 625, 627, 634–35, 640, 641
American Journal of Sciences and Arts, 331
American Literature, 105
American Magazine, 327, 380
American Medical Biographies, 270, 362, 363
American Notes, 341, 356
American Pioneer, 488, 491
American Scenery, 376

685